MIDDLEBURG CEMETERIES

Loudoun County Virginia

COMPILED
BY
THE CEMETERY COMMITTEE
OF THOMAS BALCH LIBRARY

HERITAGE BOOKS
2020

HERITAGE BOOKS

AN IMPRINT OF HERITAGE BOOKS, INC.

Books, CDs, and more—Worldwide

For our listing of thousands of titles see our website
at
www.HeritageBooks.com

Published 2020 by
HERITAGE BOOKS, INC.
Publishing Division
5810 Ruatan Street
Berwyn Heights, Md. 20740

Heritage Books by Thomas Balch Library:
Loudoun County, Virginia Cemeteries: A Preliminary Index
Middleburg Cemeteries, Loudoun County, Virginia

International Standard Book Number
Paperbound: 978-1-58549-584-9

Middleburg Cemeteries

Loudoun County, Virginia

Table of Contents

Introduction

In 1996 The Staff and Volunteers of the Thomas Balch Library for History and Genealogy published *Loudoun County, Virginia Cemeteries, A Preliminary Index*. It was intended as a tool for genealogical research in Loudoun County, Virginia. It was by no means complete, but then, no study of old cemeteries is ever complete.

Since that time the Cemetery Committee has continued investigating, finding, and cataloging the numerous cemeteries in Loudoun County. Many of the larger ones have been published separately. Hopefully all of them will be published in time.

This book covers the five public cemeteries of Middleburg, Loudoun County, Virginia. It does not include small private family cemeteries which may be found in the area. We will leave that for a later book

In all but one cemetery, the burials are grouped by lots and show the owner of the lot whenever possible. If less than half a lot (usually 4-6 burial sites) are owned by one person, the lot owner is shown as *Miscellaneous*. Epitaphs on the stones are listed if they have genealogical significance. In most cases we have left off poems and other verse.

The information included was primarily taken from grave markers in each of the five cemeteries. Information for Sharon Cemetery and Middleburg Baptist Church Cemetery was originally compiled by Mrs. Aurelia Jewell around 1950. Her information was updated by our volunteers in 1999. Some of the markers in Mrs. Jewell's listings are either no longer present or illegible, but that information is still included in this book with a notation (*) for a missing marker. Emmanuel Episcopal Church, Tyler Gore of Royston Funeral Home and Liz Wallace of Solon Cemetery Company kindly loaned us their plats of the cemeteries along with a listing of lot owners for Middleburg Memorial Cemetery.

All of the cemeteries probably have unmarked graves which unfortunately could not be included in this book. Spouses, who are still living, are also included when their names appear on a marker.

We would like to thank everyone who helped with the preparation of this book: All those who shared plats, along with John K. Gott and Eugene M. Scheel who assisted by allowing us to use historical information on the cemeteries from their books. Finally, this book would not have been completed without the computer skills of Betty Frain, the platting skills of Les Querry, and the support of Craig Scott of Willow Bend Books.

The Cemetery Committee
Of Thomas Balch Library

Jeffrey Ball
Ned Douglass
Mary Fishback
Marty Hiatt
Wynne Saffer
David Via

Abbreviations Used

B:	born
D:	died
c/o	child of
d/o	daughter of
f/o	father of
m/o	mother of
h/o	husband of
s/o	son of
w/o	wife of
ndd	no death date
*	no stone found, 1999

Emmanuel Episcopal Church Cemetery

In 1968 Alice duPont Mills gave 2.7 acres adjoining Sharon [Cemetery] to Emmanuel Church, and the same year the church bought 5.7 additional acres. Non-sectarian Emmanuel Cemetery became the largest of the town's four graveyards. – *Eugene M. Scheel*

z ←

Emmanuel
Cemetery

211 21 20 19 18 171 170 16 15 14 13 12 11 10 9 8 7 6 5 4 3 2 1

44 57
43 56 66 81
42 55 65 80 17
41 54 64 79 88 89
40 53 63 78 87 93
39 52 62 77 86 92
38 51 61 76 85 91
37 50 60 75 84 90
49 59 74 83
48 58 73 82
72

30 29 28 27
31 32

104 106 108
103 105 107

26 25
24 35 36
23 34
22 33

47
46
45

71
70
69
68
67

111

Lot: **Owner:**

Bruce D. Nichols	B: 1917	D: 1981
Jane S. Nichols	B: 1918	D: 1988

Lot: 2   Owner: Stettinius

Edward Reilly Stettinius	B: 9 Jun 1925	D: 30 Sep 1990
Edward Reilly Stettinius, III	B: 16 Dec 1927	D: 2 Jul 1969

Lot: 8   Owner: R. Thompson

Patricia Lee Thompson	B: 5 Nov 1932	D: 16 Aug 1987

Lot: 9   Owner: H. Taylor

Hobart Taylor, Jr	B: 1920	D: 1981

Lot: 10   Owner: Miscellaneous

James M. McCanless	B: 17 Nov 1925	D: 3 Nov 1981
Louis A. Montague	B: 20 May 1898	D: 16 May 1988
Ozella O. Montague	B: 30 Jan 1915	D: 13 Mar 1992
Joseph F. Kelly	B: 26 Feb 1902	D: 21 Apr 1982

Lot: 11   Owner: J.L. Wiley

James Langhorne Wiley	B: 18 Jun 1914	D: 1 Aug 1969

Lot: 12   Owner: Miscellaneous

Marius F. Villaret	B: 2 Aug 1897	D: 24 Nov 1974
Jean H. Preece	B: 6 Jun 1930	D: 15 Jun 1972
Estelle Tyler Garges	B: 21 Sep 1906	D: 18 May 1996
Charlotte B. Villaret		D: 11 Jun 1993
Philip Robison Garges	B: 1 Mar 1902	D: 14 Nov 1983

Lot: 14   Owner: White

Pamela Nanette Peppiatt	B: 7 Apr 1951	D: 25 Sep 1969

Lot: 15   Owner: Munster

Catherine Nelson Meade Munster born Fauquier County	B: 7 Sep 1890	w/o O. Walter Munster D: 25 Dec 1966
O. Walter Munster	B: 17 Feb 1891	D: 28 Dec 1961 born New York City

Lot: 18   Owner: Grasty Turner

William Montague Grasty   B: 10 Nov 1948   D: 22 Jun 1968
                                   s/o William T. & Rosalie M. Grasty

William Tippett Grasty   B: 8 Mar 1914   D: 6 May 1976

Lot: 19   Owner: D.H. Read

Caroline Read Smith   B: 3 Jun 1936   D: 22 Jan 1983

Aldona Smoluchowska Read   B: 8 Aug 1902   D: 4 Dec 1984

Duncan Hicks Read   B: 30 Oct 1896   no death date

Lot: 20   Owner: Furness

Thomas Merrill   B: 1855   D: 1932
                               h/o Elizabeth Musgrave Merrill

Elizabeth Hubbard Worrall   B: 3 Mar 1925   D: 14 Jan 1996

Elizabeth Musgrave Merrill   B: 1853   D: 1929

Elizabeth Merrill Furness   B: 1898   D: 1986
                               w/o Thomas F. Furness

Thomas Foster Furness   B: 1892   D: 1976

Lot: 21   Owner: Furness

William Ernest Worrall   B: 8 Mar 1917   D: 11 Apr 1987

Richard Pretlow Worrall   B: 1864   D: 1953

Julia Thompson Worrall   B: 25 Jul 1886   D: 6 Mar 1968

Renee Schmolck Worrall   B: 13 Apr 1918   no death date

Lot: 22A & C   Owner: Arnold

Dorothy DeGolyer Arnold   B: 1916   D: 1969
                               w/o Milton W. Arnold

Lot: 27   Owner:

Charlotte Le Ghait Peters   D: 3 Feb 1980

Thomas R. Peters   B: 10 Jun 1967   D: 3 Feb 1980
                               s/o Charlotte Peters

Lot: 32   Owner: Miscellaneous

James Clayton Webb   B: 25 Aug 1953   D: 14 Dec 1985

Gregory Campbell Webb   B: 29 Mar 1984   D: 2 Apr 1984

Abigail Leigh Webb   D: 21 Sep 1994

Lot: 37   Owner: J. & D. Lee

Dorothy Nalle Lee   B: 17 Sep 1889   D: 17 Jun 1982

Lot: 38   Owner: Reynolds

William F. Reynolds   B: 23 May 1917   no death date

Ruth E. Reynolds   B: 5 Jun 1923   D: 8 Nov 1993
                                          w/o William F. Reynolds

Lot: 39   Owner: Miscellaneous

James Samuel Kaylor   B: 21 Aug 1913   D: 14 Jul 1990
                                                        WWII

Lot: 40   Owner: Miscellaneous

Sally B. Furr   B: 13 Apr 1947   D: 3 Jan 1999
                                          w/o Wilbur R. Furr Jr

Wilbur R. Furr, Jr   B: 5 May 1941   D: 31 Oct 1990

Harold C. Furr   B: 10 Sep 1928   D: 11 May 1991

Anna H. Furr   B: 21 Jul 1930   no death date
                                  w/o Harold C. Furr, m. 1 Jan 1949

Helen Arons Olney   B: 22 Jan 1915   D: 16 Mar 1997

Lot: 41   Owner: Miscellaneous

Janis Elaine Combs   B: 20 Sep 1950   D: 27 Nov 1992

Nancy Marie Schroeder   B: 26 May 1957   D: 1 Jun 1957
                                               d/o Anna Marie

Anna Marie Schroeder   B: 16 Oct 1919   D: 1 Apr 1990
                                                 six children

Lot: 42   Owner: Miscellaneous

Katharine R. Toerge   B: 16 Mar 1897   D: 25 Jul 1978

Lida Schock Redmond   B: 15 Jun 1923   D: 25 Jan 1999

Margaret Herron McCormick B: 13 Jul 1913   D: 10 Jan 1997

Cyrus E. Jr Manierre   B: 30 Aug 1919   D: 22 Apr 1974
                                                        WWII

Lot: 48   Owner: Kelso

Anne H. Kelso	B: 9 Dec 1915	D: 13 Feb 1971 w/o Richard Kelso
Richard E. Kelso	B: 24 Nov 1910	D: 25 Mar 1971

Lot: 50   Owner:

Leon F. Crouse	B: 1892	D: 1974
Bertha M. Crouse	B: 1890	D: 1986 w/o Leon F. Crouse

Lot: 51A   Owner: Jones

Thomas Tyther Leigh Jones	B: 18 Mar 1924	D: 8 Jul 1994 Korea

Lot: 51B   Owner: Deering

Harold John Deering	B: 24 Sep 1923	D: 2 Dec 1009 WW II LT JG US Navy

Lot 51C   Owner: Diedrich

Sue Leith Diedrich	B: 1911	D: 1980 w/o John Diedrich
John Ruffing Diedrich	B: 1912	D: 1998

Lot: 57   Owner: Miscellaneous

I. Spencer Wood	B: 1924	no death date
Susan W. O'Brien	B: 1954	no death date
Leila S. Wood	B: 1929	D: 1976
Deborah W. Brown	B: 1952	D: 1981
Toni K. Saha	B: 1899	D: 1994
Gilbert W. Smith	B: 1914	D: 1999 funeral home marker
Baby Jennifer O'Brien		D: 1991
Jennifer Wood		D: 1961

Lot: 58   Owner: Miscellaneous

Charles M. Pecora	B: 26 Aug 1919	no death date
Katharine Sturges Pecora	B: 13 Jul 1921	D: 20 May 1993 w/o Charles Pecora

Lynn Pecora	B: 9 Jan 1948	D: 4 Apr 1993
	d/o Charles & Katharine Pecors	
Jacob J. Davies	B: 1920	D: 1993
J. David Welch	B: 1924	D: 1983
Sally Lou Pecora	B: 10 Apr 1949	no death date
	d/o Charles & Katharine Pecora	

Lot: 59   Owner: Miscellaneous

| Gwendolyn A. Dobson | B: 17 May 1930 | D: 28 Mar 1997 |

Lot: 63   Owner: Miscellaneous

| Herbert B. Gengler | B: 10 Nov 1908 | D: 13 Sep 1985 |
| William John Logan | B: 2 Aug 1891 | D: 29 Aug 1977 |

Lot: 65   Owner:

| Charles III Baird | B: 20 Aug 1921 | D: 11 Apr 1989 |
| | | WWII |

Lot: 66A   Owner: Miscellaneous

John P. Bodmer, Jr	B: 30 Jul 1931	no death date
Ruth M. Bodmer	B: 28 Aug 1932	D: 26 Oct 1992
		married 15 Sep 1956
Bradley J. Eden	B: 22 Mar 1973	D: 26 Jul 1995
James Preston Kem	B: 1890	D: 1965
	US senator from Missouri 1946-1952	
Mary Elizabeth Carroll Kem	B: 1898	D: 1995
w/o James P. Kem	2nd husband Alfred Edward Tarr, 1968-1983	

Lot: 75   Owner: Miscellaneous

Ann Powell Marshall	B: 10 Sep 1925	D: 29 Dec 1998
	on stone with Samuel Marshall, IV	
Samuel, Marshall, IV	B: 14 Feb 1921	D: 21 Mar 1999
Nathan Daniel Maxwell	B: 9 Nov 1992	D: 1 Dec 1992
Mary E. Harper	B: 19 Jul 1900	D: 23 May 1990
		w/o Wilmer B. Harper Sr
Wilmer B. Harper, Sr	B: 5 Apr 1900	D: 22 Feb 1991
Wilmer B. Harper	B: 22 Jan 1925	D: 17 Jan 1976

Lot: 76   Owner: Miscellaneous

| Howard F. Kesler | B: 21 Jan 1913 | D: 22 Nov 1979 |
| Sarah Elizabeth Rehm | B: 22 Nov 1998 | D: 24 Nov 1998 |

Lot: 78   Owner: Miscellaneous

| Francis Harley Sandifer | B: 29 Dec 1948 | D: 16 Mar 1994 |

Lot: 79C   Owner: Burton

| Nancy Lee Burton | B: 1936 | D: 1990 |

Lot: 79D   Owner: Schmoldt

Eleanor Woodman Schmoldt	B: 1925	D: 1988 w/o Donald H. Schmoldt
Donald Howard Schmoldt	B: 1931	no death date
Linda Schmoldt	d/o Donald & Eleanor	no dates

Lot: 80   Owner: Miscellaneous

| Gerald Schall | B: 15 Feb 1928 | D: 3 Aug 1994 |

Lot: 81   Owner: Miscellaneous

| Carolyn Ann Ramsey Boyd | B: 7 Jul 1946 | D: 4 Sep 1992 |

Lot: 82   Owner: Miscellaneous

Herman Albert Dayton	B: 26 Jul 1917	D: 3 Mar 1979 born Cornwall CT
Mark B. Hogan	B: 27 Jan 1951	no death date
Jesse W. Vandergrift	B: 18 Jun 1911	D: 25 Dec 1995
Marsha K. Hogan	B: 25 Nov 1950	D: 17 Jul 1998 on stone with Mark B. Hogan
Dorothy M. Vandergrift	B: 24 Aug 1912	D: 22 Apr 1991 on stone with Jesse W. Vandergrift
Mildred J. Erickson Batiste	B: 1895	D: 1979 w/o Wilford Batiste
Larry C. Harms	B: 22 Feb 1943	D: 18 Jul 1994
Wilford N. Batiste	B: 1893	D: 1990
Colin C. Rae	B: 20 Aug 1914	D: 22 Jun 1999

Lot: 83   **Owner: Darlington/Russell**

Jennie Hlyard Russell   B: 1900   D: 1979

Harry III Darlington   B: 1918   D: 1996

Lot: 85   **Owner: Miscellaneous**

William G. Costin, Jr   B: 1912   D: 1976
                                                                WWII

Lot: 89   **Owner: Dupont**

Edward H. Mattos   B: 6 May 1922   D: 11 Mar 1985

Philip Everett Dupont   B: 1958   D: 1979

Louise Applewhite Watson   B: 1909   D: 1988

Lot: 90   **Owner: Miscellaneous**

Emme Wick Burch   B: 1903   no death date

Preston Morris Burch   B: 1884   D: 1978

Anna Mary Cairns Polk   B: 31 Aug 1912   D: 12 May 1989

Lot: 91   **Owner: Pettibone**

John S. Pettibone   B: 20 Sep 1895   D: 11 May 1979

Rosamond Whiteside Pettibone B: 21 Jul 1895   D: 2 Aug 1984
                                                                w/o John D. Pettibone

Lot: 92   **Owner: Mills**

James Paul Mills   B: 7 Nov 1908   D: 14 Sep 1987

Lot: 93   **Owner: McKinney**

Marielle McKinney   B: 24 Dec 1921   D: 12 Jan 1998

Lot: 111   **Owner: McConnell**

Caryll Esterbrook McConnell   B: 1897   D: 1988

Robert Earll Jr McConnell   B: 1921   D: 1987

Robert Earll McConnell   B: 1889   D: 1971

Lot: 170   **Owner: Bowman**

Jean Bowman   B: 27 Sep 1917   D: 16 Aug 1994
                                        founder American Academy of Equine Art

Eleanor Holwick Bowman   B: 14 Sep 1892   D: 9 Nov 1987

Lot: 171   Owner: Morgan

Charles Morgan   B: 18 Mar 1911   D: 10 Jun 1983

Ann Cassidy Morgan   B: 14 Jan 1922   D: 16 Jul 1972

Lot: 211   Owner: Altimus

George Edward Altemus   B: 25 May 1902   D: 22 Jan 1985

Margaret Moffet Altemus   B: 3 Dec 1912   D: 27 Dec 1986

Middleburg Baptist Church Cemetery

When Burr Powell made his will in 1829, he set aside out of the land he owned a lot to be used for religious purposes. Upon his death in 1840 it passed to the trustees of the town of Middleburg. In 1844 a free church was built here, and shared by the Episcopalians, Baptists, Presbyterians and Methodists.

A cemetery was soon established on the lot surrounding the church. In 1853 the Baptists petitioned the trustees to use the "cemetery church" on two Sundays each month since the Methodists had built their own building by then. The cemetery is now known as the Baptist Church cemetery, but the people buried there didn't have to be Baptists, and the church does not maintain records of the stones.

Witnesses have reported that some markers were destroyed. An asterisk, (*) by a name indicates burials listed by Mrs. Jewell in the 1950s, for which no stone was found in 1999. This means information for those names could not be verified.

The markers in the church cemetery have been moved and are not in their original locations. Consequently, there is no plat. The names on the remaining stones are listed alphabetically.

Frances ----   D: 25 Aug 1859
                                  Our mother Frances and 4 children

Margaret Adams   Age: 69 years   D: 5 Sep 1843

Mary Jane Ball   Age: 22-11-28   D: 24 Sep 1846
                                                         w/o Franklin Ball

Mount Welby Chamblin   B: 28 Dec 1842   D: 16 Aug 1847
                                                  s/o A.G. & E.B. Chamblin

Sally Cox Chamblin   B: 3 Sep 1844   D: 18 Aug 1847
d/o A.G. & E.B. Chamblin   same stone as Mount Welby Chamblin

William H. (Rev) Chapman   Age: 52 years   D: 24 Apr 1828

Mary Thomas Dorman   Age: 0-13-19   D: 5 Nov 1832
                                                  d/o T.W. & M.P. Dorman

Thomas Robbins Dorsey   Age: 2-0-22   D: 4 Nov 1832
s/o Rev T.J. & J.P.P. Dorsey   Eldst son / lies cold in death

John Fletcher French   B: 28 May 1821   D: 29 Jul 1821
                                                         s/o John C. French

An Catharine Frey   B: 10 May 1776   D: 22 Jan 1854
                                  w/o John P. Frey   Age: 77- 8-12

John P. Frey   Age: 66- 3-17   D: 30 Nov 1841

James H. Furlong   Age: 3-11-28   D: 20 Apr 1833
s/o H. & J.S. Furlong   same stone as Sarah J. Furlong

Sarah J. Furlong   Age: 2- 1-19   D: 6 May 1833
d/o H. & J.S. Furlong   same stone as James H. Furlong

Ellen Garson   Age: 56- 1- 5   D: 7 Nov 1853
                                                         w/o Nelson Garson

Nancy Gibson   Age: 62 years   D: 10 Oct 1831

*Isaac Gochnauer   Age: 73- 4-18   D: 29 Oct 1837

*Nancy Gochnauer   Age: 72- 5-20   D: 1 Jul 1847
                                                  w/o Isaac Gochnauer

Ann Catherine Hereford   Age: 78 years   D: 6 Dec 1830
                                                  w/o Francis Hereford

Francis Hereford   Age: 54 years   D: 16 Oct 1821

Catherine Hoffman   Age: 34 years   D: 23 Oct 1847
                 w/o C.W. Hoffman, d/o R.S. & M. Buckey of MD

Virginia Hoffman   Age: 6- 4- 3   D: 7 Nov 1846
                                                          d/o C.W. & C.S. Hoffman

Hannah I. Hough   B: 17 Jan 1817   D: 23 Nov 1848
                                                          w/o Thomas Hough

Ann Mariah Johnson   B: 30 Oct 1825   D: 8 Jan 1844
d/o Thomas & Thurza Johnson   Born in Washington

John S. Johnson   B: 8 Aug 1837   D: 25 Apr 1841
                                                          s/o Thomas & Thurza Johnson

* Mary Jones   Age: 82 years   D: 22 Nov 1825

Hannah Maddux   Age: 86 years   D: 25 Sep 1845
                                                          w/o William Maddux

---- Mcveigh   Age: 8 days   D: 6 Jul 1830
                                  s/o Townsend & K.H. McVeigh infant

Jane A. Mcveigh   Age: 32 years   D: 26 Dec 1833
                                                          w/o Hiram McVeigh

Jane A.E. Mcveigh   Age: 0-10-17   D: 19 Jan 1830
                                                          d/o Hiram & Jane A. McVeigh

Richard Watson Mcveigh   Age: 0- 5-28   D: 2 Dec 1836
                                                          s/o J.H. & C.A. McVeigh

Virginia Mcveigh   Age: 10 days   D: 6 Aug 1829
                                                          d/o Townsend & K. H. McVeigh

*Ann Catherine Merchant   Age: 78 years   D: 6 Dec 1839
                                                          w/o Francis Merchant

Mary R. Newman   Age: 6- 1-27   D: 26 Mar 1845
                                                          d/o W. G. & Mary Newman

Robert Newman   Age: 3- 5-11   D: 29 Mar 1845
                                                          s/o W. G. & Mary Newman

Aaron Rawlings   Age: 57-11-22   D: 22 Feb 1816

Elizabeth Rawlings   Age: 65- 7- 9   D: 4 Apr 1836

Minnervy Ann Rawlings   Age: 4 years   D: 24 Sep 1825

*Stephen Rawlings   Age: 43 years   D: 26 Apr 1832

*Mary Jane Ritzer   Age: 29- 2-25   D: 26 Mar 1844
                                                          w/o H. Ritzer

Gabriel Skinner   Age: 54 years   D: 5 Jul 1839

| Mary Speats | Age: 22-10-26 | D: 26 Dec 1845 |
| | | w/o Thomas Speats |

| E. Towperman | Age: 27-10-18 | D: 14 Nov 1834 |

| Kitty Turner | Age: 60 years | D: 3 Feb 1859 |
| | | In memory of our mammy |

| Catharine Wharton | | D: Jan 1815 |

| *Elizabeth E. Young | | no dates |

| *Julious H. Young | | no dates |

| Rebecca Young | Age: 28 years | D: 6 Apr 1827 |
| | | w/o John M. Young |

| Teresa Young | w/o John M. Young | D: 29 Aug 1831 |

Middleburg Memorial Cemetery

Middleburg Memorial Cemetery was incorporated in 1938, when the trustees, Harry J. Duffey, Paul Adams, and Thomas Walter Fred bought seven acres for a new cemetery. Norris Royston's undertaking parlor, established 1932, assumed responsibility for upkeep of the burial grounds in 1958.

The older, traditional stones are in plots numbered 1-143. To keep the view from Federal Street open, grave markers west of the Baptist Church, with the higher numbers, are ground level bronze plaques.

Middleburg Memorial Cemetery

First Section

Baptist Church

Second Section

Road

Federal Street

Third Section

Middleburg Memorial Cemetery
First Section

N ◄———

Gate

Gate

							98	111	126	
			40	54	68	82	97	112	127	
1	14	27	41	55	69	83	98	113	128	
2	15	28	42	56	70	84	99	114	129	
3	16	29	43	57	71	85	100	115	130	
4	17	30	44	58	72	86	101	116	131	
5	18	31	45	59	73	87	102	117		
6	19	32	46	60	74	88	103	118		
7	20	33	47	61	75	89	104	119	132	
8	21	34	48	62	76	90	105	120	133	143
9	22	35	49	63	77	91	106	121	134	144
10	23	36	50	64	78	92	107	122	135	145
11	24	37	51	65	79	93	108	123	136	146
12	25	38	52	66	80	94	109	124	137	147
13a	26a	39a	53a	67a	81a	95a	110a	125a	138a	148a
13	26	39	53	67	81	95	110	125	138	148

Middleburg Memorial Cemetery
Second Section

N

```
                                                    | 199 | 198 | 197 |
                                                    | 202 | 201 | 200 |

                                                    | 205 | 204 | 203 |
                                              | 209 | 208 | 207 | 206 |

                                              | 212a | 212 | 211 | 210 |
                                              | 216  | 215 | 214 | 213 |

                                  | 221a | 221 | 220 | 219 | 218 | 217 |
                                  | 227  | 226 | 225 | 224 | 223 | 222 |

                      | 234a | 234 | 233 | 232 | 231 | 230 | 229 | 228 |
               | 241b | 241a | 241 | 240 | 239 | 238 | 237 | 236 | 235 |

               | 249a | 249 | 248 | 247 | 246 | 245 | 244 | 243 | 242 |
        | 258a | 258 | 257 | 256 | 255 | 254 | 253 | 252 | 251 | 250 |

| 268a | 268 | 267 | 266 | 265 | 264 | 263 | 262 | 261 | 260 | 259 |
| 277c | 277b | 277a | 277 | 276 | 275 | 274 | 273 | 272 | 271 | 270 | 269 |

| 288a | 288 | 287 | 286 | 285 | 284 | 283 | 282 | 281 | 280 | 279 | 278 |
| 299b | 299a | 299 | 298 | 297 | 296 | 295 | 294 | 293 | 292 | 291 | 290 | 289 |

| 311a | 311 | 310 | 309 | 308 | 307 | 306 | 305 | 304 | 303 | 302 | 301 | 300 |
| 324  | 323 | 322 | 321 | 320 | 319 | 318 | 317 | 316 | 315 | 314 | 313 | 312 |

| 337 | 336 | 335 | 334 | 333 | 332 | 331 | 330 | 329 | 328 | 327 | 326 | 325 |
| 350 | 349 | 348 | 347 | 346 | 345 | 344 | 343 | 342 | 341 | 340 | 339 | 338 |

| 364 | 363 | 362 | 361 | 360 | 359 | 358 | 357 | 356 | 355 | 354 | 353 | 352 | 351 |
| 378 | 377 | 376 | 375 | 374 | 373 | 372 | 371 | 370 | 369 | 368 | 367 | 366 | 365 |

| 391 | 390 | 389 | 388 | 387 | 386 | 385 | 384 | 383 | 382 | 381 | 380 | 379 |
| 404 | 403 | 402 | 401 | 400 | 399 | 398 | 397 | 396 | 395 | 394 | 393 | 392 |

| 417 | 416 | 415 | 414 | 413 | 412 | 411 | 410 | 409 | 408 | 407 | 406 | 405 |
| 430 | 429 | 428 | 427 | 426 | 425 | 424 | 423 | 422 | 421 | 420 | 419 | 418 |

| 443 | 442 | 441 | 440 | 439 | 438 | 437 | 436 | 435 | 434 | 433 | 432 | 431 |
| 456 | 455 | 454 | 453 | 452 | 451 | 450 | 449 | 448 | 447 | 446 | 445 | 444 |

        | 468 | 467 | 466 | 465 | 464 | 463 | 462 | 461 | 460 | 459 | 458 | 457 |
              | 479 | 478 | 477 | 476 | 475 | 474 | 473 | 472 | 471 | 470 | 469 |
```

N ←

Middleburg Memorial Cemetery
Third Section

Lot: Unidentified

Mary Louise Greer	B: 16 Aug 1914	D: 24 Dec 1985
Robert L. Kerns, Jr	B: 1935	D: 1992
Annabelle Walker	B: 1916	D: 1996
Barbara Jean Furr Waugerman	B: 4 Mar 1938	no death date

Lot: 1   **Lot Owner: Walter Leith**

Gertrude Wright Leith	B: 10 May 1898	D: 26 Nov 1980
Walter Gregg Leith	B: 27 Jul 1897	D: 6 Apr 1971
Peggy Leith Schneider	B: 21 Oct 1924	D: 16 Nov 1986
Ray Schneider	B: 21 May 1917	no death date

Lot: 2   **Lot Owner: Walter Leith**

Ada F. Leith	B: 17 May 1896	D: 18 Oct 1979
Arthur L. Leith	B: 20 Feb 1892	D: 17 Jun 1974
Francis Marion Leith	B: 22 Aug 1910	D: 24 Jan 1985
Harriet McGregor Leith	B: 4 Aug 1908	D: 10 Jan 1970
Henrietta Tiffany Leith	B: 17 Nov 1890	D: 12 Oct 1982
Mamie E. Leith	B: 11 Sep 1896	D: 9 Oct 1986
Randolph H. Leith	B: 8 May 1895	D: 17 Dec 1981
Theodric Bryant Leith	B: 4 Jan 1894	D: 1 Feb 1974

Lot: 3(1-4)   **Lot Owner: Roberta Seipp**

Ellen Seipp Mackethan	B: 30 Sep 1932	D: 6 Aug 1974
John Tyrrell, Esq	B: 14 Oct 1870	D: 11 Dec 1957

Lot: 3(5-8)   **Lot Owner: Thomas Kirby**

Anne S. Kirby	B: 1 Aug 1905	D: 27 Oct 1992 w/o Thomas
Thomas Kirby	B: 20 Dec 1907	no death date h/o Anne S. Kirby
Jean K. Leonard	B: 11 Sep 1931	D: 9 Feb 1982 w/o Robert G. Leonard Jr
Robert G. Leonard, Jr	B: 2 Dec 1930	no death date

Lot: 4   Lot Owner: Roberta Seipp

Roberta Tyrrell Seipp	B: 4 Dec 1902	D: 27 Aug 1994
William Conrad Seipp	B: 18 Oct 1889	D: 26 Jul 1962 born Chicago

Lot: 5(1-4)   Lot Owner: Lewis Gibb

Jean Regan Gibb	B: 3 May 1908	D: 29 Dec 1983
Lewis Mills Gibb	B: 30 Oct 1902	D: 24 Jan 1971

Lot : 5(5-8)   Lot Owner: Carlton Rutledge

Elias Ball Rutledge	B: 1860	D: 1939
Emmeline Rutledge	B: 1895	D: 1936
Marie Rose Rutledge	B: 1912	D: 1994
Mary Isabel Rutledge	B: 1861	D: 1951

Lot: 6   Lot Owner: Archie Smith

Archie Magill Smith	B: 1877	D: 1953
Mary Turner Smith	B: 3 Sep 1884	D: 29 Jul 1939

Lot: 7(1-4)   Lot Owner: Otto Furr

Dallas Otto Furr	B: 6 Jan 1886	D: 31 Oct 1947
Daniel Otto Furr, Jr	B: 20 Jul 1919	D: 19 Oct 1963
Elizabeth S. Furr	B: 4 Jul 1897	D: 26 Oct 1958

Lot: 7(1-4)   Lot Owner: Edward Waddell

Frances Waddell Rash	B: 20 Sep 1931	D: 28 Jul 1951
Roy Lee Rash	B: 3 Dec 1929	D: 28 Jul 1951
Edward Thomas Waddell	B: 14 Jul 1909	D: 1 Oct 1983
Helen Jeffries Waddell	B: 21 Jan 1910	D: 24 Feb 1979

Lot: 8   Lot Owner: Grover Hatcher

Amelia R. Hatcher	B: 19 Feb 1896	D: 8 Sep 1980
Benton S. Hatcher	B: 20 Feb 1921	D: 7 Oct 1967 WWII
Grover C Hatcher, Jr	B: 17 Sep 1919	D: 16 Feb 1991
Grover C. Hatcher	B: 18 Oct 1885	D: 24 Sep 1951

Martha L. Hatcher	B: 22 Jan 1923	D: 20 Jun 1969

Lot: 9   Lot Owner: Robert L. Humphrey

Ethel Boss Humphrey	B: 30 Aug 1896	D: 23 Sep 1988 "Mudea"
Gladys J. Humphrey	B: 9 Jul 1923	D: 15 Dec 1994 WWII
Dr Robert Lee Humphrey	B: 1883	D: 1954
	s/o William Lodge & Rose Moore	
William Rufus Humphrey	B: 30 Aug 1923	D: 14 Mar 1993 Korea

Lot: 10   Lot Owner: Mrs. Lula Powell & Robert Powell

Robert L. Campbell	B: 2 Mar 1932	D: 23 Mar 1994 Children on marker
Virginia L. Campbell	B: 19 Mar 1933	no death date
Bertie A. Powell	B: 6 Nov 1887	D: 5 Nov 1950
George C. Powell	B: 5 May 1885	D: 19 Sep 1954 Children on marker
Lula A. Powell	B: 2 Jun 1913	no death date
Robert Lee Powell	B: 7 Apr 1907	D: 17 Jan 1948

Lot: 11   Lot Owner: Ernest Dawson, Jr.

Ernest Lynwood Dawson	B: 16 Jun 1918	D: 29 Mar 1994 WWII
Marjorie B. Dawson	B: 18 Feb 1919	D: 4 May 1979
Thomas Earl Sacra	B: 13 Apr 1925	D: 8 Mar 1996

Lot: 12(1-4)   Lot Owner: Ernest Dawson, Sr.

Frances D. Canard	B: 30 Mar 1924	D: 6 Feb 1968
Robert M. Canard	B: 4 Dec 1923	D: 7 Oct 1974
Catherine A. Dawson	B: 13 Jun 1891	D: 1 Dec 1974
Ernest L. Dawson, Sr	B: 10 Aug 1889	D: 22 Nov 1947

Lot: 12(5-8)   Lot Owner: Alfred T. Patterson, Jr.

A.T. Patterson	B: 21 Apr 1913	D: 24 Dec 1950
Dorothy D. Sacra	B: 30 Mar 1915	D: 16 Dec 1964

Lot: 13A   Lot Owner: Furr

George W. Furr	B: 1886	D: 1947
Maudie R. Furr	B: 1913	no death date
Nettie K. Furr	B: 1887	D: 1980
Thomas F. Furr	B: 1911	D: 1981
Wilmer G. Hunsberger	B: 1917	D: 1976 WWII

Lot: 15   Lot Owner: Walter Leith

Wallace Friestedt	B: 1923	D: 1974
Frances M. Leith	B: 18 Oct 1941	D: 10 Oct 1987
Joseph E. Leith	B: 20 May 1899	D: 11 Apr 1976

Lot: 16   Lot Owner: Westfelt

| Frances Heyworth Westfelt | B: 1903 | D: 1969
born Lake Forest, IL |
| Pamela Westfelt | B: 1943 | D: 1960 |

Lot: 17   Lot Owner: Mae Frances Heflin

| Clarence Grimsley Heflin | B: 15 Mar 1886 | D: 27 Aug 1954 |
| Matilda Frances Heflin | B: 10 Jun 1887 | D: 22 Jan 1967 |

Lot: 18   Lot Owner: Livingston Johnson

Elizabeth Mayo Johnson	B: 16 Dec 1913	no death date w/o Livingston Lee Johnson
Livingston Lee Johnson	B: 1 Oct 1908	D: 11 Aug 1992 h/o Elizabeth Mayo
Livingston S. Johnson	B: 24 Jun 1877	D: 12 Mar 1957
Nellie Lee Johnson	B: 10 May 1880	D: 20 Oct 1964
Edmund G. Whitehead	B: 10 Jul 1909	D: 13 Sep 1985
Marion J. Whitehead	B: 12 Jun 1912	D: 10 Jan 1993

Lot: 19   Lot Owner: Clarence Furr

Clarence Furr	B: 28 Aug 1910	D: 30 Oct 1992
Claudia Furr	B: 28 Aug 1910	D: 11 Jan 1952
Louise Furr	B: 15 Jan 1879	D: 6 Mar 1945

Sally Carter Furr	B: 15 Dec 1914	no death date
Walter C. Furr	B: 16 Jun 1922	D: 19 May 1970
Woodrow Wilson Furr	B: 28 Aug 1918	D: 22 Jun 1960 WWII
Helen Alice Smith	B: 28 Jul 1904	D: 9 Jul 1965
Roley H. Smith	B: 10 May 1895	D: 19 Dec 1970

Lot: 20   Lot Owner: Nettie Byrne

Everett M. Byrne	B: 10 Sep 1883	D: 6 May 1956
Nettie A. Byrne	B: 10 Sep 1889	D: 29 Aug 1986

Lot: 22   Lot Owner: Richard & Terry Bell

Pamela Kay Bell	B: 5 May 1971	D: 7 Mar 1972

Lot: 23   Lot Owner: Mrs. Lula Powell

William Hayward Powell	B: 11 Jan 1911	D: 1 Feb 1965
William Henry Powell	B: 19 Feb 1920	D: 20 Nov 1971

Lot: 25   Lot Owner: Miscellaneous

Lee F. Hammer	B: 3 Nov 1870	D: 27 Apr 1953 Sp Am War
Anthony M. Soto	B: 28 Dec 1900	D: 4 Jul 1965
Verlene Mary Soto	B: 22 Sep 1914	D: 8 Jun 1986

Lot: 26A(1-4)   Lot Owner: John L. McIntyre

Annie V. McIntyre	B: 1913	D: 1982
Blanche G. McIntyre	B: 1876	D: 1951
J Lewis McIntyre	B: 1865	D: 1954
John W. McIntyre	B: 1915	no death date
Robert L. McIntyre	B: 24 Jan 1911	D: 14 Dec 1974

Lot: 26A(5-8)   Lot Owner: Grimes

John T. Grimes	B: 1889	D: 1948

Lot: 31   Lot Owner: Philip Connors

Constance Regan Connors	B: 18 Jun 1906	D: 3 Nov 1958
Philip Connors	B: 26 Jan 1903	D: 4 Jul 1972

Lot: 32   Lot Owner: Craun

Thomas Jesse Bell, III	B: 25 Jun 1967	D: 15 Dec 1986
Preston Hampton Craun	B: 7 Feb 1890	D: 19 Dec 1953 WWI
Mae Craun Dunbar	B: 11 Sep 1903	D: 24 Apr 1983
John Thomas Furr	B: 4 May 1907	D: 17 Jun 1963

Lot: 33   Lot Owner: Robert Sinclair

Lucille White Kerns	B: 9 May 1910	D: 20 Oct 1974
Annie G. Sinclair	B: 12 Jul 1906	D: 16 Feb 1971
George B. Sinclair	B: 22 Dec 1902	D: 28 May 1977

Lot 34(3-4)   Lot Owner: Jack A. Walters

| Jack Arthur Walters | B: 21 May 1905 | D: 4 Oct 1994 |
| Sabina Mae Walters | B: 3 May 1905 | D: 11 Feb 1990 |

Lot: 34(5-8)   Lot Owner: Elizabeth Ann Cockrell

| Dorothy L. Cockrell | B: 1911 | D: 1965 |
| J. Warren Cockrell | B: 1912 | D: 1965 |

Lot: 35(3-4)   Lot Owner: Stanley Edmond Wilson

| Stanley Edmund Wilson | B: 3 Feb 1909 | D: 29 Oct 1971 |
| Winifred Vansickler Wilson | B: 16 Jan 1910 | no death date |

Lot: 35(5-8)   Lot Owner: Betty Glascock

| Bettie Elizabeth Glascock | B: 27 Jul 1906 | D: 15 Oct 1992 |
| Beverly Earl Glascock | B: 13 Aug 1929 | D: 11 Sep 1997 |

Lot: 36   Lot Owner:

| Militza Maryann Hunter | B: 1 Mar 1923 | D: 30 Jun 1990 |

Lot 37(1-4)   Lot Owner: John Mitchell

| Hildegarde Mitchell | B: 1909 | D: 1975 |
| John Mitchell | B: 15 Oct 1895 | D: 26 Jan 1968 WWI & WWII |

Lot: 37   **Lot Owner: Vaino & Ruth Ala**

Ruth Polen Ala	B: 13 Oct 1917	D: 15 Jul 1992
Vaino Jonathan Ala	B: 1913	D: 1982
		WWII

Lot: 38   **Lot Owner: Norris A.L. Royston**

Anna Elizabeth Haga Edwards	B: 1941	D: 1996
Charles R. Haga	B: 24 Oct 1911	D: 17 Sep 1968
Mary Jane Haga	B: 10 Sep 1910	D: 12 Oct 1971
Bertha Warren Royston	B: 1912	D: 1985
Lewis H. Royston	B: 1871	D: 1951
Mamie E. Royston	B: 1887	D: 1972
Norris Royston	B: 1902	D: 1970
		Masonic

Lot: 39   **Lot Owner: Joseph Mulford**

Joseph Minot Mulford	B: 26 Oct 1889	D: 31 Jul 1970
Laura Jan McMartin Mulford	B: 11 Jun 1903	D: 1 Sep 1979
Elizabeth Van Schuylenburgh	B: 10 Aug 1930	D: 5 Sep 1954

Lot: 39A   **Lot Owner: Not Given**

G.R. Tartiere	B: Mar 1892	D: Mar 1993
R.F. Tartiere	B: Jul 1881	D: Aug 1950

Lot: 40   **Lot Owner: Not Given**

Barrington E. Basil Hall	B: 7 Jun 1895	D: 20 Oct 1961
Constance M. Hall	B: 6 Sep 1866	D: 18 Dec 1949
G. Basil Hall	B: 1 Jan 1863	D: 26 Jan 1943
V. Mary D. Hall	B: 4 Oct 1896	D: 18 Jan 1954

Lot: 43   **Lot Owner: Louis C. Dimos**

Louis C. Dimos	B: 28 Mar 1897	D: 23 Oct 1966
		born in greece
Vasiliki M. Dimos	B: 28 Oct 1905	D: 16 Jul 1991

Lot: 44   **Lot Owner: Miscellaneous**

Dorothy Lee Miller   B: 5 Apr 1932   D: 16 Aug 1990

Lot: 45   **Lot Owner: Miscellaneous**

Alcernon S. Davy   B: 11 Nov 1894   D: 5 Sep 1964

Mary W. Davy   B: 29 May 1905   D: 28 Feb 1988

Christopher M. Greer   B: 1898   D: 1960

Marguerite Greer   B: 1894   D: 1976

Lot: 46   **Lot Owner: Florence Howdershell**

Margaret Ann Gregg   B: 27 Nov 1928   D: 3 Nov 1993

Florence M. Howdershell   B: 3 Dec 1916   no death date

Nellie K. Howdershell   B: 1894   D: 1974

Robert D. Howdershell   B: 1891   D: 1976

Lot: 47   **Lot Owner: Payne**

Bettie Melvilla Melton Payne   B: 23 Mar 1907   D: 1 Aug 1987
                                        w/o Lucien Thomas Payne Sr

Llewellyn Eugene Payne   B: 20 Jun 1932   D: 1 Sep 1983
                                        s/o Lucien & Bettie Payne

Lucien Thomas Payne, Sr   B: 27 Jul 1899   D: 28 Oct 1995
                                        Children named on marker

Lot: 48   **Lot Owner: Lawrence D. & Darlane L. Payne**

Darlane L. Payne   B: 1935   no death date

Lawrence D. Payne   B: 1930   D: 1996

Lot: 50   **Lot Owner: Robert B. Young**

Robert B. Young   B: 23 Jul 1907   D: 10 Apr 1980

Sybil W. Young   B: 3 Nov 1910   D: 12 Apr 1977

Lot: 52   **Lot Owner: Miscellaneous**

Hugh Duncan Brown   B: 23 Apr 1954   D: 16 Dec 1989

Lot: 53   **Lot Owner: Miscellaneous**

Elizabeth Fishback Wine   B: 28 Jul 1918   D: 20 Dec 1993

Walter Wesley Wine   B: 6 Aug 1916   D: 3 Nov 1993

Lot: 53A   Lot Owner: Miscellaneous

David Mark McCready	B: 2 Feb 1955	D: 31 Jul 1995
		h/o Linda Marie
Linda Marie McCready	B: 15 Apr 1952	no death date
		w/o David Mark

Lot: 68   Lot Owner: Miscellaneous

Dorothy Jones	B: 1894	D: 1945
		w/o William Empson Jones
Dorothy Margaret Jones	B: 27 May 1923	D: 1 Mar 1998
William Empson Jones	B: 1888	D: 1953

Lot: 82   Lot Owner: Miscellaneous

Eleanor Nichols Sharp	B: 24 Feb 1914	D: 27 Sep 1996
Freda G. Sharp	B: 1884	D: 1963
Frederick W. Sharp	B: 1880	D: 1957
Frederick W. Sharp, Jr.	B: 2 Mar 1911	D: 15 Nov 1998

Lot: 97   Lot Owner: Pauline King

Allen T. Edmonds	B: 1 Oct 1927	D: 19 Dec 1969
Carroll Edmonds	B: 2 May 1884	D: 25 Nov 1957
Phil W. Edmonds	B: 7 Nov 1921	D: 29 Sep 1975
George E. King	B: 30 Jan 1942	D: 20 Feb 1967
Hazel V. Smith	B: 5 Sep 1943	D: 18 Nov 1973

Lot: 112   Lot Owner: Miscelleneous

Frank C. Edmonds	B: 24 Sep 1907	D: 10 Nov 1970
Mildred L. Edmonds	B: 1925	no death date
Wilson D. Edmonds	B: 1918	D: 1992
		h/o Mildred L.
Philip F. German	B: 24 Apr 1928	D: 15 Dec 1989

Lot: 127   Lot Owner: Miscellaneous

Garland Fields	B: 31 Aug 1936	D: 11 Jan 1987
Carter F. Riley	B: 19 Jul 1914	D: 21 Dec 1984

Lot: 206   **Lot Owner: Miscellaneous**

Wilmer Russel Kerns   B: 6 Dec 1937   D: 28 Apr 1976

Lot: 210   **Lot Owner: Josephine Swart Lanham**

Josephine Swart Lanham   B: 7 Apr 1896   D: 18 Feb 1985

Walter Scott Woodward   B: 20 Nov 1916   D: 31 Dec 1985
                                                    WWII

Lot: 213   **Lot Owner: Miscellaneous**

Edward Lynn Dodson   B: 29 Jun 1946   D: 18 Oct 1992

Lot: 236   **Lot Owner: Frederick A. Crisman, Jr.**

Arvilla E. Crisman   B: 8 Oct 1926   D: 13 Jul 1982

Frederick A. Crisman, Jr   B: 9 Mar 1923   D: 2 May 1989
                                                    WWII

Lot: 236   **Lot Owner: Alice Fowble**

Alice M. Fowble   B: 1909   D: 1995

J. Alex Fowble   B: 1905   D: 1984

Lot: 237   **Lot Owner: Hazel & Roy Lanham**

Hazel L. Lanham   B: 1930   no death date

Roy F. Lanham   B: 1920   D: 1992

Lot: 237   **Lot Owner: Minnie P. Leonard**

Harry Lee Leonard   B: 12 Aug 1903   D: 3 Nov 1982

Minnie Payne Leonard   B: 23 Jun 1908   no death date

Lot: 238   **Lot Owner: Miscellaneous**

Harry Tullos Dunn   B: 18 Aug 1894   D: 23 Jan 1995

Lot: 244   **Lot Owner: Philo Cockerille**

Daisy D. Cockerille   B: 9 Sep 1882   D: 18 Sep 1969

Lot: 248   **Lot Owner: Mary M. Brown**

James Arnold Benton   B: 8 Oct 1909   D: 11 Apr 1991

Alton G. Brown   B: 1918   D: 1985

Mary M. Brown   B: 1917   D: 1994

Lot: 249   Lot Owner: Delbert Cain

Delbert Wilson Cain, Sr   B: 2 Aug 1945   D: 31 Dec 1984

Lot: 249   Lot Owner: Edward G. Williams

Aaron C. Williams   B: 16 Nov 1982   D: 28 Oct 1986

Tabitha S. Williams   B: 26 Mar 1984   D: 28 Oct 1986

Lot: 250   Lot Owner:

Mary Catherine Spurlock   B: 15 Jul 1960   D: 22 Aug 1995

Lot: 251   Lot Owner: Gertrude Herger

Eleonor L. Herger   B: 1878   D: 1967

Frances H. Herger   B: 1880   D: 1954

Gertrude L. Herger   B: 1892   D: 1961

Lot: 252   Lot Owner: Philo Cockerille

Eula I. Cockerille   B: 1914   D: 1987

Philo C. Cockerille   B: 1912   D: 1980

Richard J. Cockerille   B: 8 Jun 1938   D: 3 Oct 1955

Lot: 255   Lot Owner:Janet Faye Suddueth

Beverley S. Suddueth   B: 18 Jun 1917   D: 2 Feb 1980

Janet Faye Suddueth   B: 2 Jan 1938   no death date

Lot: 256   Lot Owner: Ira Raymond Kestner

Ira Raymond Kestner   B: 7 Oct 1898   D: 15 Mar 1974
                                                                          WWI

Lot: 256   Lot Owner: Zachary Taylor

Bryant Leach   B: 3 Dec 1903   D: 29 Oct 1979

Rush M. Leach   B: 19 Nov 1908   D: 1 Oct 1974

Virginia C. Taylor   B: 1908   D: 1989

Wade Leith Taylor   B: 25 Dec 1931   D: 28 Sep 1995
                                                                          Korea

Zachary Taylor, Sr   B: 1902   D: 1977

Lot: 257   Lot Owner: Charles Kirk

Charles Elmer Kirk   B: 22 Jan 1898   D: 24 May 1984

Lot: 261   Lot Owner: Lois Diane Leonard

Clarence C. Leonard	B: 17 May 1927	D: 10 Apr 1980
Lois Diane Leonard	B: 5 Dec 1955	D: 4 Apr 1956
Lois E. Leonard	B: 1931	no death date
Richard O. Leonard	B: 1922	D: 1988
Bobby Iden Jr Popkins		D: 5 Jan 1979

Lot: 264   Lot Owner: William Canard

| Nellie Ann Canard | B: 23 Jul 1932 | D: 23 Jul 1973 |
| William Canard | B: 1926 | D: 1976 Korea |

Lot: 264   Lot Owner: Joseph Cornell

| Joseph W. Cornell, Jr | B: 1910 | D: 1984 |
| Nellie L. Cornell | B: 1914 | D: 1975 |

Lot: 265   Lot Owner: William E. Kirk, Sr.

| William E. Kirk, Jr | B: 2 Mar 1952 | D: 16 Jul 1973 |

Lot: 269   Lot Owner: J.S. Buck

| James S. Buck | B: 1901 | D: 1991 |
| Wanda P. Buck | B: 1903 | D: 1991 |

Lot: 269   Lot Owner: Strother White

| Gillie White | B: 1914 | D: 1977 |
| Strother T. White | B: 1913 | no death date |

Lot: 270   Lot Owner: Alfred G. Leonard

William Bolt	B: 1937	D: 1997
Alfred G. Leonard	B: 7 Apr 1913	no death date
Calvin Lee Leonard	B: 5 Apr 1948	D: 16 Jun 1952

Lot: 271   Lot Owner: Alfred Leonard

| Margaret A. Leonard | B: 21 Feb 1925 | no death date |

Lot: 272   Lot Owner: James Humphrey Leonard

| J Humphrey Leonard | B: 1883 | D: 1963 |
| Larry M. Leonard | B: 10 Feb 1959 | D: 26 Mar 1988 |

| Lester M. Jr Leonard | B: 28 Aug 1966 | D: 10 Jun 1967 |
| Levie C. Leonard | B: 1881 | D: 1962 |

Lot: 274   Lot Owner: Miscellaneous

Jack L. Leonard	B: 1936	no death date
Ruth A. Leonard	B: 1934	D: 1993
Elmo Thomas Sr Wines	B: 19 Apr 1912	D: 10 Apr 1992 WWII
Pearl M. Wines	B: 29 Sep 1906	D: 29 Apr 1996

Lot: 275   Lot Owner: Luther Costello

| Emma Katherine Costello | B: 1 Apr 1913 | D: 28 Dec 1995 |
| Luther L. Costello | B: 1904 | D: 1954 |

Lot: 278   Lot Owner: Ruth Ellen Bolt

| Charlie T. Bolt | B: 16 Dec 1905 | D: 25 Oct 1971 |
| Ruth E. Bolt | B: 13 Nov 1906 | D: 10 Sep 1984 |

Lot: 279   Lot Owner: Daniel Bolt

Cecil C. Bolt	B: 21 Jan 1897	D: 5 Aug 1954
Daniel J. Bolt	B: 13 Feb 1918	D: 23 May 1945 WWII
Lucy M. Bolt	B: 25 Nov 1878	D: 13 Oct 1949
Walter L. Bolt	B: 21 Nov 1916	D: 15 May 1970 WWII

Lot: 280   Lot Owner: Page Howdershell

Leila T. Howdershell	B: 1892	D: 1989
Page Howdershell	B: 1896	D: 1983
Ethel M. Rhodes	B: 6 Sep 1901	D: 8 May 1965
John W. Rhodes	B: 30 Sep 1894	D: 1 Apr 1952 WWI

Lot: 281   Lot Owner: Miscellaneous

| Kennard C. Bolt | B: 4 Jan 1915 | D: 29 Mar 1968 |
| Marie D. Bolt | B: 4 Mar 1916 | no death date |

John William Rhodes, Jr   B: 23 Sep 1922   D: 10 Jan 1989
WWII

Lot: 282   Lot Owner: Roberta Ann Edwards

Amon S. Edwards   B: 22 Nov 1884   D: 15 Sep 1973

Roberta G. Edwards   B: 1 Feb 1883   D: 16 Jan 1953

Lot: 283   Lot Owner: Miscellaneous

Betty Simpson Howdershell   B: 1929   no death date

Charles L. Howdershell, Sr   B: 1927   no death date

Charles Lee Howdershell, Jr   B: 1968   D: 1987

Hattie Mae Stream   B: 16 Jun 1906   D: 6 Jul 1995

Lot: 284   Lot Owner: Pierre Gruen

Pierre Gruen   B: 21 Apr 1916   D: 10 Jun 1977

Lot: 284   Lot Owner: William Francis Pearson

Dorothy H. Pearson   B: 1918   no death date

W Francis Pearson   B: 1914   D: 1991

Lot: 285   Lot Owner: Aranka L. Mehely

Aranka L. Mehely   B: 22 Sep 1900   D: 8 May 1981

Lot: 289   Lot Owner: Fred Griffith

Fred W. Griffith   B: 7 Mar 1872   D: 15 Aug 1946

Pamela B. Griffith   B: 19 Oct 1874   D: 6 Mar 1965

Lot: 290   Lot Owner: John S. Cole

Charity B. Cole   B: 19 Jun 1911   D: 21 Oct 1986

Earlie S. Cole   B: 2 Jan 1928   D: 14 Apr 1947
WWII

John S. Cole   B: 2 Sep 1906   D: 7 Jul 1975

John Thomas Cole   B: 1 Dec 1929   D: 2 Nov 1968

Lot: 292   Lot Owner: William Collie

Charles Tibbs Cockerille   B: 1883   D: 1954

Lucy Summers Cockerille   B: 1874   D: 1949

Agnes McBey Collie   B: 11 Jan 1882   D: 25 May 1948

Lot: 293   **Lot Owner: James W. Ashton**

James Ware Roger Ashton   B: 1 Sep 1912   D: 18 Dec 1994

Lot: 295   **Lot Owner: Joseph Huffman**

Yu Lee Jeanette Huffman   B: 5 Mar 1952   D: 7 Aug 1952

Lot: 296   **Lot Owner: Miscellaneous**

John Foster Bolt   B: 21 Aug 1901   D: 2 Mar 1957

Lot: 297   **Lot Owner: Miscellaneous**

Stephan Ross Ames   B: 12 Oct 1960   D: 11 Oct 1991

Lot: 300   **Lot Owner: Nelson Warren**

Nelson P. Warren, Jr   B: 1939   D: 1979

Lot: 301   **Lot Owner: Walter Kirk**

Ida V. Kirk   B: 1876   D: 1960

Walter Elmer Kirk   B: 17 Nov 1876   D: 16 Nov 1939

Lot: 302   **Lot Owner: Charles Triplett**

Annie L. Triplett   B: 25 Jun 1901   D: 30 May 1976

Charles B. Triplett   B: 11 Aug 1860   D: 22 Jun 1942

Emma Lee Triplett   B: 8 Sep 1868   D: 7 Mar 1959

Lot: 303   **Lot Owner: Willie Jenkins**

Mary B. Jenkins   B: 29 May 1910   D: 9 Dec 1996

Willie Jenkins   B: 19 Jan 1912   D: 15 Nov 1976

Lot: 304   **Lot Owner: Robert Skinner**

Robert I. Skinner   B: 12 Jan 1890   D: 15 Feb 1966

Virginia H. Skinner   B: 29 Nov 1886   D: 7 Apr 1974

Lot: 305   **Lot Owner: Webb & Catherine Kirkpatrick**

Catherine M. Kirkpatrick   B: 1910   D: 1994

Webb D. Kirkpatrick   B: 1913   D: 1995

Lot: 306   **Lot Owner: John Alexander**

John Alexander   B: 1907   D: 1982
WWII

Lot: 307   Lot Owner: Linda Griffith Jenkins

Linda Griffith Jenkins   B: 29 Apr 1952   D: 21 Jun 1985

Lot: 313   Lot Owner: Miscellaneous

Nora Lee Benton   B: 7 Nov 1866   D: 15 May 1945

Henrietta Carter   B: 1 Jan 1875   D: 23 Apr 1956

Lot: 314   Lot Owner: William Alexander

Bertha E. Alexander   B: 1886   D: 1971

William Alexander   B: 1871   D: 1945

Lot: 316   Lot Owner: Humphrey O. Dodson

Humphrey O. Dodson   B: 1908   D: 1973

Louise P. Kloeppinger   B: 1909   D: 1985

Milton Kloeppinger   B: 1903   D: 1993

Lot: 317   Lot Owner: Robert L. Frazier, Sr.

Irene Frazier   B: 1920   D: 1972

Robert L. Frazier   B: 1922   D: 1992

Lot: 318   Lot Owner: Margaret W. Gordon

Margaret W. Gordon   B: 1921   no death date

Raymond M. Jr Gordon   B: 1923   D: 1975
                                                                  WWII

Lot: 318   Lot Owner: Clayton Tinsman

Andrew Clayton Tinsman, Sr   B: 1908   D: 1989

Helen B. Tinsman   B: 1918   no death date

Lot: 319   Lot Owner: Richard Griffith

Agnes S. Cornell   B: 1908   D: 1988

John W. Cornell   B: 1902   D: 1963

Richard M. Griffith   B: 16 Aug 1912   D: 21 Dec 1952
                                                                  WWII

Lot: 320   Lot Owner: James W. Waddell, Sr.

Fannie M. Waddell   B: 1917   no death date

James W. Waddell, Sr   B: 1912   D: 1981

Lot: 321   Lot Owner: Randall Ballenger

| Betty Jane Ballenger | B: 26 Dec 1943 | D: 1 May 1982 |
| Donna Renea Warring | B: 7 Dec 1967 | D: 1 May 1982 |

Lot: 325   Lot Owner: Miscellaneous

| James Edward Leonard | B: 25 Feb 1907 | D: 21 Feb 1986 |
| Pauline G. Leonard | B: 8 Oct 1914 | D: 5 Oct 1945 |

Lot: 326   Lot Owner: Miscellaneous

| Hunton G. Leonard | B: 8 May 1914 | D: 15 Mar 1992 |
| Madie M. Leonard | B: 9 Jul 1920 | D: 8 Oct 1957 |

Lot: 327   Lot Owner: Charles Orebaugh

| Charles C. Orebaugh | B: 1888 | D: 1958 |
| Roberta L. Orebaugh | B: 1904 | D: 1985 |

Lot: 328   Lot Owner: Edna Payne

| Edna E. Payne | B: 1894 | D: 1985 |

Lot: 329   Lot Owner: Norman E. Kirk, Sr.

Annie S. Kirk	B: 7 Jan 1899	D: 18 May 1972
Norman E. Kirk, Jr	B: 1925	D: 1950
Norman E. Kirk, Sr	B: 20 Jan 1896	D: 15 Apr 1980

Lot: 330   Lot Owner:

| Katherine K. Cornish | B: 1915 | no death date |
| James F. Young | B: 9 Jan 1906 | D: 13 Aug 1980 |

Lot: 331   Lot Owner: William & Eleanor Gordon

| William Lee Mickie Gordon | B: 29 Sep 1927 | D: 2 Jun 1996 WWII |
| Myrtle F. Monroe | B: 1907 | D: 1996 |

Lot: 332   Lot Owner: William T. Gray

| Dorothy K. Gray | B: 1914 | D: 1996 |
| William T. Gray | B: 1914 | D: 1951 |

Lot: 338   Lot Owner: Miscellaneous

Mollie Leonard Kelly	B: 1876	D: 1958
Frieda A.K. Leonard	B: 1926	no death date
Sam Leonard	B: 1929	D: 1988

Lot: 339   Lot Owner: Jenkins

Charles C. Downs	B: 1909	D: 1958
Lucy C. Downs	B: 1904	D: 1974
Charles Jenkins	B: 1861	D: 1946
Susie Jenkins	B: 1872	D: 1948

Lot: 340   Lot Owner: Ernest Lee Leonard

| Ernest Lee Leonard | B: 22 Feb 1942 | D: 3 Oct 1979 |
| Fannie B. McDavid | B: 18 May 1914 | D: 20 Apr 1970 |

Lot: 341   Lot Owner: Francis P. Moffett

| Betty A. Moffett | B: 1930 | no death date |
| Francis P. Moffett | B: 1930 | D: 1987 |

Lot: 342   Lot Owner: Lula Bridge

Bennie Bridge	B: 13 Mar 1910	D: 29 Jan 1969
Lula Bridge	B: 15 Apr 1870	D: 2 Jun 1953
Rixey Bridge	B: 4 May 1905	D: 24 Feb 1956
Willie Bridge	B: 29 May 1899	D: 12 Dec 1955

Lot: 343   Lot Owner: Mrs. Alma Bridge

Alma Ann Bridge	B: 6 Dec 1916	no death date
Preston Bridge	B: 4 Apr 1913	D: 14 Apr 1959
Rose Lee Payne	B: 1935	no death date
Wyatt E. Payne	B: 1928	no death date

Lot: 344   Lot Owner: Elith Larsen

| Elith V. Larsen | B: 19 Sep 1891 | D: 24 Aug 1949 |
| Mabel I. Larsen | B: 12 May 1918 | D: 21 Dec 1975 |

Lot: 345   Lot Owner: Miscellaneous

A. Marie Elkins	B: 3 Oct 1935	D: 20 Nov 1995
Cecil E. Sr Elkins	B: 1 Sep 1934	no death date
Leetha E. Embrey	B: 1905	D: 1951
Maurice T. Embrey	B: 1904	D: 1991

Lot: 351   Lot Owner: Frances Leonard

Brandon Corey Lee Aikens	B: 16 Dec 1994	D: 12 Jan 1995
Frances L. Leonard	B: 1917	D: 1985
Noah W. Leonard	B: 24 Dec 1897	D: 31 Dec 1966
Robert L. Leonard	B: 1909	D: 1978
Ruby J. Leonard	B: 1935	D: 1979

Lot: 352   Lot Owner:Gordon C. Purvis

| Gordon Charles Purvis | B: 12 Nov 1907 | D: 9 Apr 1946 |

Lot: 353   Lot Owner: Miscellaneous

| Josephine Waddell Burton | B: 13 May 1918 | D: 14 Jan 1952 |

Lot: 354   Lot Owner: Thomas & Nettie Hancock

Harvey L. Downs	B: 1904	D: 1971
Nettie Lee Hancock	B: 1898	D: 1990
Thomas W. Hancock	B: 1921	D: 1989

Lot: 355   Lot Owner: Raymond Kirk

| Annie E. Kirk | B: 8 May 1903 | D: 2 Feb 1989 |
| Raymond E. Kirk | B: 25 Feb 1900 | D: 24 Apr 1982 |

Lot: 356   Lot Owner: Marvin Hitt

| Marvin M. Hitt | B: 1896 | D: 1971 |
| Melissa C. Hitt | B: 1898 | D: 1960 |

Lot: 357   Lot Owner: Stuart Otis Burton

Nellie B. Burton	B: 20 May 1898	D: 1 Feb 1987
Nora F. Burton	B: 15 Jun 1928	D: 16 Jul 1989
Stuart E. Burton	B: 8 Oct 1922	D: 5 Feb 1975

Stuart O. Burton	B: 11 Sep 1898	D: 7 Jan 1974

Lot: 358   Lot Owner: Lester R. Bennett

Lesley Jean Bennett	B: 21 Sep 1962	D: 10 Mar 1975
Lester Raymond Bennett	B: 8 Mar 1898	D: 12 Jul 1990
Minnie Aliene Bennett	B: 15 Aug 1901	D: 26 Oct 1993

Lot: 365   Lot Owner: Wesley Leonard

Keith F. Leonard	B: 1973	D: 1996 s/o Paul & Violet
Paul Wesley Leonard	B: 1915	D: 1995
Violet B. Leonard	B: 1916	D: 1997

Lot: 366   Lot Owner: Nancy & Allen Lee

Allen Louis Lee	B: 1921	no death date
Nancy Baxter Lee	B: 7 Sep 1943	D: 1 Apr 1946
Peggy Alice Polen Lee	B: 1925	D: 1994

Lot: 367   Lot Owner: A.S. Downs

Adlai Stevenson Downs	B: 3 Nov 1891	D: 17 Jul 1955
Margaret M. Downs	B: 15 Feb 1895	D: 25 Feb 1973
Alice Baxter Polen	B: 24 Jan 1885	D: 11 May 1954
Clayton L. Polen	B: 4 Apr 1878	D: 30 Nov 1959

Lot: 368   Lot Owner: Joseph C. Polen

Joseph Clayton Polen	B: 11 Jan 1922	D: 6 May 1971

Lot: 369   Lot Owner: Harry Lambert

Dollie E. Lambert	B: 1914	D: 1985
Harry S. Lambert	B: 1914	D: 1992

Lot: 370   Lot Owner: William Leach

James L. Lambert	B: 28 Jul 1935	D: 21 Sep 1954
William M. Leach	B: 20 Aug 1872	D: 13 Mar 1957

Lot: 370   Lot Owner: Woodville & Hazel Price

Hazel R. Price	B: 26 Feb 1910	D: 24 Dec 1992
Woodville G. Price, Sr	B: 6 Aug 1906	D: 9 Dec 1987

Lot: 371   Lot Owner: Miscellaneous

| Callie C. Furr | B: 13 Apr 1882 | D: 21 Nov 1949 |
| Warren J. Furr | B: 25 Sep 1881 | D: 13 Sep 1949 |

Lot: 372   Lot Owner: Carlton L. Shackelford

| Anita M. Shackelford | B: 1909 | D: 1983 |
| Carlton L. Shackelford | B: 1908 | D: 1985 |

Lot: 374   Lot Owner: Thomas & Leeta Cherrix

| Thomas Kallen Cherrix | B: 7 Apr 1982 | D: 16 Apr 1982 |

Lot: 379   Lot Owner: Harry Leonard

Alice C. Leonard	B: 22 Aug 1912	D: 2 Sep 1986
Elisha M. Leonard	B: 17 Jul 1900	D: 28 May 1967
Harry Leonard	B: 1903	D: 1972
Nettie M. Leonard	B: 1904	D: 1973

Lot: 380   Lot Owner: William H. Downs

Mary Alice Downs	B: 10 Jan 1875	D: 7 Nov 1939
Mary Elizabeth Downs	B: 1912	D: 1989
Willard A. Downs	B: 13 Mar 1910	D: 23 Nov 1967
William H. Downs	B: 15 Aug 1876	D: 2 Oct 1946

Lot: 381   Lot Owner: William R. & Hattie Jackson

| John Edward Jackson | B: 31 May 1943 | D: 2 Jun 1943 |
| William R. Jackson | B: 1 Dec 1913 | D: 8 Mar 1987 |

Lot: 382   Lot Owner: William Byrne

| Florence G. Byrne | B: 10 Jun 1889 | D: 22 Nov 1973 |
| William N. Byrne | B: 1862 | D: 1944 |

Lot: 383   Lot Owner: Albert Leith

Albert H. Leith	B: 1884	D: 1967
Bennie F. Sr Leith	B: 1914	D: 1964
Mary L. Leith	B: 1888	D: 1978
Patricia A. Leith	B: 1919	D: 1978

Lot: 385   Lot Owner: Miss Lula Powell

Harry T. Powell   B: 11 Apr 1923   D: 30 Oct 1977

Lot: 386   Lot Owner: Preston Joseph Bridge

Fern M. Bridge   B: 1944   no death date

Preston J. Bridge   B: 1940   no death date

Wanda L. Bridge   B: 1966   D: 1985

Jessie Dawson   B: 1928   no death date

W. Warren Dawson   B: 1927   D: 1990

Lot: 387   Lot Owner: Marjory Leonard

Timothy Wayne Dodson   B: 16 Jan 1958   D: 19 Dec 1990
                                                        Bubby

Katie Marjory Leonard   B: 1 Oct 1916   D: 24 Feb 1981

Nevel L. Leonard   B: 9 Oct 1911   D: 21 Nov 1980

Lot: 388   Lot Owner: Miscellaneous

Rosalie Nash   B: 25 Jun 1933   D: 24 Feb 1985

Lot: 392   Lot Owner: Miscellaneous

Harry A. Dunn   B: 5 Jan 1874   D: 28 Jul 1947

Lot: 393   Lot Owner: William H. Downs

Gordon L. Downs   B: 1919   no death date

Mabel S. Downs   B: 1916   no death date

Phillip Lindsey Downs   B: 26 Oct 1915   D: 9 Jan 1991
                                                         WWII

Lot: 395   Lot Owner: Vivian R. Cameron

Jennitt F. Cameron   B: 2 Jun 1902   D: 14 Mar 1981

Vivian R. Cameron   B: 3 Jan 1899   D: 16 Mar 1990

Lot: 396   Lot Owner: James R. Jenkins

Helen C. Jenkins   B: 1924   D: 1975

James R. Jenkins   B: 1921   no death date

Lot: 397   Lot Owner: Zachary Clemens

Catherine G. Clemens	B: 1924	D: 1991
Zachary T. Clemens	B: 1914	D: 1991

Lot: 398   Lot Owner: Astor & Mattie Godwin

Mattie Griffith Godwin	B: 21 Feb 1914	D: 7 Feb 1991

Lot: 399   Lot Owner: Miscellaneous

Lewis D. Glascock	B: 1928	D: 1995
Louise E. Woodward	B: 1924	no death date

Lot: 401   Lot Owner: Miscellaneous

Jedidiah William Law	B: 26 Oct 1981	D: 16 Jan 1987

Lot: 405   Lot Owner: Claudius Poland

Claudius E. Poland	B: 1901	D: 1958
Cornelius F. Poland	B: 1875	D: 1945
Dorothea S. Poland	B: 1902	D: 1991

Lot: 406   Lot Owner: John W. Rhodes

Margaret R. Farrow	B: 13 Jan 1942	D: 8 Nov 1977
John Rhodes	B: 11 Jan 1914	D: 2 Jul 1994 WWII
John Richard Rhodes		D: 1946
Orville Neilson Rhodes		D: 1947
Marion L. Shannon	B: 1888	D: 1967

Lot: 407   Lot Owner: Henry Houchins

Elsie Louise Houchins	B: 1 Sep 1937	D: 10 Dec 1946
Henry R. Houchins	B: 1913	D: 1986
James Russell Houchins	B: 28 Jun 1941	D: 27 Jul 1969
Mary M. Houchins	B: 1917	D: 1996

Lot: 408   Lot Owner: Charles Sinclair

Charles N. Sinclair	B: 18 Nov 1898	D: 26 May 1968
Frances Ashby Sinclair	B: 17 Apr 1862	D: 9 Jan 1948

| Virginia Pearl Sinclair | B: 25 Sep 1913 | D: 13 Feb 1995 |
| Turner F. Sudduth | B: 7 Jan 1912 | D: 9 Apr 1981 |

Lot: 410   Lot Owner: Fayette Downs

| Fayette Downs | B: 1879 | D: 1965 |
| Zella P. Downs | B: 18 Oct 1882 | D: 6 Jan 1974 |

Lot: 411   Lot Owner: Miscellaneous

| Mark Allen Byrne | B: 25 Sep 1957 | D: 15 Sep 1989 |

Lot: 412   Lot Owner: Miscellaneous

| Charles R. Sr Duncan | B: 1921 | D: 1989 |
| Kathaline L. Duncan | B: 1927 | no death date |

Lot: 418   Lot Owner: George Rhodes

| George W. Rhodes | B: 1896 | D: 1963 |
| Julia K. Rhodes | B: 1903 | D: 1985 |

Lot: 419   Lot Owner: John Rhodes

Benjamin F. Rhodes	B: 5 Oct 1905	D: 4 Nov 1972
C. Frank Rhodes	B: 8 Apr 1876	D: 27 Feb 1967
Katie W. Rhodes	B: 28 Apr 1878	D: 2 Oct 1951

Lot: 420   Lot Owner: Miscellaneous

| Fannie Elizabeth Houchins | B: 28 Feb 1871 | D: 7 Jan 1948 |
| Margaret R. Tinsman | B: 12 Aug 1907 | D: 25 Mar 1980 |

Lot: 421   Lot Owner: William Utterback

| Elsie A. Utterback | B: 28 Apr 1887 | D: 22 Apr 1968 |
| William Utterback | B: 1 Apr 1879 | D: 14 Jan 1955 |

Lot: 422   Lot Owner: William Barney Utterback

| William H. Utterback | B: 12 Dec 1905 | D: 31 Mar 1981 WWII |

Lot: 423   Lot Owner: Doris Utterback

| Doris Utterback Canard | B: 5 Oct 1925 | D: 10 Jun 1984 |
| Charles M. Utterback | B: 25 Jan 1907 | D: 9 Feb 1975 |

Lot: 424   Lot Owner: Miscellaneous

Ellwood D. Cameron	B: 5 Mar 1925	no death date
Mary E. Cameron	B: 15 Apr 1928	D: 13 Oct 1987

Lot: 431   Lot Owner: Melvin & Agnes Warren

Agnes Riddle Warren		no dates
Melvin A. Warren, Jr	B: 22 Jul 1940	D: 16 Jul 1966 Green Beret
Melvin Amor Warren, Sr	B: 1905	D: 1985

Lot: 432   Lot Owner: George & Donna Zacko

Dorothy Damon Zacko	B: 21 Nov 1958	D: 24 Nov 1973

Lot: 434   Lot Owner: John & Edna Deavers

Edna M. Deavers	B: 1917	D: 1984
John S. Deavers	B: 1905	no death date

Lot: 444   Lot Owner: Miscellaneous

Charles B. Rhodes	B: 3 Jan 1932	D: 14 Jul 1991 Korea

Lot: 446   Lot Owner: Miscellaneous

Patricia Shepherdson Arwine	B: 21 Jan 1945	D: 8 Apr 1986
Mary Powell Choate	B: 29 Oct 1883	D: 3 Mar 1983

Lot: 457   Lot Owner: Mary L. Atwell

Eugene S. Atwell	B: 2 Aug 1921	D: 19 Nov 1982

Lot: 458   Lot Owner: V.M. Johnson

Mary M. Johnson	B: 11 Aug 1963	D: 30 Dec 1972 Toss up
Sylvia M. Johnson	B: 1900	D: 1961
V. Mason Johnson, Jr	B: 1902	D: 1987

Lot: 459   Lot Owner: Jack Hutchison

John Hanson Hutchison	B: 1903	D: 1993
Marjorie Tyler Hutchison	B: 1902	D: 1979

Lot: 459   Lot Owner: William E. Tyler

Ruth Ferguson Tyler	B: 14 Sep 1899	D: 19 Apr 1990
William E. Tyler, Jr	B: 26 Nov 1898	D: 27 Mar 1962 WWI

Lot: 460   Lot Owner:Carty

John H. Carty	B: 10 Jun 1910	D: 4 Mar 1965 WWII
Belle P. Field	B: 31 Dec 1920	no death date
Thomas E. Field	B: 17 Oct 1920	D: 12 Nov 1983

Lot: 461   Lot Owner: Miscellaneous

Daniel Boone Ridgeway	B: 1948	D: 1996
Edward Fenton Ridgeway, Sr	B: 23 Dec 1917	D: 12 Sep 1987 Buzz

Lot: 470   Lot Owner: Edith J. Thompson

Harry S. Lewis	B: 1914	D: 1987
Violet G. Lewis	B: 1923	D: 1995
Damond Seyl Thompson	B: 27 Jun 1916	D: 31 May 1968

Lot: 471   Lot Owner: Miscellaneous

Rodney Charles Hibner	B: 17 Sep 1927	D: 17 Oct 1991 WWII
Emma R. Waddell	B: 1917	D: 1987
William H. Waddell	B: 1915	D: 1985 WWII

Lot: 472   Lot Owner: Miscellaneous

Galen Franklin Comer	B: 17 Jun 1919	D: 17 Nov 1994 WWII

Lot: 702   Lot Owner: Miscellaneous

Hackley Embrey Ashby	B: 22 Dec 1920	D: 13 Aug 1994 WWII
Nancy C. Ashby	B: 16 Jan 1924	D: 21 Feb 1991

Lot: 712 **Lot Owner: Mark W. Gordon**

Mark W. Gordon	B: 1956	D: 1972
Robert Blair Gordon	B: 27 Dec 1925	D: 8 May 1991 WWII
Elijah Griffith	B: 7 Aug 1919	D: 2 Mar 1994 WWII

Lot: 713 **Lot Owner: Julius Craun**

Cecil D. Craun	B: 1924	D: 1976 Korea
Dovie W. Craun	B: 18 Jun 1902	D: 8 Jun 1989
Julius Daniel Craun	B: 30 May 1890	D: 17 Nov 1966 WWI

Lot: 714 **Lot Owner: William D. Piggott, Sr.**

Rebie C. Piggott	B: 1904	D: 1985
William D. Piggott	B: 1902	D: 1972
William D. Piggott, Jr	B: 23 Aug 1932	D: 22 Jan 1985 Korea

Lot: 715 **Lot Owner: Shirley Ryan**

Othie S. Presgraves	B: 24 Dec 1902	D: 27 May 1981
Dorothy M. Ryan	B: 18 Oct 1924	no death date
Shirley T. Ryan	B: 11 Jun 1925	D: 17 Mar 1981 Korea

Lot: 716 **Lot Owner: Bobby Lynn Byington**

| Bobby L. Byington | B: 1953 | D: 1973 |
| Ronny L. Byington | B: 1953 | D: 1973 |

Lot: 717 **Lot Owner: Lonnie & Alma Sutphin**

| Alma Ann Sutphin | B: 1910 | D: 1990 |
| Lonnie D. Sutphin | B: 1902 | D: 1973 |

Lot: 717   **Lot Owner: Charlotte & Buk Waddell**

Charlotte R. Waddell   B: 29 Jul 1915   D: 15 Apr 1995

Isaac M. Waddell, Jr   B: 26 Mar 1914   D: 3 Apr 1994
                                                                      WWII

Lot: 718   **Lot Owner: Irene E. Amos**

Walter T. Amos   B: 17 Apr 1924   D: 2 Dec 1975

Lot: 719   **Lot Owner: Hugh A. & Kathryn Orndoff**

Betty Lee Bolton   B: 2 Jul 1928   D: 2 Mar 1980

Joseph E. Burdette, Sr   B: 4 Sep 1943   D: 23 Jun 1993
                                                                      Vietnam

Harrison Riley Orndoff   B: 23 Mar 1937   D: 14 Dec 1997

Hugh Harrison Orndoff   B: 1920   D: 1984
                                                                      WWII

Lot: 721   **Lot Owner: Helen Louise Anderson**

Helen R. Anderson   B: 1914   D: 1980

Joseph B., Sr Anderson   B: 1913   D: 1975

Lot: 722   **Lot Owner: Clarence E. Tinsman, Jr.**

Clarence E. Tinsman, Jr   B: 26 May 1940   D: 17 Jul 1971

Katherine Rhodes Tinsman   B: 15 Apr 1923   D: 2 Mar 1994

Lot: 723   **Lot Owner: Charles E. Duggan**

Edith B. Duggan   B: 1921   no death date

Lot: 723   **Lot Owner: David Rhodes**

David O. Rhodes   B: 7 Apr 1901   D: 22 Mar 1979

Leona R. Rhodes   B: 6 Aug 1908   no death date

Lot: 724   **Lot Owner: Miscellaneous**

Annie G. Glascock   B: 1927   no death date

Howard J. Glascock   B: 1927   D: 1994

Lot: 725   **Lot Owner: Miscellaneous**

Calvin C. Lloyd   B: 1918   no death date

Gladys R. Lloyd   B: 1921   D: 1991

| Albert O'Neal Varner | B: 31 Jul 1938 | D: 17 Oct 1991 Vietnam |

Lot: 728   Lot Owner: Louis Sutphin

| Louis R. Sutphin | B: 6 Jan 1907 | D: 8 Nov 1958 Buddy |

Lot: 729   Lot Owner: Linwood A. Sutphin

| Linwood A. Sutphin | B: 1911 | D: 1985 |
| Pauline G. Sutphin | B: 1917 | D: 1975 |

Lot: 736   Lot Owner: William & Bertha Madden

| Bertha V. Madden | B: 1906 | no death date |
| William F. Madden | B: 1902 | D: 1981 |

Lot: 740   Lot Owner: Miscellaneous

| Edgar R. Surface, Sr | B: 7 Oct 1934 | D: 28 Feb 1991 |
| Glenn Aubrey Surface | B: 23 Jan 1907 | D: 12 Feb 1987 |

Lot: 741   Lot Owner: Miscellaneous

| Betty L. Green | B: 1939 | no death date |
| Kenneth W. Sr Green | B: 1934 | D: 1988 |

Lot: 745   Lot Owner: Miscellaneous

| Mary M. Eckert | B: 27 Mar 1897 | D: 31 May 1976 |
| Raymond Lee Gray, Sr | B: 28 Jan 1923 | D: 4 Feb 1994 WWII |

Lot: 746   Lot Owner: Leo & Patti R. Raybits

| Leo C. Raybits | B: 4 Nov 1917 | D: 16 Jul 1993 |
| Patti R. Raybits | B: 15 Oct 1934 | no death date |

Lot: 746   Lot Owner: Nace Rhodes

| Nace C. Rhodes | B: 1898 | D: 1981 |
| Nora L. Rhodes | B: 1894 | D: 1979 |

Lot: 749   Lot Owner: Henry Clay Dunivan

| Henry Clay Dunivan | B: 14 Mar 1921 | D: 28 Jul 1982 |

Lot: 749   Lot Owner: Alice & Bus Lloyd

Alice D. Lloyd	B: 25 Sep 1932	no death date
Wilmer L. Lloyd	B: 11 Apr 1921	D: 25 Jan 1991

Lot: 750   Lot Owner: J.C. Dunivan

Jake C. Dunivan	B: 1898	D: 1988
Victoria S. Dunivan	B: 1901	D: 1980
Robert Lee Varner	B: 1915	D: 1979 WWII

Lot: 751   Lot Owner: Linwood Lawrence

Lynwood Lee Lawrence	B: 15 Mar 1893	D: 17 Apr 1960

Lot: 752   Lot Owner: Miscellaneous

Clarence B. Moffett	B: 26 Apr 1896	D: 17 Jul 1967 WWI

Lot: 753   Lot Owner: Carter Byrne

Annie Gertrude Byrne	B: 15 Feb 1892	D: 18 Jul 1968
Travis Carter Byrne	B: 14 Jun 1891	D: 1 Jun 1962

Lot: 754   Lot Owner: Earl Boxwell

Earl W. Boxwell	B: 14 Jul 1906	D: 20 Dec 1966
Mabel B. Boxwell	B: 17 Jan 1914	D: 3 Feb 1982

Lot: 755   Lot Owner: Althea C. St. Clair

Althea Cook St Clair	B: 8 Jun 1908	D: 27 Oct 1996
Gilbert L. St Clair, Jr	B: 18 Jun 1939	D: 24 Jan 1974
Gilbert L. Sr St Clair	B: 15 Jul 1911	D: 10 Mar 1973

Lot: 756   Lot Owner: Wade Rodham

Kathleen B. Rodham	B: 1913	D: 1989
Wade J. Rodham	B: 1912	D: 1983
Mary A. Yauger	B: 1911	no death date
Wilbert S. Yauger	B: 1911	D: 1996

Lot: 760   Lot Owner: Della Embrey

Della Embrey	B: 1899	D: 1962
George Meredith Embrey	B: 29 Mar 1895	D: 11 Oct 1978 WWI
Norman Fletcher	B: 2 Oct 1889	D: 12 Feb 1963
Mattie Summers	B: 1874	D: 1963

Lot: 761   Lot Owner: Harvey & Emma Moore

Emma Moore	B: 1909	D: 1964
Harvey Moore	B: 1902	D: 1977

Lot: 763   Lot Owner: J. Marshall Campbell

Catherine A. Campbell	B: 1913	D: 1978
James M. Campbell, Jr	B: 1 Aug 1948	D: 27 Oct 1993

Lot: 764   Lot Owner: George Bettis

George S. Bettis	B: 1898	D: 1962
Jennie V. Bettis	B: 1904	D: 1980

Lot: 764   Lot Owner: Eva E. Surface

Eva Evelyn Surface	B: 8 May 1912	D: 23 Jun 1969

Lot: 765   Lot Owner: Eugene Griffith

Judy Ann Griffith	B: 28 Jul 1962	D: 24 May 1963
Claudia E. Johnson	B: 16 Apr 1886	D: 27 Nov 1963
Hosea Upton Johnson	B: 23 Sep 1884	D: 1 Mar 1970

Lot: 766   Lot Owner: Eugene Griffith

Clara Gillespie	B: 17 Jun 1915	D: 7 Oct 1996
Luther C. Gillespie	B: 18 Aug 1906	D: 15 Feb 1969
Thomas Neville Griffith, Sr	B: 30 Sep 1910	D: 7 Apr 1984

Lot: 768   Lot Owner: Cleveland Jenkins

Cleveland F. Jenkins	B: 14 Sep 1906	D: 17 Jan 1967
Margaret H. Jenkins	B: 6 Feb 1902	D: 12 Sep 1986

Lot: 769   Lot Owner: Rebecca Hayton

John H. Hayton	B: 30 Apr 1926	D: 11 Mar 1983 WWII
Rebecca R. Hayton	B: 13 Apr 1928	D: 4 Apr 1993

Lot: 770   Lot Owner: Melvin Dailey

Anderson E. Dailey		D: 4 Jun 1962
Edward A. Dailey		D: 4 Jun 1962
Thomas Jay Dailey		D: 18 Dec 1964
James Douglas Waddell	B: 1942	D: 1964 h/o Janet

Lot: 772   Lot Owner: Matt Hayes

Matthias J. Hayes	B: 1909	D: 1977 WWII
Jessica Stockton McMann	B: 1890	D: 1957
John Robert Welsh	B: 9 Jan 1887	D: 8 Feb 1958

Lot: 773   Lot Owner: John Steele

James C. Sr Dunivan	B: 10 Feb 1920	D: 24 Apr 1987 WWII
John Wm Steele	B: 1882	D: 1959
Viola Steele	B: 1897	D: 1990

Lot: 774   Lot Owner: Norris Payne

James Milton Payne	B: 8 Dec 1917	D: 24 Feb 1973 WWII
Mamie Payne	B: 21 Mar 1891	D: 20 Jul 1977
Norris Payne	B: 9 May 1888	D: 30 Aug 1982
Virginia M. Payne	B: 18 Oct 1914	D: 15 Dec 1991

Lot: 775   Lot Owner: Preston Middleton

Glenna L. Middleton	B: 9 Sep 1898	D: 25 Jul 1975
J Preston Middleton	B: 10 Nov 1891	D: 15 Jan 1957
Courtney Taylor	B: 1903	D: 1983

Lot: 776   Lot Owner: Martha Saffer

Delbert Thornton Saffer, MD	B: 1904	D: 1953
Martha G. Saffer	B: 1908	D: 1972

Lot: 777   Lot Owner: Fred Byrne

Annie S. Byrne	B: 1895	D: 1989
Frederick H. Byrne	B: 1887	D: 1978

Lot: 778   Lot Owner: Thomas & Jennie Jeffries

Jennie G. Jeffries	B: 1922	no death date
Thomas H. Sr Jeffries	B: 1914	D: 1980

Lot: 780   Lot Owner: Miscellaneous

Maude R. Putnam	B: 22 May 1897	D: 8 Jul 1972
Winter W. Putnam	B: 4 Jun 1892	D: 11 Apr 1975

Lot: 782   Lot Owner: Miscellaneous

Annie K. White	B: 1925	D: 1995
Donald R. Sr White	B: 1920	D: 1989

Lot: 784   Lot Owner: Miscellaneous

Betty Ann Pullen	B: 10 Dec 1956	D: 26 Aug 1976

Lot: 785   Lot Owner: Frank Berkley Owens

Frank B. Owens, Jr	B: 14 Mar 1926	D: 17 Sep 1976

Lot: 786   Lot Owner: Walter C. Simmons

Bessie Pearl Simmons	B: 8 Aug 1907	D: 14 Oct 1980
Walter Clark Simmons	B: 25 Dec 1889	D: 8 Apr 1982

Lot: 787   Lot Owner: Nettie Arnold

Nettie Lee Arnold	B: 14 Apr 1923	D: 5 Mar 1963

Lot: 787   Lot Owner: Richard Legge

Bessie C. Legge	B: 1913	no death date
Lewis Legge	B: 1899	D: 1963

Lot: 789   Lot Owner: Earl Powell

Earl S. Powell	B: 1919	D: 1991

Evelyn V. Powell	B: 1923	D: 1981

Lot: 790   Lot Owner: Preston Gregg

Clifton C. Gregg	B: 30 Oct 1918	D: 13 Sep 1970 WWII
Willard R. Gregg	B: 27 Apr 1910	D: 7 Dec 1963

Lot: 793   Lot Owner: Miscellaneous

Robert King Lawson	B: 1 Jun 1939	D: 10 Jul 1994

Lot: 798   Lot Owner: James McCormick

Elizabeth M. McCormick	B: 22 Jun 1890	D: 8 Jun 1972
James K. McCormick	B: 14 Oct 1883	D: 7 Feb 1957
Joseph C. McCormick	B: 1918	D: 1977 WWII

Lot: 799   Lot Owner: Thomas Darling

Thomas Neil Darling	B: 1895	D: 1955

Lot: 799   Lot Owner: Leo Robinson

Claudia Robinson	B: 19 Oct 1906	D: 2 Oct 1956
Leonard C. Robinson	B: 30 Jun 1910	D: 19 Jan 1977
Linda Jane Robinson	B: 24 Aug 1958	D: 16 Nov 1958

Lot: 800   Lot Owner: Kemper Houchins

Matilda H. Ferguson	B: 31 Aug 1885	D: 14 Mar 1964
William M. Ferguson	B: 16 Aug 1885	D: 26 Dec 1953
Kemper A. Houchins	B: 16 Nov 1873	D: 2 Oct 1954

Lot: 801   Lot Owner: Robert Maddox

Robert M. Maddox	B: 1892	D: 1948

Lot: 801   Lot Owner: Ruth Nicholls

James C. Nickolls	B: 26 Jun 1908	D: 25 Aug 1956
Ruth S. Nickolls	B: 1 Nov 1909	D: 26 Aug 1986

Lot: 802   Lot Owner: Mary Flournoy

Halle S. Flournoy	B: 3 Oct 1904	D: 1 Mar 1961 WWII

Lot: 803   Lot Owner: Alice Edwards

Charles Wesley Edwards   B: 31 Jul 1917   D: 5 Aug 1961
                                                                                    WWII

Lot: 804   Lot Owner: Mrs. Alice Wilson

W Stanley Wilson   B: 15 Dec 1911   D: 3 Feb 1962

Lot: 805   Lot Owner: James Frank Bell

James Frank Bell   B: 18 Oct 1903   D: 13 Jun 1970

Sarah E. Bell   B: 10 Feb 1919   no death date

Lot: 806   Lot Owner: James E. Bell

Henry Franklin Bell   B: 1927   D: 1979

James Edward Bell   B: 31 Oct 1924   D: 18 Feb 1987
                                                                                    WWII

Lot: 809   Lot Owner: Marshall T. Campbell, Sr.

Marshall T. Campbell, Sr   B: 31 Mar 1925   D: 5 Sep 1972L

Lot: 809   Lot Owner: Hallie Grimes

Hallie W. Grimes   B: 1 Sep 1897   D: 19 Mar 1971

Ruth M. Grimes   B: 25 Jul 1910   D: 22 Oct 1992

Lot: 810   Lot Owner: Ezra B. Owens

Ezra B. Owens   B: 12 Aug 1921   D: 14 Dec 1986

Louise V. Owens   B: 18 Nov 1915   D: 29 Aug 1969

Lot: 810   Lot Owner: Robert & Margaret Wharton

Robert E. Wharton   B: 5 Oct 1930   D: 25 Apr 1995

Lot: 811   Lot Owner: William Walter Tumblin

Pheba Tumblin   B: 1884   D: 1968

W. Walter Tumblin   B: 1880   D: 1966

Lot: 812   Lot Owner: Robert L. Campbell

Edna L. Campbell   B: 25 Jul 1914   D: 24 Sep 1965

Lot: 812   Lot Owner: Robert Triplett Washington

Robert Triplett Washington   B: 1912   D: 1978
                                                                                    WWII

Lot: 813   Lot Owner: Charles W. George

| Charles W.W. George | B: 1912 | no death date |
| Lucy U. George | B: 1914 | D: 1971 |

Lot: 814   Lot Owner: Thomas & Frances Henry

| Russell William Henry | B: 27 Mar 1900 | D: 30 Nov 1976 WWI |

Lot: 815   Lot Owner: Alecia Craig

| Alecia J. Craig | B: 15 Jun 1915 | no death date |
| Roy S. Craig, Sr | B: 9 Mar 1913 | D: 13 Mar 1983 |

Lot: 824   Lot Owner: Curtis Ambler

Curtis R. Ambler	B: 26 May 1906	D: 4 Feb 1960
Mae Kimes Ambler	B: 17 Sep 1905	D: 1 Apr 1970
Ann J. Kimes	B: 20 May 1883	D: 23 Dec 1958
James M. Kimes	B: 16 Jan 1871	D: 20 Jan 1957

Lot: 825   Lot Owner: Skip Scholl

Francis E. Sholl	B: 4 May 1940	D: 6 Aug 1958
Andrew Lee Sisk, Sr	B: 1913	D: 1991
Mary Irene Sisk	B: 1921	D: 1987

Lot: 825   Lot Owner: Strother

| Charles E. Strother | B: 3 Dec 1919 | D: 12 May 1991 WWII |

Lot: 827   Lot Owner: Harry & Mabel James

| Harry T. James, Sr | B: 6 Feb 1914 | D: 24 Apr 1981 WWII |
| Mabel W. James | B: 18 Sep 1914 | no death date |

Lot: 828   Lot Owner: Bradshaw Edwards

| Bradshaw Edwards | B: 3 Dec 1893 | D: 16 Jun 1974 |
| Lucy Inez Edwards | B: 28 Sep 1895 | D: 26 Feb 1964 |

Lot: 829   Lot Owner: Lucille Funk

| Lucille V. Funk | B: 1918 | D: 1972 |

Lot: 830   Lot Owner: Robert L. Allder

Patsie M. Allder	B: 1912	D: 1971
Robert Lee Allder	B: 1902	D: 1985 WWII

Lot: 835   Lot Owner: Ruby Ridgeway

Roland T. Ridgeway	B: 23 May 1917	D: 26 Feb 1967 WWII

Lot: 836   Lot Owner: Floyd Tumblin

Paul Daniel Tumblin	B: 24 Dec 1942	D: 9 Jul 1968

Lot: 837   Lot Owner: Floyd H. Tumblin, Jr.

Floyd H. Tumblin	B: 1906	D: 1971
Lillie Tumblin	B: 1914	D: 1985

Lot: 838   Lot Owner: Miscellaneous

Paul Trail Spieles	B: 27 Aug 1939	D: 12 Jan 1993 Cowboy
Shirley Ann Spieles	B: 20 Dec 1940	no death date

Lot: 839   Lot Owner: Thomas & Frances Henry

Frances E. Henry	B: 1916	D: 1988
Thomas J. Henry	B: 1906	D: 1990

Lot: 844   Lot Owner: Fred B. Simpson

Adam L. Simpson	B: 1900	D: 1972
Fred B. Simpson, Jr	B: 15 Jan 1965	D: 21 May 1970

Lot: 845   Lot Owner: Fred B. Simpson

Mary Lockhart Simpson	B: 25 Mar 1915	D: 4 Jul 1990
Katie salyers Vencill	B: 4 May 1896	D: 16 Dec 1991

Lot: 847   Lot Owner: Maurice Cockrille

Ethel M. Cockrell	B: 29 Nov 1908	D: 22 Feb 1996
Maurice Elmo Cockrell	B: 11 May 1888	D: 13 Aug 1956

Lot: 849   Lot Owner: Lee Griffith

Charles Oliver Attmanspacher	B: 4 Mar 1904	D: 24 Jul 1985

Ellen G. Attmanspacher	B: 31 Jan 1916	D: 30 Jun 1994
Lee Abner Griffith	B: 15 Nov 1878	D: 17 Dec 1962
Mary Bertha Griffith	B: 16 Sep 1884	D: 17 Jun 1955

Lot: 849   Lot Owner: Tullose Teele

William Tulloss Teele	B: 28 May 1885	D: 9 May 1965

Lot: 850   Lot Owner: Tullose Teele

Jennie Lee Teele	B: 18 Jan 1887	D: 7 Sep 1961

Lot: 850   Lot Owner: Frank Van Deman

Frank E. Van Deman, Jr	B: 7 Apr 1907	D: 17 May 1962

Lot: 851   Lot Owner: Charles Martz

Charles F. Martz	B: 9 May 1873	D: 30 Jan 1956
Charles William Martz	B: 28 Jun 1908	D: 7 May 1991
Lona E. Martz	B: 29 Mar 1879	D: 11 Jun 1968

Lot: 852   Lot Owner: Homer K. Barrett

Homer Kenneth Barrett	B: 22 May 1903	D: 23 Feb 1983

Lot: 852   Lot Owner: John R. & Marion Thomas

John Rector Thomas	B: 28 Oct 1908	D: 6 Jul 1983

Lot: 853   Lot Owner: Miscellaneous

Barbara Jean Leonard	B: 21 Sep 1950	D: 12 Aug 1992

Lot: 854   Lot Owner: Donald Bachman

Dennis Lee Bachman	B: 22 May 1954	no death date
Doris C. Bachman	B: 23 Dec 1923	D: 12 Nov 1982
Joseph G. Cunningham	B: 30 Mar 1894	D: 30 Jul 1967

Lot: 859   Lot Owner: Dudley C. Webb

Laura Idell Webb	B: 22 Apr 1916	D: 29 Apr 1967

Lot: 860   Lot Owner: Lawrence Walker

Lawrence R. Walker	B: 12 Oct 1900	D: 25 Jun 1966

Lot: 861   Lot Owner: James Arbogast

James Dale Arbogast	B: 10 Feb 1949	D: 21 Nov 1969

Lot: 861   Lot Owner: Edgar N. Waddell

Edgar Neville Waddell	B: 5 Oct 1905	D: 8 Jan 1966
George N. Waddell	B: 16 Jan 1931	D: 7 Jan 1982 Korea
Martha Virginia Waddell	B: 6 Feb 1908	D: 5 Jan 1965

Lot: 862   Lot Owner: Lillian Denny

| Lillian Denny | B: 1879 | D: 1966 |

Lot: 862   Lot Owner: Cary Fletcher

| Carrie Fletcher | B: 1875 | D: 1965 |

Lot: 862   Lot Owner: Lena Furr

| Lena G. Furr | B: 1907 | D: 1993 |

Lot: 863   Lot Owner: Thomas Green

Druscilla T. Green	B: 7 Apr 1918	D: 3 Aug 1978
Horace Elmore Green	B: 23 Aug 1922	D: 13 Feb 1981 WWII
Thomas A. Green	B: 3 May 1910	D: 13 Jan 1966 WWII

Lot: 863   Lot Owner: Sadie Trammell

Edward A. Trammell	B: 1916	D: 1978 WWII
Sadie C. Trammell	B: 26 Jun 1895	D: 7 May 1971
Dora Green Trussell	B: 6 Jun 1888	D: 26 Jan 1967

Lot: 864   Lot Owner: Marshall Green

| Grace E. Green | B: 1911 | D: 1972 |
| James M. Green | B: 1908 | D: 1991 |

Lot: 864   Lot Owner: Thomas Washington

Frank V. Washington	B: 16 Dec 1938	D: 20 Dec 1994
Helen C. Washington	B: 1928	no death date
Thomas M. Washington	B: 1916	D: 1967

Lot: 865   Lot Owner: Charlotte Green

Amos R. Green   B: 1915   D: 1982
                                                                          WWII

Lot: 869   Lot Owner: Emma Darnell

Emma M. Darnell   B: 16 Nov 1914   D: 1 Oct 1965

Lot: 870   Lot Owner: Thomas W. Sudduth

Mabel Lee Sudduth   B: 18 Feb 1918   D: 9 Jan 1981

Lot: 873   Lot Owner: Alice Flynn

Luther L. Flynn   B: 17 Nov 1898   .   D: 13 Jul 1957

Lot: 874   Lot Owner: James Milton Lawson

Alice Virginia Lawson   B: 4 Jul 1918   D: 1 Nov 1986

James Milton Lawson   B: 7 Aug 1912   D: 28 Jul 1958

Lot: 875   Lot Owner: Miscellaneous

Helen Hasson Conover   B: 1906   D: 1995

James Dwyer Conover   B: 1908   D: 1989

Lot: 876   Lot Owner: Manly Ray Johnston

Forrest Ray Johnston   B: 26 Feb 1891   D: 18 Mar 1965

Mamie L. Johnston   B: 11 Dec 1893   D: 25 Nov 1962

Lot: 877   Lot Owner: Albert S. Orrison, Jr.

Joanne Orrison   B: 6 Jun 1948   D: 3 Jun 1972

Lot: 878   Lot Owner: Miscellaneous

John Weaver Slingerland   B: 10 Sep 1922   D: 27 Aug 1994
                                                                          WWII

Lot: 880   Lot Owner: H.A. & Lucy A. Martz & Gilbert Martz

Gilbert A. Martz   B: 1923   no death date

Herbert A. Martz   B: 1898   D: 1990

Lucy Ann Martz   B: 1905   D: 1976

Thomas Lee Martz   B: 10 Mar 1901   D: 14 Aug 1976

Lot: 881   Lot Owner: John Mack Klepper

| Doris L. Klepper | B: 1934 | no death date |
| John M. Klepper | B: 1923 | D: 1983 |

Lot: 884   Lot Owner: Edward Hawes

Lafayette M. Hawes	B: 1890	D: 1979
Maisie Hawes	B: 1904	no death date
Walter Smith Hawes	B: 20 Jun 1886	D: 24 Jan 1971 WWI

Lot: 885   Lot Owner: Richard Sudduth

| Joseph A. Suddueth | B: 8 Sep 1920 | D: 15 Mar 1974 |
| Richard H. Sudduth | B: 18 Jul 1922 | D: 22 Jan 1967 |

Lot: 886   Lot Owner: Dorothy Hunter

| Birthon Hunter | B: 1902 | D: 1976 |
| Dorothy Hunter | B: 1908 | no death date |

Lot: 886   Lot Owner: James & Nellie Signor

| James H. Signor | B: 1917 | D: 1972 |
| Nellie S. Signor | B: 1918 | D: 1982 |

Lot: 887   Lot Owner: Lloyd Kirkpatrick

| Kathleen S. Kirkpatrick | B: 1909 | no death date |
| Lloyd C. Kirkpatrick | B: 1904 | D: 1985 |

Lot: 888   Lot Owner: Edith Gray Wiggins

| William Lewis Sutphin | B: 10 Mar 1915 | D: 28 May 1970 |
| Edith Gray Wiggins | B: 1902 | D: 1968 |

Lot: 889   Lot Owner: Thomas M. Edwards

| Juanita M. Edwards | B: 22 May 1940 | no death date |
| Thomas M. Edwards, Jr | B: 16 Sep 1942 | D: 2 Mar 1968 |

Lot: 894   Lot Owner: Payne (Miscellaneous)

| Welby E. Payne | B: 1907 | D: 1965 |

Lot: 896   Lot Owner: Ackley Williams

| Evelyn V. Williams | B: 6 Jun 1919 | D: 7 Nov 1960 |
| Mollie F. Williams | B: 14 Mar 1894 | D: 9 Mar 1957 |

Lot: 897   Lot Owner: Major Kannard

| Alice V. Kannard | B: 25 Jul 1913 | D: 26 Aug 1963 |
| Major Kannard | B: 3 Apr 1906 | no death date |

Lot: 898   Lot Owner: Edith Ashby

Charles C. Ashby	B: 1889	D: 1974
Edith Irene Ashby	B: 18 Feb 1896	D: 27 Aug 1957
Edith O. Ashby	B: 1918	no death date
Harvey W. Ashby	B: 1914	D: 1988

Lot: 899   Lot Owner: John Campbell

| John H. Campbell | B: 31 Jul 1916 | D: 27 Jul 1961 |
| Mary A. Campbell | B: 15 Feb 1910 | D: 29 Jan 1996 |

Lot: 899   Lot Owner: Eva Henderson

| Evelyn V. Henderson | B: 3 Aug 1889 | D: 9 Jan 1963 |
| Armond E. Starkey | B: 7 Apr 1906 | D: 9 Oct 1971 |

Lot: 900   Lot Owner: Eugual Schulz

| Eugual B. Schulze | B: 22 Jul 1909 | D: 16 Feb 1975 |
| Harry E.C. Schulze | B: 1 Apr 1890 | D: 19 Sep 1962 |

Lot: 903   Lot Owner: Margaret Pearson

| George R. Pearson | B: 1918 | D: 1965 |
| Margaret S. Pearson | B: 1927 | D: 1995 |

Lot: 904   Lot Owner: Edgar Holmes

| Edgar Penn Holmes | B: 10 Sep 1897 | D: 4 Sep 1967 WWI |
| Lillian R. Holmes | B: 27 Nov 1896 | D: 30 Jul 1971 |

Lot: 904   Lot Owner: Cecil Rhodes

| Bessie M. Rhodes | B: 1914 | no death date |
| Cecil L. Rhodes | B: 1905 | D: 1992 |

Lot: 905   Lot Owner: Forrest Rhodes

| Forrest E. Rhodes | B: 1897 | D: 1978 |
| Julia L. Rhodes | B: 1904 | D: 1973 |

Lot: 907   Lot Owner: Mattie E. Ridgeway

| Mattie E. Ridgeway | B: 31 Jan 1910 | D: 11 Dec 1972 |

Lot: 908   Lot Owner: Guy G. Glass

Bessie M. Glass	B: 1910	D: 1978
Guy G. Glass	B: 1900	D: 1974
Catherine B. Leach	B: 4 May 1897	D: 21 Jun 1973

Lot: 910   Lot Owner: Roland S. Sowers

James W. Sowers	B: 1937	D: 1996
Julia T. Sowers	B: 1912	no death date
Patricia A. Sowers	B: 1940	no death date
Roland S. Sowers	B: 1895	D: 1972

Lot: 912   Lot Owner: Russell & Mary Walton

| Stephen Michael Walton | B: 19 Mar 1960 | D: 8 Jun 1973 |

Lot: 913   Lot Owner: William P. Robertson

| William Paul Robertson, Jr | B: 1963 | D: 1970 Toot |

Lot: 922   Lot Owner: John Pyne

| Margie Elaine Pyne | B: 31 Dec 1937 | D: 21 Nov 1969 |

Lot: 923   Lot Owner: Miscellaneous

Catherine C. Fletcher	B: 18 Aug 1930	D: 19 Jan 1987
Charles W. Fletcher	B: 9 Oct 1927	no death date
James C. Kirk	B: 1913	D: 1967 Dick
Nellie W. Kirk	B: 1914	no death date

Lot: 924   Lot Owner: Burns H. Robertson

| Angela Rae Robertson | d/o Burns & Rachel | D: 1959 |

Lot: 925   Lot Owner: Betty S. Kirk

| Francis Edward Kirk | B: 3 Oct 1929 | D: 12 Nov 1959 Korea |
| Aubrey E. Lloyd | B: 1882 | D: 1975 |

Lot: 926   Lot Owner: Nancy Cooper

James Roland Cooper	B: 10 May 1933	D: 17 Jan 1969
Mildred M. McCormick	B: 25 Jan 1916	D: 24 Dec 1986 Nannie
Thomas E. Swain	B: 13 Dec 1902	D: 27 Jan 1960

Lot: 927   Lot Owner: Miscellaneous

Hilda L.l Armstrong	B: 10 Jul 1910	D: 4 Dec 1986
Bessie Lee Lloyd	B: 21 Sep 1910	D: 1 Nov 1988
Thomas Alvin Lloyd	B: 15 May 1905	D: 4 Dec 1961

Lot: 932   Lot Owner: William L. Ryan

| James S. Ryan | B: 3 Oct 1901 | D: 3 Apr 1970 |
| William Douglass Ryan | B: 13 Aug 1973 | D: 20 Jun 1996 Boo |

Lot: 933   Lot Owner: Miscellaneous

| Clyde Linden Baxter | B: 24 May 1920 | D: 17 May 1986 WWII |
| Mary D. Baxter | B: 5 Aug 1921 | no death date |

Lot: 935   Lot Owner: Richard Earl Alexander

Marion Amos Alexander	B: 5 Feb 1926	D: 29 Mar 1986 WWII
Nellie G. Alexander	B: 1900	D: 1994
R. Earl Alexander	B: 1894	D: 1976 WWI

Lot: 936   Lot Owner: Miscellaneous

Forrest S. Lisenbee	B: 1924	D: 1992
		WWII
Donald Oscar Sutphin, Sr	B: 1 Feb 1946	D: 9 Sep 1971

Lot: 937   Lot Owner: Charles R. Waddell, Jr.

Bertie M. Waddell	B: 1884	D: 1972
Charles Rozier Waddell, Jr	B: 19 Feb 1946	D: 28 Dec 1992

Lot: 944   Lot Owner: Miscellaneous

Paul Thomas Crouch	B: 29 Aug 1916	D: 28 Apr 1976
Walter Lee Crouch	B: 12 Aug 1943	D: 7 Mar 1964
Robert L. Waddell	B: 2 Mar 1892	D: 4 Aug 1969
Sadie F. Waddell	B: 1892	D: 1957

Lot: 945   Lot Owner: Miscellaneous

Verna P. Bozelle	B: 3 Sep 1911	D: 22 Dec 1957
Lucy L. Waddell	B: 1908	D: 1986
Robert W. Waddell	B: 1916	D: 1987

Lot: 946   Lot Owner: Miscellaneous

C. Walter Fletcher	B: 1896	D: 1958
Mary S. Fletcher	B: 1905	D: 1964
Ruby E. Kirby	B: 18 Nov 1913	D: 20 Dec 1964

Lot: 947   Lot Owner: Claude Leith

B. Franklin Leith, Jr	B: 1882	D: 1961
Claude Gibson Leith, Jr	B: 22 Nov 1956	D: 8 Oct 1958
		Gippy
Claude Gibson Leith, Sr	B: 22 Apr 1920	D: 1 Mar 1991
		WWII

Lot: 948   Lot Owner: Claude Leith

Raymond W. Noonan	B: 1 Aug 1896	D: 22 Aug 1978
Va D. Leith Noonan	B: 5 Oct 1901	D: 18 Aug 1978

Lot: 949   Lot Owner: Wharton Hall

Estelle A. Hall	B: 30 Aug 1903	D: 26 Oct 1990
Wharton E. Hall	B: 2 Feb 1898	D: 11 Mar 1971
James McCall	B: 1927	D: 1982
Mary McCall	B: 1936	no death date
William Russell Underwood	B: 4 Jan 1902	D: 1 Mar 1993

Lot: 950   Lot Owner: George W. & E. Robertson

Edna H. Robertson	B: 1906	D: 1992
George W. Robertson	B: 1897	D: 1977

Lot: 951   Lot Owner: Miscellaneous

Charles Edward Jr Craun	B: 22 Jul 1947	D: 28 Sep 1996 Vietnam
Olga R. Craun	B: 22 Jan 1924	D: 8 Dec 1995

Lot: 954   Lot Owner: Lucy Locke

Frances A. Jeffries	B: 24 Aug 1929	D: 2 Jun 1993
Edward F. Locke	B: 22 Jun 1938	no death date
Lucy L. Locke	B: 26 Jan 1936	D: 9 Mar 1992
Charles F. Owens	B: 15 May 1901	D: 4 May 1982
Nealia K. Owens	B: 28 Jan 1906	D: 2 Feb 1972

Lot: 955   Lot Owner: Richard Lee Williams

Dorothy A. Williams		no dates
Richard L. Williams	B: 1940	D: 1971

Lot: 956   Lot Owner: Miscellaneous

Catherine M. Ballenger	B: 1913	D: 1985
E. Russell Sr Ballenger	B: 1912	D: 1975
Catherine B. Embrey	B: 1917	D: 1994
Fred H. Embrey	B: 1913	D: 1974

Lot: 957   Lot Owner: James Hall

Elizabeth P. Hall	B: 1918	D: 1978
James G. Hall	B: 1912	D: 1975

Lot: 959   **Lot Owner: Mrs. Alice Ball**

Alice Marie Ball	B: 19 Nov 1915	D: 19 Feb 1983
William Ernest Ball	B: 6 Aug 1914	D: 2 Feb 1972 WWII
Chester Earl Finchum	B: 1894	D: 1981 WWI
Nannie C. Finchum	B: 1 Jun 1896	D: 14 May 1991

Lot: 960   **Lot Owner: Mary Ruth Jenkins**

Mary Ruth Jenkins	B: 20 Mar 1913	D: 12 May 1978
Walter C. Jenkins	B: 27 Jan 1909	D: 19 Nov 1975

Lot: 961   **Lot Owner: Miscellaneous**

Richard D. Milbourne	B: 1941	D: 1997

Lot: 967   **Lot Owner: Elmer Harriss**

Elmer F. Harriss	B: 26 Sep 1889	D: 17 Sep 1965
Lucy Pearson Harriss	B: 3 Apr 1886	D: 25 Feb 1959
Thomas F. Harriss	B: 25 Jul 1919	D: 6 Jun 1974

Lot: 968   **Lot Owner: F. Gorman Hatcher**

F. Gorman Hatcher, Jr	B: 1903	D: 1974

Lot: 969   **Lot Owner: Miscellaneous**

Ethel Jeffries Edwards	B: 29 Aug 1905	D: 7 Feb 1987
William H. Edwards, Sr	B: 1899	D: 1980 WWI

Lot: 970   **Lot Owner: Thomas Soaper**

Elwood Waldo Carter	B: 19 Aug 1926	D: 8 Jul 1987 WWII
Elwood Lee Soaper	B: 9 Dec 1956	D: 7 Mar 1960

Lot: 971   **Lot Owner: Miscellaneous**

Cora L. Edwards	B: 1919	D: 1993
Golder F. Edwards	B: 1927	D: 1980
Pauline E. Edwards	B: 1917	no death date
Philip T. Edwards	B: 1908	D: 1986

Lot: 972   Lot Owner: Miscellaneous

Vena M. Bettis   B: 1922   D: 1985

Lot: 974   Lot Owner: Miscellaneous

Arthur Leon Sr Sommers   B: 31 May 1927   D: 30 Oct 1983

Lucy Bell Sommers   B: 1 Mar 1923   D: 10 Apr 1973

Lot: 979   Lot Owner: Miscellaneous

Lemuel F. Owens   B: 1932   D: 1986

Lot: 980   Lot Owner: Russell Owens

Katie V. Owens   B: 1900   D: 1983

Lenny Owens   B: 1938   no death date

Lot: 980   Lot Owner: Miscellaneous

Duane A. Hall   B: 1966   D: 1993

Linda A. Hall   B: 1944   no death date

Wayne G. Hall   B: 1941   no death date

Lot: 989   Lot Owner: Cecil T. Campbell

Cecil Thomas Campbell   B: 12 Aug 1898   D: 6 Jul 1974

Grace Riley Campbell   B: 15 Jun 1902   D: 6 Mar 1981

Richard L. Campbell   B: 4 May 1932   D: 21 Jun 1982
                                                                Korea

Mary S. Kees   B: 25 Dec 1926   D: 20 Dec 1991

Lot: 990   Lot Owner: Miscellaneous

Bessie Virginia Baker   B: 24 Mar 1898   D: 27 Aug 1967

James H. Baker, Jr   B: 12 Aug 1923   no death date

James Henry Baker   B: 25 Mar 1891   D: 25 Oct 1966

Mary M. Baker   B: 30 Jan 1926   D: 27 May 1986

Lot: 991   Lot Owner: Clarence Waddell

Clarence E. Waddell   B: 1898   D: 1975

Clarence E. Waddell, Jr   B: 22 Dec 1938   D: 31 Dec 1959

Donald H. Waddell   B: 1946   D: 1975

Mary H. Waddell   B: 1902   D: 1980

Lot: 992   Lot Owner: Miscellaneous

Ghorley R. Hatcher   B: 6 Mar 1898   D: 19 Oct 1961

Harry H. Hatcher   B: 12 Mar 1896   D: 1 Jun 1962

Katherine N. Hatcher   B: 8 Feb 1900   D: 17 Dec 1988

Granville D. Jacobs   B: 28 Sep 1919   D: 6 Apr 1973
                                                                  WWII

Lot: 993   Lot Owner: Golder Edwards

Golder I. Edwards   B: 26 Mar 1884   D: 15 May 1960

Virginia J. Edwards   B: 21 Sep 1886   D: 4 Jan 1966

Clarence B. Jennings   B: 11 Aug 1901   D: 28 Nov 1964

Hubert R. Leverette   B: 14 Feb 1919   D: 4 Jul 1967

Louise Edwards Leverette   B: 13 Jan 1915   D: 13 Dec 1996

Lot: 1002   Lot Owner: Miscellaneous

Katherine H. Forsyth   B: 14 Aug 1892   D: 12 Nov 1989

Lot: 1012   Lot Owner: Miscellaneous

Agnes Waddell Robertson   B: 28 Mar 1940   D: 23 May 1993

Joseph Elwood Weeks   B: 16 Mar 1930   D: 20 Jan 1994
                                                                  Korea

Richard B. Weeks   B: 23 Mar 1880   D: 18 Jan 1968

Lot: 1014   Lot Owner: Miscellaneous

John W. Gray   B: 1919   D: 1961

Samuel F. Gray   B: 1892   D: 1972

Lot: 1031   Lot Owner: Miscellaneous

Hugh Adams MacDougall   B: 11 Jul 1933   D: 29 Aug 1964

Lot: 1032   Lot Owner: Miscellaneous

Daren M. Kauffman   B: 18 Dec 1974   D: 4 Jan 1975

Lot: Gate   Lot Owner: Miscellaneous

Carrie Anna Draisey   B: 3 May 1923   no death date

Paul Draisey   B: 5 May 1924   D: 19 May 1987

| Kathleen R. Gore | B: 1912 | D: 1976 |
| Ray C. Michael, Sr | B: 28 May 1917 | D: 25 Apr 1987 |

Sharon Cemetery

By the late 1840's the acre graveyard surrounding the Free Church had become crowded, so on February 24, 1849 seventeen citizens of the County of Loudoun, their names headed by Humphrey Brooke Powell, incorporated as the Sharon Cemetery Company "for the purpose of establishing a public cemetery." In November, 1850 they bought four and one-half acres from Marietta F. Powell for $520, with the 1857 deed noting that the Free Church and its graveyard were "now in the occupancy of the said company." *–Eugene M. Scheel*

* Indicates burials listed by Mrs. Jewell for which no stone was found. This means the information could not be verified.

The circle with CSA in the center is a memorial grave for Confederate soldiers. The church was used as a hospital during the war, and soldiers who died in the hospital were probably buried in random graves throughout the cemetery. If their graves were ever marked, the wooden boards or crosses are now gone. The United Daughters of the Confederacy erected the monument, in the center of the circle, with eighty markers of known burials.

In areas where graves were found outside of the mapped sites, they have been identified using the closest lot number and the "A" indicator.

| 346 | 347 | 350 | | 351 | 354 | 355 | 358 | 359 | 362 | 363 | 366 | 367 | 370 |
| 345 | 348 | 349 | | 352 | 353 | 356 | 357 | 360 | 361 | 364 | 365 | 368 | 369 |

344	343												
341	342	1		29	56	57	84	85		108	109	136	137
340	339	2	27	30 55	58	83	86			107 106	110	135 A	138 A
337	338	3	26	31	54	59	82	87		111	134	139
336	335	4	25	32	53	60	81	88		105	112	133	140

333	334	5	24	33	52	61	80		113	132	141
332	331	6	23	34	51	62	79		114	131	142
329	330	7	22	35	50	63				130	143
328	327										
325	326	8	21	36	49	64				129	144
324	323	9	20	37	48	65	76		117	128	145
321	322	10	19	38	47	66	75		118	127	146

320	319	11	18	39	46	67	74	93		100	119	126	147
317	318	12	17	40	45	68	73	94		99	120	125	148
316	315	13	16	41	44	69	72	95				124	149
313		14	15	42	43	70	71	96				123	150
312	314												

	309	307	306		303	302	299	298	295	294	291	290	287
311	310	308	305		304	301	300	297	296	293	292	289	288
379	381	383	385		387	389	391	393	395	397	399	401	403
380	382	384	386		388	390	392	394	396	398	400	402	404

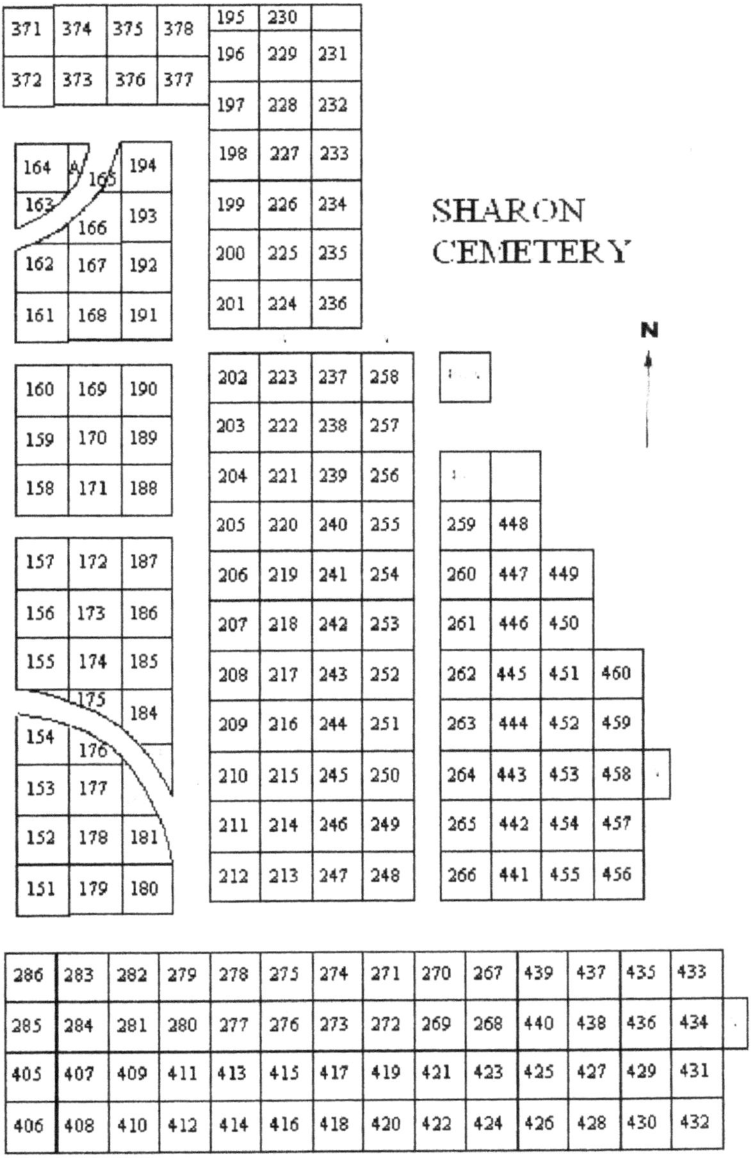

SHARON CEMETERY

N

Top-left block:

371	374	375	378
372	373	376	377

164	166	194
163	166	193
162	167	192
161	168	191
160	169	190
159	170	189
158	171	188
157	172	187
156	173	186
155	174	185
175		184
154	176	
153	177	
152	178	181
151	179	180

Center block:

195	230		
196	229	231	
197	228	232	
198	227	233	
199	226	234	
200	225	235	
201	224	236	
202	223	237	258
203	222	238	257
204	221	239	256
205	220	240	255
206	219	241	254
207	218	242	253
208	217	243	252
209	216	244	251
210	215	245	250
211	214	246	249
212	213	247	248

Right block:

259	448		
260	447	449	
261	446	450	
262	445	451	460
263	444	452	459
264	443	453	458
265	442	454	457
266	441	455	456

Bottom block:

286	283	282	279	278	275	274	271	270	267	439	437	435	433
285	284	281	280	277	276	273	272	269	268	440	438	436	434
405	407	409	411	413	415	417	419	421	423	425	427	429	431
406	408	410	412	414	416	418	420	422	424	426	428	430	432

Lot: 1   1898 Owner: H.B. Powell

Ellen Boyd Powell	B: 11 Sep 1840	D: 1 Nov 1841
Sarah Harrison Powell	B: 1737	D: 20 Oct 1812
	w/o Col. Leven Powell, d/o Hon. Burr Harrison, III	
Mary Elizabeth Powell	B: 16 Jul 1831	D: 16 Sep 1833
Maria Loudonia Powell	B: 3 Dec 1832	D: 17 Aug 1834
Ann R. H. Powell	B: 18 Jan 1807	D: 2 Apr 1895
		w/o H. B. Powell
Burr Powell	B: 11 May 1768	D: 14 Oct 1839
Catharine Powell	B: 9 Jun 1770	D: 18 May 1851
Humphrey Brooke Powell	B: 18 Feb 1795	D: 6 Apr 1859
Edward Burr Powell	B: 1 Sep 1802	D: 29 Oct 1823
Humphrey Powell Harrison	Age: 11 mos	D: 9 Aug 1856
	s/o E. J. & S. P. Harrison	

Lot: 2   1898 Owner: H.B. Powell

Laura Harrison	B: 14 Dec 1824	D: 21 Aug 1825
	d/o B. W. & S. H. Harrison	

Lot: 3   1898 Owner: J.B. & J.T. Skinner

John Turner Skinner	B: 1901	D: 1963
Florence Pizzini Reed	B: 22 Nov 1905	D: 25 Oct 1984
James B. Skinner	B: 8 Jul 1887	D: 8 May 1974
Margot LeLong Skinner	B: 1884	D: 1957
Anne Pizzini Barbour	B: 29 Jun 1875	D: 14 Jun 1968

Lot: 4   1898 Owner: J.S. Myers

Louise C. Warren	B: 23 Feb 1920	
Braddie B. Myers	Age: 3 yrs	D: 3 Dec 1881
Frederick F. Warren	B: 30 Nov 1915	D: 6 Aug 1999

Lot: 5   1898 Owner: Asa & Nancy Rector

Ann F. Rector	B: 14 Nov 1837	D: 28 Sep 1923
Asa H. Rector	B: 9 Sep 1839	D: 24 Jan 1911
		CSA: 6th VA Cavalry, Co. A

Clarence H. Rector	B: 31 Aug 1870	D: 3 Mar 1939
R. H. Rector	B: 9 Mar 1833	D: 9 Jun 1888
Minnie Nelson Rector	B: 25 Sep 1872	D: 22 Oct 1943

Lot: 6   1898 Owner: Dawson

Carroll Franklin Dawson	B: 25 May 1879	D: 26 Jun 1884
		s/o B. F. & J. R. Dawson
Maude E. Dawson	B: 1882	D: 1967
B. F. Dawson	B: 23 Aug 1851	D: 7 Nov 1929
Irma E. Dawson	B: 1885	D: 1972
Jeanette R. Dawson	B: 6 Apr 1856	D: 23 Sep 1930
		w/o B. F. Dawson
J. Copeland Dawson	B: 22 Aug 1880	D: 18 Jun 1950

Lot: 8   1898 Owner: Jno. H. Griffith

| Annie Cornell Griffith | B: 1884 | D: 1972 |
| John H. Griffith | B: 1883 | D: 1941 |

Lot: 9   1898 Owner: L.M. Downs

Lawrence M. Downs	B: 7 Apr 1884	D: 31 Jan 1951
Hattie A. Lunceford Downs	B: 15 Feb 1879	D: 10 Mar 1951
Robert L. Allison	B: 17 Apr 1876	D: 3 Jun 1936

Lot: 10   1898 Owner: S.G.A. Roszell

Sarah DeButts Roszel	B: 2 Dec 1855	D: 11 Oct 1913
		w/o George A. Roszel
S. Sam Roszel	B: 28 Oct 1882	D: 21 Sep 1961
Rosa D. H. Roszel	B: 12 Jan 1889	D: 11 Jun 1981
George Asbury Roszel	B: 3 Sep 1850	D: 12 Mar 1906
Rosa Roszel McGill	B: 1 Jul 1884	D: 20 Jul 1948
James Page Roszel	B: 6 Mar 1925	D: 28 Jan 1976

Lot: 11   1898 Owner: Fritz Reuter

Adolfine Sophie Reuter	B: 24 Dec 1860	D: 15 Sep 1929
		w/o Frederick W. Reuter
Frederick August Reuter	B: 9 Nov 1891	D: 16 Sep 1975

| Frederick William Reuter | B: 30 Sep 1861 | D: 29 Jan 1906 |
| Martha Turner Reuter | B: 22 Feb 1893 | D: 28 Aug 1961 |

Lot: 12   1898 Owner: Ida Craun

| Lawrence Craun | | D: 1 May 1895 |
| | s/o D. H. & I. E. Craun | Age: 1 yr |

Lot: 13   1898 Owner: W.M. Waddell

Isaac M. Waddell	B: 1870	D: 17 May 1943
Bulah L. Yates	B: 11 Dec 1902	D: 13 Mar 1903
	d/o Willie L. & Louise K. Yates	
William A. Waddell	B: 16 Apr 1837	D: 6 Nov 1907
Frances Downs Waddell	B: 1876	D: 1956

Lot: 14   1898 Owner: L.W. Waddell

Beverly Royal Waddell	B: 4 Jun 1899	D: 25 Jul 1902
	s/o Lemuel & Lillie Waddell	
Lillie Kerns Waddell	B: 1878	D: 1957
James T. Leach	B: 30 Sep 1905	D: 16 Mar 1980
W. Lemuel Waddell	B: 1868	D: 1941

Lot: 15L   1898 Owner: Thos. Pearson

Forest Pearson		D: 1930
	s/o T. F. & E. F. Pearson	Age: 9 days
Thomas F. Pearson	B: 1884	D: 1958
Elizabeth H. Pearson	B: 1886	D: 1970
Murray R. Pearson	B: 4 Jul 1922	
Norma B. Pearson	B: 15 Mar 1933	

Lot: 15U   1898 Owner: Mrs. Edw. Griffith

Mary Pearson Griffith	B: 5 Dec 1852	D: 5 Aug 1932
Edward Griffith	B: 2 Oct 1849	D: 19 Apr 1934
Sarah E. Griffith	B: 9 Oct 1885	D: 1 Mar 1936
Ella Griffith	B: 30 Jan 1889	D: 11 Jan 1947

Lot: 16L   1898 Owner: Harry Underwood

Elmer F. Guy Pearson	B: 22 Oct 1910	D: 17 Apr 1995
Evelyn P. Tiffany	B: 24 Aug 1927	D: 12 Jan 1993
Marian F. Pearson	B: 3 Mar 1918	D: 10 Apr 1977
L. Aaron Byrne	B: 12 Aug 1946	D: 23 Sep 1975
Dorothy Pearson Byrne	B: 6 Oct 1924	D: 10 Jan 1988
Stanley M. Byrne	B: 20 Dec 1947	D: 28 Jun 1964
Clyde H. Sutphin	B: 25 Jun 1913	D: 21 May 1975
Mattie L. Sutphin	B: 25 Jan 1910	D: 8 Feb 1986

Lot: 16U   1898 Owner: W. Creel

Wellington Creel	B: 1878	D: 1960
Mattie L. Creel	B: 1880	D: 1953
		w/o Wellington Creel
Milton G. Creel	B: 28 Jul 1911	D: 1 Feb 1948
Ruby May Creel	B: 28 Aug 1913	D: 5 Aug 1926
Alice M. Creel	B: 20 Sep 1917	D: 5 Jun 1918

Lot: 17L   1898 Owner: W.K. Risdon

William K. Risdon	B: 17 Jul 1889	D: 12 Jul 1958
Cennie E. Risdon	B: 5 Apr 1896	D: 26 Jul 1931
		w/o W. K. Risdon

Lot: 17U   1898 Owner: D.A. Ferguson

Marie Ferguson Waff	B: 6 Apr 1921	D: 19 Apr 1996
Pearl I. Ferguson	B: Sep 1891	D: Sep 1968
		d/o Asbery & Elizabeth Ferguson
Leslie Daniel Ferguson	B: 28 Apr 1898	D: 18 Feb 1965
Daniel A. Ferguson	B: 1858	D: 1936
M. Elizabeth Ferguson	B: 1856	D: 1929

Lot: 18L   1898 Owner: Elmer Manuel

Caroline V. Manuel	B: 20 Mar 1863	D: 22 Sep 1936

Lot: 18U   1898 Owner: Albert F. Smith

James M. Smith	B: 12 Nov 1906	D: 12 Apr 1968
Edith Claire Tavenner	B: 21 May 1899	D: 24 Oct 1967
Dorothea I. Maddox	B: 12 Apr 1912	D: 25 Jun 1983
Albert Franklin Smith	B: 7 Nov 1871	D: 11 Jan 1929
Lessie Pearl Keyes	B: 9 Nov 1876	D: 22 Feb 1961
Mamie Smith	B: 19 Aug 1900	D: 10 Sep 1901
Milton Murray Smith	B: 28 Dec 1901	D: 3 Apr 1902
Flora Estelle Smith	B: 10 Dec 1897	D: 30 Mar 1922
Lena Francis Smith	B: 23 Aug 1910	D: 18 Dec 1916
Mary Marguerite Smith	B: 21 Nov 1922	D: 22 Aug 1923

Lot: 19   1898 Owner: Sadie Ward

| Elizabeth G. Ward | B: 1869 | D: 1947 |
| Rosie Blanch Ward | B: 1872 | D: 1949 |

Lot: 21   1898 Owner: Elmer Thomas

Lucius Elmer Thomas	B: 22 Dec 1896	D: 10 Dec 1971
Tarlton B. Thomas	B: 25 Mar 1858	D: 24 Dec 1934
Martha W. Thomas	B: 18 Jan 1897	D: 13 Sep 1974
Katherine B. Thomas	B: 30 Jan 1872	D: 16 Sep 1943
Annie Megeath Thomas	B: 22 Sep 1924	D: 8 Mar 1930
	d/o Elmer & Martha Thomas	

Lot: 22   1898 Owner: G.W. Cocke

Hunton Foster Cocke	B: 11 Jul 1865	D: 6 Oct 1939
	s/o Rufus Taylor & Sarah E. Cocke	
Kemp F. Cocke	Age: 74 yrs	D: 8 May 1885
Gourley Wellington Cocke	B: 1 Jul 1844	D: 13 Feb 1906

Lot: 23   1898 Owner: W.J. Luck

| S. Preston Luck | B: 14 Aug 1874 | D: 7 Sep 1938 |
| Lucile Ashton Luck | B: 18 Jul 1884 | D: 25 Jan 1955 |

William J. Luck, MD	B: 23 Apr 1836	D: 3 Dec 1906
	CSA: 4th NC Cavalry, Surgeon	
William J. Luck	B: 14 Dec 1906	D: 30 Apr 1944
Marion C. Luck	B: 21 Apr 1909	D: 29 Dec 1964
Roberta R. Luck	B: 1 Dec 1846	D: 7 Apr 1909
Roszier R. Luck	B: 2 Oct 1872	D: 3 Feb 1901
W. W. Luck, MD	B: 28 May 1871	D: 21 Feb 1898

Lot: 24   1898 Owner: W.A. Rector

Mary R. Cole	B: 13 Sep 1875	D: 29 Jul 1959
		w/o James M. Cole
Sarah J. Rector	B: 6 Mar 1844	D: 5 Nov 1920
		w/o W. A. Rector
James M. Cole	B: 15 Mar 1880	D: 13 Dec 1961
Kathryne O. Rector	B: 13 Feb 1882	D: 7 Oct 1903
		w/o Lewis E. Rector
W. A. Rector	B: 10 Apr 1837	D: 13 Sep 1911

Lot: 25L   1898 Owner: Hamilton

| H. H. Hamilton | Age: 19 yrs | D: 24 Sep 1851 |
| Willie Hamilton | | Age: 1 yr |

Lot: 25U   1898 Owner: E.A. Tyler

Lucy Mary Watson	B: 15 Sep 1870	D: 13 Feb 1949
Alice Elizabeth Watson	B: 1 May 1875	D: 31 Jan 1902
	d/o Joseph T. & Mary E. Watson	
Mary E. Watson	B: 15 May 1840	D: 13 Mar 1927
		w/o J. T. Watson
J. T. Watson	B: 12 Aug 1839	D: 31 Jan 1908

Lot: 26   1898 Owner: F.W. Luckett

| F. W. Luckett | Age: 83 yrs | D: 5 Mar 1869 |

Lot: 27   1898 Owner: Miss P. Waugh

| Sarah H. Chilton | Age: 61 yrs | D: 24 May 1838 |
| Mary Peyton Waugh | | D: Aug 1865 |

Lot: 28U   1898 Owner: J. Cullen

Armstead Cullen   B: 4 Aug 1856   D: 29 Dec 1856
                                            s/o John & Winifred Cullen

Lot: 29   1898 Owner: W.F. Dowell

Sonoro Dowell   B: 5 Jan 1823   D: 23 Mar 1891
                                            w/o William Dowell

William F. Dowell, Jr.   B: 24 Nov 1848   D: 12 Oct 1885

Lot: 30   1898 Owner: Not Listed

Margaret H. Hall   B: 13 Apr 1880   D: 12 Dec 1917

Lot: 31   1898 Owner: L. Luckett

Mary Luckett Miller   D: 19 Feb 1916

Nannie Glass   Age: 26 yrs   D: 19 Aug 1861
                                            w/o William W. Glass

Ludwell Luckett   B: 13 Mar 1796   D: 13 May 1875

Ludwell H. Luckett   B: 9 Nov 1826   D: 9 Oct 1891

Evalina Luckett   B: 3 Oct 1823   D: 16 Mar 1887
                                            d/o Ludwell & Ann C. Luckett

Ann C. Luckett   D: 14 Nov 1852
                               w/o Ludwell Luckett   Age: 50 yrs

*Dr. G.T. Luckett   Age: in 35th yr   D: 28 Apr 1868

Lot: 32   1898 Owner: Mrs. S. Skillman

Cora L. Benton   B: 7 Nov 1866   D: 6 Nov 1889
                                            d/o R. H. & M. A. Benton

Dora L. Benton   B: 25 Aug 1860   D: 24 Aug 1889
                                            d/o R. H. & M. A. Benton

T. H. Benton   B: 7 Apr 1871   D: 11 Nov 1903

Martha A. Benton   B: 25 May 1837   D: 21 Oct 1889
                                            w/o Richard H. Benton

Lot: 33   1898 Owner: Mrs. H.P. Sughner

Mary J. Surghnor   d/o James & Harriett P. Surghnor

James Surghnor   Age: 53 yrs   D: 25 Feb 1838

Harriet P. H. Surghnor   D: 16 Dec 1870
                                   w/o James Surghnor   Age: 85 yrs

Florence W. Shuman   w/o S. T. Shuman

George W. Shuman   no dates

Harriett Peyton Shuman   w/o George W. Shuman

Septimus T. Shuman   c/o George W. & Harriett P. Shuman

Shuman   c/o George W. & Harriett P. Shuman

Frances A. Surghnor   d/o James & Harriett P. Surghnor

Lot: 34   1898 Owner: Jas. Warren

Arthur Amor   B: 20 Feb 1881   D: 8 Mar 1904
                                                        s/o J. & E. S. Amor

Rosina W. Baldwin   B: 5 Dec 1885   D: 8 Jul 1967

Sarah Stone Warren   B: 2 Jul 1846   D: 2 Jan 1910
                                                        w/o James A. Warren

George A. Warren   B: 15 Oct 1879   D: 12 Jul 1937

Louise Maud Mary Warren   B: 7 May 1870   D: 31 May 1916
                                 d/o James A. & Sarah Stone Warren

Jane Warren   B: 12 Jul 1881   D: 7 Oct 1881
                                 d/o James A. & Sarah Stone Warren

James A. Warren   B: 26 Jun 1845   D: 29 Mar 1932

Emily F. Warren   B: 5 Jul 1888   D: 15 Jul 1934
                                 d/o James A. & Sarah Stone Warren

Lot: 35   1898 Owner: Harry Hatcher

Sophy Dowell Hatcher   B: 1852   D: 1922

William Claude Hatcher   B: 1882   D: 30 Sep 1947

Harry Hatcher   Age: 54 yrs   D: 23 Apr 1895
                                          CSA: 43rd VA Cavalry, Co. A

Florence Dibrell Hatcher   B: 1888   D: 1939

Lot: 38   1898 Owner: A.B. Moore

Alexander Beard Moore   B: 2 Jul 1836   D: 21 Jan 1914
s/o John & Martha B. Moore   CSA: 8th VA Infantry, Co. D

Francis Berkeley Moore	B: 8 Oct 1892	D: 15 Dec 1911
	s/o Alexander B. & Lucy B. Moore	
George E. Moore	B: 16 Jul 1895	D: 22 Feb 1928
	s/o Alexander B. & Lucy B. Moore	
Lucy Beverley Moore	B: 29 Mar 1855	D: 12 Jan 1916
	w/o Alexander Beard Moore	
Rosanna Douglass Moore	B: 21 Nov 1882	D: 2 Sep 1919
	w/o G. F. Moore	
Ann B. Moore	B: 14 Dec 1881	D: 3 Apr 1953
	d/o Alexander B. & Lucy B. Moore	

Lot: 39   1898 Owner: W.P. Burgess

George Moffett Burgess	B: 1889	D: 1958
Virginia S. Burgess	B: 1892	D: 1983
Field Burgess	B: 1888	D: 1962
Oscar W. Burgess	B: 1899	D: 1965
Louise V. Burgess	B: 1861	D: 1925
Winter P. Burgess	B: 1861	D: 1932

Lot: 40L   1898 Owner: A.M. Waddell

Mabel Waddell Monroe	B: 8 Aug 1911	D: 21 Dec 1994
Alice Wine Waddell	B: 7 Sep 1881	D: 4 Nov 1964
Asa Noland Waddell	B: 16 Apr 1873	D: 20 Nov 1940
William Dulaney Monroe	B: 21 May 1899	D: 29 Sep 1972

Lot: 40U   1898 Owner: Mrs. J.H. Davis

Ewell A. Sutphin	B: 15 Sep 1876	D: 6 May 1934
	h/o Mabel C. Sutphin	
Mabel C. Sutphin	B: 22 May 1882	D: 23 Apr 1963
	w/o Ewell A. Sutphin	
Everlee Mae Sutphin	B: 31 Mar 1909	D: 30 Oct 1992
	d/o E. A. & M. C. Sutphin	
James H. Davis	B: 3 Jan 1849	D: 13 Nov 1906

Lot: 41   1898 Owner: Mrs. E.H. Gibson

Edward Carter Gibson	B: 1839	D: 1909
		CSA: 8th VA Infantry, Co. A
Mary C. Hutchison	B: 13 Aug 1879	D: 23 Nov 1929
		w/o G. T. Hutchison
Joseph R. Turner	B: 4 Jun 1912	D: 17 Sep 1993
George T. Hutchison	B: 15 Oct 1881	D: 28 Nov 1966
Frances R. Gibson	B: 1847	D: 1919
		w/o E. C. Gibson
Joseph R. Turner	B: 17 Oct 1873	D: 5 Mar 1926
Dagmar K. Turner	B: 2 Feb 1919	D: 13 Dec 1988
Annie Turner Hutchison	B: 2 Feb 1887	D: 11 Nov 1954

Lot: 42L   1898 Owner: G.A. Pearson

George Albert Pearson	B: 29 Oct 1882	D: 4 Feb 1968
Elwood Pearson	B: 16 Aug 1894	D: 31 Oct 1971
Randolph Pearson	B: 3 Jun 1891	D: 26 Nov 1967

Lot: 42U   1898 Owner: T.J. Pearson

Annie E. Pearson	B: 17 Sep 1887	D: 8 Dec 1965
		d/o J. T. & M. E. Pearson
J. T. Pearson	B: 27 Jan 1854	D: 12 Dec 1919
Mary E. Pearson	B: 18 Jan 1855	D: 4 Jun 1916
		w/o J. T. Pearson

Lot: 43   1898 Owner: Mrs. S.E. Pearson

Mazie B. Pearson	B: 1884	D: 1945
Milton M. Pearson	B: 1886	D: 1953
J. C. Pearson	B: 1828	D: 1865
		CSA: Loudoun Artillery
S. H. Pearson	B: 1851	D: 1922
Sarah E. Pearson	B: 1828	D: 1906
		w/o John C. Pearson
W. F. Pearson	B: 1856	D: 1882
Ollie M. Pearson	B: 1882	D: 1943

Amanda B. Pearson	B: 1853	D: 1888
		w/o S. H. Pearson
Elizabeth C. Pearson	B: 1865	D: 1937
Alice H. Pearson	B: 1862	D: 1929

Lot: 44   1898 Owner: Dr. Fred Hutchison

Mary Louisa Hutchison	B: 13 Nov 1884	D: 5 Jul 1904
	d/o Frederick & Mary T. Hutchison	
Mary T. Hutchison	B: 13 Jun 1862	D: 15 Mar 1929
William L. Adams	B: 1940	
Robert Perrington Adams	B: 26 Jul 1927	D: 30 Jul 1983
Paul A. Adams	B: 1899	D: 1986
Eleanor G. Adams	B: 1905	D: 1994
Frederick Ludwell Hutchison	B: 26 Aug 1891	D: 15 Dec 1977
Frederick Hutchison, MD	B: 2 Dec 1852	D: 20 Feb 1933

Lot: 45   1898 Owner: F.A. Ish

Robert A. Ish	B: 23 Apr 1882	D: 29 Jan 1901
		s/o F. A. & A. L. Ish
Milton A. Ish	B: 11 Jun 1884	D: 20 Sep 1969
Frank A. Ish	B: 3 Jul 1847	D: 21 Oct 1923
Alice L. Ish	B: 29 Mar 1853	D: 3 Jan 1914
		w/o Frank A. Ish
Robert Francis Ish	B: 5 Jul 1917	D: 17 Aug 1941
		s/o M. A. & Elizabeth A. Ish
Elizabeth A. Ish	B: 3 Mar 1884	D: 1 Feb 1965

Lot: 46   1898 Owner: M. Zimmerman

Hannah Lee Zimmerman	B: 9 Jun 1880	D: 19 Jul 1977
John M. Zimmerman	B: 10 Nov 1876	D: 29 Dec 1894
Milton Zimmerman	B: 6 Nov 1840	D: 6 May 1902
Amanda Allison Zimmerman		D: 17 Dec 1913
Nellie Zimmerman	B: 23 Jan 1882	D: 7 Feb 1966

Lot: 47   1898 Owner: Hugh Brent

| Joseph Warren Brent | B: 23 Dec 1840 | D: 21 Jun 1863 |
| | | CSA: died at Upperville |

| Juliet P. Brent | B: 28 Sep 1815 | D: 13 Jun 1889 |

| Lafayette Brent | B: 11 Jan 1816 | D: 3 Aug 1895 |

| Nannie J. Brent | B: 1 Aug 1857 | D: 30 Nov 1893 |

| Sallie E. A. Brent | Age: 79 yrs | D: 31 Dec 1931 |

| William A. Brent | B: 3 Apr 1842 | D: 4 Oct 1904 |
| | | CSA: 7th VA Cavalry, Co. A |

| *Anabel Beattie | B: 18 Nov 1871 | D: 18 Sep 1874 |
| | | d/o Fountain & Annie E. Beattie |

1898 Owner: C.G. Hathaway

| Elizabeth F. Russell | B: 1908 | D: 1960 |

| Elizabeth Hathaway | B: 11 Mar 1882 | D: 28 Nov 1886 |
| | | d/o C. G. & Blanche Hathaway |

| Blanchie Hathaway | B: 12 Jan 1888 | D: 15 Nov 1963 |

| Blanche Hathaway | B: 14 Jan 1855 | D: 30 Dec 1937 |

| Charles G. Hathaway | B: 6 Feb 1850 | D: 8 May 1929 |

| M. Lucile Hathaway | B: 12 Jul 1890 | D: 15 May 1973 |

Lot: 49   1898 Owner: John Doyle

| John Doyle | B: 1838 | D: 1906 |
| | | CSA: 8th VA Infantry, Co. D |

| John J. Roche | B: 1865 | D: 1928 |

Lot: 50   1898 Owner: G.R. Hatcher

| Mary J. Hatcher | | D: 21 Feb 1890 |
| | | w/o Gourley R. Hatcher |

| Hattie E. Hatcher | Age: 61 yrs | D: 26 May 1909 |
| | | d/o Gourley & Mary J. Hatcher |

| Gourley R. Hatcher | B: 1 Oct 1810 | D: 26 Nov 1884 |

Lot: 51   1898 Owner: Wm Crouch

| Callie C. Davis | B: 14 Jun 1849 | D: 6 Oct 1910 |

| Charles E. Davis | B: 1845 | D: 1933 |

Annie M Davis	B: 20 Nov 1889	D: 7 Dec 1890
		d/o C. E. & C. Davis
William Crouch	B: 12 Aug 1812	D: 26 Apr 1878
Mary Virginia Crouch	B: 9 Apr 1850	D: 21 Jan 1918
*Joseph M. Davis	Age: 23-1-2	D: 17 Jan 1915
Arrena Crouch	B: 19 Dec 1810	D: 15 Sep 1883
		w/o William Crouch

Lot: 52L   1898 Owner: Miscellaneous

*Marietta F. Tyler	B: 7 Dec 1829	D: 5 Oct 1900
	only d/o Joseph P. & Elizabeth McGeath of this county	
John James Tyler	B: 2 Mar 1831	D: 7 Dec 1910
		CSA: 8th VA Infantry, Co. D
William H. Smallwood	Age: 18 yrs	D: 7 Jul 1864
		CSA: 43rd VA Cavalry, Co. A

Lot: 52U   1898 Owner: T.J. Skinker

Thomas Julian Skinker	B: 1819	D: 1900
Ann E. Hite Skinker	B: 1830	D: 1912
Howard Skinker	B: 17 Feb 1861	D: 20 Dec 1889
		s/o T. J. & A. E. Skinker

Lot: 53   1898 Owner: E.A. Tyler (some stones removed from the Tyler family graveyard near Aldie)

Ellen P. Tyler	B: 2 Jan 1878	D: 1 Jun 1880
		d/o Edmund A. & Ellen T. Tyler
Edmund Tyler	B: 9 Aug 1792	D: 3 Apr 1844
Flora E. Tyler	B: 9 Sep 1882	D: 9 Jun 1883
		d/o Edmund A. & Ellen T. Tyler
Edmond A. Tyler	B: 15 Jul 1832	D: 4 May 1911
		CSA: 8th VA Infantry, Co. D
Dr. Thomas M. Boyle	Age: 64 yrs	D: 2 Sep 1872
Henry J. Tyler	B: 10 May 1872	D: 2 Oct 1878
		s/o Edmund A. & Ellen T. Tyler
Joseph A. Tyler	B: 27 Nov 1867	D: 20 Oct 1868
		s/o Edmund A. & Ellen T. Tyler

Isabell Tyler	Age: 60 yrs	D: 30 Apr 1835
John Tyler	Age: 60 yrs	D: 10 Aug 1809
Ellen Tuttle Davis Tyler	B: 11 Feb 1839	D: 2 Mar 1907
		w/o Edmund A. Tyler
Mary L. Tyler	B: 5 Dec 1874	D: 9 Dec 1875
		d/o Edmund A. & Ellen T. Tyler
Lewis C. Tyler	B: 6 Jan 1870	D: 6 Jun 1870
		s/o Edmund A. & Ellen T. Tyler
Mary K. Tyler	Age: 61 yrs	D: 7 Oct 1884
infant Tyler	B: 6 Jun 1881	D: 6 Jun 1881
		c/o Edmund A. & Ellen T. Tyler

Lot: 54   1898 Owner: F.W. Powell

Matilda Jane Neville	B: 1833	D: 1926
Richard Wilmer Powell	B: 21 Aug 1851	D: 16 Apr 1853
Mary Powell	B: 9 Mar 1842	D: 3 Jun 1842
Lucia Powell	B: 4 Feb 1841	D: 22 Feb 1841
Harry Richard Neville	B: 22 Mar 1866	D: 7 Apr 1927
Dr. E. F. Powell	B: 24 Apr 1850	D: 25 Oct 1911
Charles Bell Powell	no dates	Age: 10 mos

Lot: 55   1898 Owner: A.S. Jones

| H. Van Dyke Johns | Age: 4 mos | D: 11 Sep 1878 |

Lot: 56   1898 Owner: Ann Dowell

James A. Dowell	B: 1 Mar 1814	D: 27 Apr 1822
Elizabeth A. Dowell	B: 24 Mar 1810	D: 25 Nov 1825
Elisha Dowell	B: 10 Aug 1770	D: 24 Jul 1847
Catherine L. Dowell	B: 22 May 1806	D: 15 Nov 1825
Ann Dowell	B: 22 Dec 1782	D: 1 Aug 1867
*Elisha B. Dowell	B: 20 Mar 1825	D: 20 Apr 1825
		Age: 1 mo.
*Bushrod W. Dowell	B: 22 Feb 1816	D: 11 Jul 1829
		Age: 4-4-19

John A. Dowell   B: 29 Mar 1808   D: 21 Mar 1832

Lot: 57   1898 Owner: A. Woolf

Ann C. Woolf   B: 22 Feb 1819   D: 23 Sep 1896
                                                        w/o Andrew Woolf

Rev. James A. Woolf   B: 10 Aug 1848   D: 8 Aug 1900
                                                        s/o Andrew & Ann C. Woolf

infants Woolf   B: 20 Jan 1880   D: 1 Jan 1881
                                                        c/o Thomas E. & Lizzie F. Woolf

Rev. William E. Woolf   B: 29 Apr 1851   D: 16 Sep 1919

Clara H. Woolf   Age: 3 mos   D: 5 Aug 1860

Andrew Woolf   B: 7 Feb 1812   D: 11 Oct 1901

Mary Cornelia Fletcher   B: 29 Jan 1845   D: 16 Feb 1899
                                                        w/o F. Marion Fletcher

Albert D. Woolf   Age: 6 mos   D: 16 May 1857

Lot: 58   1898 Owner: Col. Holliday

Mary J. Redmond   B: 3 Jan 1849   D: 10 May 1926
                                                        w/o Wilford Redmond

Colwell Holiday   B: 1 Apr 1820   D: 1 Jun 1874

Ernest Lynwood Redmond   B: 23 Apr 1878   D: 18 Sep 1958

Lot: 59   1898 Owner: F. Littleton

John K. Littleton   B: 1 Apr 1791   D: 27 Dec 1852

Catherine M. Littleton   B: 9 Aug 1822   D: 19 May 1901
                                                        w/o Richard C. Littleton

Fielding Littleton   Age: 59 yrs   D: 31 Mar 1857

Richard C. Littleton   B: 3 Mar 1820   D: 23 Jan 1900

Hannah Littleton   B: 20 Aug 1793   D: 2 Jun 1861
                                                        w/o John K. Littleton

Frances Washington Ball d/o Burgess & Frances Ball   Age: 84 yrs

Lot: 60   1898 Owner: J. Thompson

Frances T. Thompson   B: 29 Apr 1799   D: 7 Jan 1892

Israel B. Thompson   B: 3 May 1792   D: 14 Dec 1882

C. Peyton Thompson   B: 10 Oct 1834   D: 13 Jun 1859

| *S. Louisa Thompson | B: 27 May 1830 | D: 5 Mar 1883 |
| Laura J. Thompson | B: 4 May 1833 | D: 9 Aug 1861 |

Lot: 62   1898 Owner: T. Middleton

Sarah McDonald Middleton	B: 16 May 1845	D: 14 May 1935
John Wiley Middleton	B: 21 Mar 1838	D: 30 Mar 1893
		CSA: 7th VA Cavalry, Co. K

Lot: 63   1898 Owner: Miscellaneous

Yates Middleton	B: 9 Jun 1870	D: 16 May 1877
Mary E. Murray	B: 19 Dec 1813	D: 22 Jan 1907
James Gilham	Age: 68 yrs	D: 18 Apr 1875

Lot: 65   1898 Owner: Estate of Jas H. Hathaway

James H. Hathaway	B: 27 Apr 1812	D: 2 Jul 1892
James Adams	Age: 84 yrs	D: 14 Dec 1849
Virginia W. Adams	Age: 7 yrs	D: 8 Dec 1847
		d/o Gustavus & Elizabeth Adams
Elizabeth Adams	Age: 27 yrs	D: 19 Sep 1841
		w/o Gustavus Adams
Mary Ann Hathaway	B: 21 Apr 1811	D: 28 Aug 1854
		w/o J. H. Hathaway
Gustavus Adams	Age: 39 yrs	D: 13 Mar 1846
James A. Hathaway	B: 5 Apr 1848	D: 28 Feb 1892
Sallie Ashby	B: 13 May 1809	D: 1 Dec 1885
		w/o John J. Ashby
Elizabeth Hathaway	B: 16 Jul 1812	D: 7 Dec 1892
		w/o J. H. Hathaway
Charles S. Adams	Age: 45 yrs	D: 1 Feb 1850
Elizabeth Adams	Age: 71 yrs	D: 30 Nov 1840
		w/o James Adams
*Levenia Adams	B: 1 Oct 1833	D: 22 Sep 1907
		w/o J.W. Adams

Lot: 66 **1898 Owner: Mrs. D.C. Hatcher**

Daniel Cocke Hatcher	B: 1837	D: 1912
		CSA: 7th Va Cavalry, Major
Edwin Chunn Hatcher	B: 1874	D: 1946
Meta Hatcher Green	B: 1882	D: 1973
Meta Chunn Hatcher	B: 1850	D: 1941

Lot: 67L **1898 Owner: John J. Currell**

John J. Currell	B: 31 Mar 1829	D: 19 Aug 1886
Mary A. Currell	B: 26 Oct 1819	D: 27 Sep 1894
		w/o John J. Currell
Eveline Dawes		D: 17 Jul 1887
		d/o James E. & Amanda F. Dawes

Lot: 67U **1898 Owner: Lynn Humphrey**

J. Humphrey Lynn	B: 4 Sep 1852	D: 5 Jun 1929
Parilia F. Lynn	B: 12 Oct 1850	D: 9 May 1927
Leslie A. Lynn	B: 7 Oct 1881	D: 5 Sep 1886

Lot: 68 **1898 Owner: L.A. Turner**

Georgianna T. Hutchison	B: 18 Jan 1899	D: 14 Nov 1983
B. H. Werner	B: 22 Jun 1919	D: 31 Oct 1993
Ludwell T. Hutchison	B: 2 Aug 1897	D: 14 Jan 1961
Lucy Adams Turner	B: 7 Oct 1856	D: 23 Jan 1923
		w/o Lyttleton A. Turner
Lyttleton Adams Turner	B: 16 May 1859	D: 17 Nov 1925
Margaret Turner	B: 16 May 1857	D: 30 Mar 1937
Fannie R. Adams	B: 8 Feb 1854	D: 30 Apr 1937
Alice Ish Werner	B: 15 Sep 1915	D: 11 Nov 1987

Lot: 69 **1898 Owner: Ed. Wilson**

Rachel Wilson Adams	B: 1 Jan 1862	D: 19 Jun 1937
Margaret E. Wilson Sowers	B: 2 Sep 1897	D: 15 Jan 1939
		w/o Herbert J. Sowers

Mosby Wilson   B: 27 Dec 1866   D: 23 Jul 1900
                                  s/o Edward & M. A. Wilson

Margaret Ann Sowers   B: 20 Dec 1923   D: 4 Nov 1934
                                  d/o H. J. & Margaret W. Sowers

Margaret Parker Wilson   B: 1 Apr 1829   D: 13 Oct 1914
                                  w/o Edward Wilson

Edward Wilson   B: 27 Jun 1831   D: 3 Jul 1919

John F. Adams   B: 9 Mar 1854   D: 6 Jun 1940

Rachel Parker   B: 22 Dec 1809   D: 22 Apr 1897
                                  w/o Robert Parker

Lot: 70N   1898 Owner: A.B.C. Whitacre

Fannie Whitacre   B: 21 Nov 1835   D: 12 Jun 1929

Robert Whitacre   B: 23 Apr 1827   D: 27 Jan 1901

Ella Whitacre   B: 1 Feb 1866   D: 24 Dec 1934

Elma J. Whitacre   B: 28 Feb 1878   D: 26 Jun 1969

Lot: 70S   1898 Owner: N. Lynn/Forest Dishman

Eugenia D. Dishman   B: 1899   D: 1993

B. Forrest Dishman   B: 1898   D: 1969

T. Noel Lynn   B: 13 Mar 1877   D: 28 Dec 1939

Carrie W. Lynn   B: 11 Sep 1884   D: 22 Feb 1948

Lot: 71L   1898 Owner: Mrs. Lena Haxall

Bolling Walker Barton   B: 1845   D: 1924

Bolling Walker Haxall   B: 1851   D: 1919

Lena Noland Haxall   B: 1852   D: 1920
                                  w/o Bolling Walker Haxall

Bolling Walker Haxall, Jr.   B: 1884   D: 1919

Katharine McClure Haxall   B: 1878   D: 1958

Lot: 72   1898 Owner: Mrs. S. Hutchison

T. Gales Hutchison   B: 8 Nov 1888   D: 28 Jan 1954

Elizabeth L. Hutchison   B: 13 Jan 1876   D: 14 Feb 1969

| Henry Hanson Hutchison | B: 29 Mar 1874 | D: 5 Jun 1896 |
| | | s/o H. B. & S. E. Hutchison |

| Henry B. Hutchison | B: 3 Jun 1822 | D: 3 Feb 1890 |

| Sarah E. Hutchison | B: 6 Apr 1843 | D: 22 Feb 1921 |

| Henry H. Wilson | B: 11 Nov 1902 | D: 18 Oct 1928 |
| | | s/o W. P. & Fanny H. Wilson |

| Thomas Drury Hutchison | B: 10 Feb 1878 | D: 31 May 1898 |
| | | s/o H. B. & S. E. Hutchison |

| Fannie Hutchison Wilson | B: 17 Aug 1872 | D: 12 Mar 1911 |

Lot: 73   1898 Owner: R. Howdershell

| Laura V. Howdershell | Age: 33 yrs | D: 11 Apr 1887 |
| | | w/o R. A. Howdershell |

| R. A. Howdershell | B: 15 Jun 1840 | D: 6 Aug 1917 |

Lot: 74   1898 Owner: C.W. Simpson

| Caroline E. Stewart Simpson | B: 1841 | D: 1926 |
| | | w/o Charles W. Simpson |

| Charles W. Simpson | B: 1816 | D: 1884 |

| Richard C. Simpson | B: 1875 | D: 1934 |

Lot: 75   1898 Owner: Sam Field

| Marie Wood Field | B: 29 May 1864 | D: 4 Sep 1943 |
| | | w/o S. S. Field |

| George Harris Field | B: 1868 | D: 1937 |

| Martha Ellen Field | B: 29 Sep 1858 | D: 18 Nov 1865 |
| | | d/o Samuel & Sarah V. Field |

| S. S. Field | B: 14 Dec 1864 | D: 17 Apr 1920 |

| Samuel Field | B: 18 Jun 1821 | D: 29 Jan 1900 |

| Susie K. Woodward Field | B: 1861 | D: 1931 |
| | | w/o G. Harris Field |

| Sarah Virginia Field | B: 28 Mar 1831 | D: 25 Sep 1904 |
| | | w/o Samuel Field |

| S. Edmonia Field | B: 25 Apr 1856 | D: 17 Feb 1880 |
| | | d/o Samuel & Sarah V. Field |

Lot: 76   1898 Owner: L. Carter

| Landon Carter | B: 1810 | D: 1888 |

| Ann Eliza Carter | B: 1814 | D: 1892 |
| | | w/o Landon Carter |

Lot: 77   1898 Owner: Miss Skinner

| Bettie Jackson Skinner | B: 22 Jan 1837 | D: 14 Jan 1914 |

| Elizabeth Skinner | Age: 90 yrs | D: 23 Mar 1884 |
| | | w/o Gabriel Skinner |

| Fanny Skinner | | D: 1869 |

| Jane P. Skinner | | D: 14 Mar 1883 |

| Mary Skinner | | D: 1867 |

Lot: 78   1898 Owner: R.W. Christie

| Ann Crupper | B: 17 Feb 1827 | D: 4 Jan 1900 |
| | | w/o Thomas A. Crupper |

| Thomas A. Crupper | B: 3 Dec 1826 | D: 28 Mar 1905 |
| | | s/o John B. & Elizabeth Crupper |

Lot: 79   1898 Owner: Mrs. A. Grimsley

| Mary V. Davis Marshall | B: 1886 | D: 1937 |
| | | w/o Richard H. Marshall |

| Richard H. Marshall | B: 1870 | D: 1927 |

Lot: 80   1898 Owner: Sarah Violet

| C. W. Jeffries | B: 10 Sep 1832 | D: 24 Dec 1916 |

| Walter S. Jeffries | B: 26 Jun 1874 | D: 11 Oct 1898 |

| Edith E. Jeffries | B: 19 Jun 1836 | D: 14 Apr 1892 |

| Ashford Violett | B: 2 Mar 1807 | D: 2 Jan 1841 |

Lot: 81   1898 Owner: R.S. Chinn

| Ida Eliza Chinn | B: 28 Dec 1855 | D: 22 Apr 1897 |
| | | w/o J. Stretchley Chinn |

| Margaret Catharine Griffith | B: 19 Mar 1837 | D: 13 Jul 1882 |

| Sarah Metta Chinn | Age: 19 yrs | D: 9 Sep 1872 |
| | | d/o R. S. & Sallie Chinn |

| Sallie Beatty Chinn | B: 3 May 1825 | D: 31 Dec 1912 |
| | | w/o R. S. Chinn |

| R. S. Chinn | Age: 68 yrs | D: 12 May 1888 |

Lot: 82   1898 Owner: Sam Chinn

| Millie Chinn | Age: 50 yrs | D: 27 Jul 1846 |

| Samuel Chinn | Age: 75 yrs | D: 25 Jan 1854 |

| Frances C. Beaty | Age: 44 yrs | D: 4 Jul 1861 |
| | | w/o John Beaty |

| Sue V. Chinn | | D: 21 Nov 1876 |

Lot: 83   1898 Owner: W.J. Stephens/Thos. Welsh

| Bessie E. Stephens | B: 18 Dec 1880 | D: 10 Feb 1938 |
| | | w/o W. J. Stephens |

| Thomas H. Welch | B: 20 Apr 1886 | D: 1 Apr 1923 |

| Erma E. Stephens | B: 26 Jul 1909 | D: 23 Mar 1911 |
| | d/o W. J. & Bessie Welch Stephens | |

Lot: 84   1898 Owner: H. Kincheloe

| James M. Kincheloe | B: 29 May 1836 | D: 26 Aug 1861 |

| Hardwick Kincheloe | B: 26 Sep 1803 | D: 14 Nov 1846 |

| John W. Kincheloe | B: 12 Oct 1833 | D: 31 Oct 1912 |
| | | CSA: 7th VA Cavalry, Co. A |

| Kate S. Kincheloe | B: 29 Oct 1854 | D: 19 Jan 1938 |
| | | w/o Thomas J. Kincheloe |

| Mary A. Kincheloe | Age: 66 yrs | D: 2 May 1877 |
| | | w/o Hardwick Kincheloe |

| Thomas J. Kincheloe | B: 15 Aug 1839 | D: 18 Dec 1920 |

| Annie Turner Kincheloe | B: 7 Nov 1852 | D: 12 Mar 1893 |
| | | w/o John W. Kincheloe |

Lot: 85L   1898 Owner: F.S. Warren

| Bertha Pearson Warren | B: 1880 | D: 1939 |

| Frederick Samuel Warren | B: 1876 | D: 1953 |

Lot: 85U   **1898 Owner: G.W. Summers**

William Ludwell Summers   D: 3 Jun 1895

Lucy C. C. Summers   B: 15 Apr 1825   D: 8 Oct 1888
                                                     w/o G. W. Summers

Lot: 86   **1898 Owner: L.H. Herndon**

George Love   Age: 72 yrs   D: 9 Sep 1853

Louisa H. L. Herndon   Age: 86 yrs   D: 3 Jan 1890
                                          w/o Rev. Traverse Herndon

Traverse D. Herndon   Age: 44 yrs   D: 10 Sep 1854

Mary S. Love   Age: 79 yrs   D: 21 Nov 1862
                                          w/o Rev. George Love

Lot: 87U   **1898 Owner: A. Beavers**

Christiana Leith   Age: 64 yrs   w/o W. G. Leith
                                               2nd husband

John A. Beavers   B: 1 Mar 1816   D: 2 Aug 1858

Lot: 88   **1898 Owner: B.D. Barlett**

Guley E. Bartlett   B: 24 Jan 1806   D: 25 Jul 1865

Elizabeth B. Bartlett   B: 30 May 1852   D: 13 Oct 1922
                                          d/o B. D. & Armenia Bartlett

Burgess D. Bartlett   B: 30 May 1807   D: 16 Sep 1880

Sallie Anna C. Bartlett   B: 12 Aug 1849   D: 12 Mar 1947

Armenia Bartlett   B: 24 Jul 1812   D: 9 Feb 1883
                                          w/o Burgess D. Bartlett

Bennina M. Bartlett Glover   B: 30 Jan 1854   D: 18 Apr 1940
                                          w/o William M. Glover

Sanford Henry Bartlett   B: 18 Dec 1846   D: 16 Jul 1858
                                          s/o Burgess D. & Armenia Bartlett

Lot: 89   **1898 Owner: J.M. Luck**

*Drusilla A. Luck   Age: 5-4-5   D: 18 Oct 1860

                                          d/o John M. & Mary A. Luck

Dausilla A. Moran   Age: 74 yrs   D: 6 May 1889

                                          w/o John M. Moran

| John M. Moran | Age: 81 yrs | D: 21 Jun 1890 |

Lot: 92   1898 Owner: J.E. Brenner

William Frederick Brenner	B: 19 Oct 1868	D: 4 Mar 1903
Fannie Crissey Brenner	B: 26 Jul 1841	D: 12 Jul 1873
		w/o J. E. Brenner
Lillian Brenner	B: 19 Jul 1878	D: 22 Feb 1881
		d/o J. E. & J. M. Brenner

Lot: 93A   1898 Owner: Not Listed

John Douglass Moore	B: 1915	D: 1961
Mary Weems Chinn Moore	B: 21 Jun 1876	D: 16 Jun 1961
d/o Chloe Adams & John Lyttleton Chinn		
John Douglass Moore	B: 20 Feb 1879	D: 5 Jan 1936
	s/o Robert L. & Isabella Tyler Moore	
Mary Chinn Moore Darling	B: 23 Jun 1912	
	w/o Dashwood Peyton Darling	
Robert L. Moore	B: 15 Jul 1910	D: 8 Jun 1935

Lot: 93L   1898 Owner: Thos. Wyncoop

Hunton Wynkoop	Age: 13 yrs	D: 15 Aug 1888
		s/o J. T. & Fannie Wynkoop
Willie S. Wynkoop	B: 14 Nov 1870	D: 15 Jan 1876
		s/o J. T. & Fannie Wynkoop

Lot: 93U   1898 Owner: G.W. Dear

George W. Dear	Age: 67 yrs	D: 24 Aug 1883
H. Clay Dear	B: 31 Aug 1848	D: 1 Sep 1905
		CSA: 43rd VA Cavalry, Co. D
Sarah A. Dear	Age: 73 yrs	D: 15 Feb 1892
		w/o George W. Dear

Lot: 94   1898 Owner: Geo Wynkoop

| Corbin Wynkoop | Age: 15 yrs | D: 11 Oct 1876 |
| | | s/o G. W. & J. E. Wynkoop |

Lot: 95   1898 Owner: Sam Skinner

| Annie E. Skinner | B: 3 Jul 1837 | D: 28 Feb 1891 |

Annie E. Skinner   B: 3 Jul 1837   D: 28 Feb 1891

William Friench Gulick   B: 6 Mar 1841   D: 23 Sep 1902
CSA: 8th VA Infantry, Co. D

Fanny Skinner Gulick   B: 9 Jul 1843   D: 17 Feb 1909
w/o W. F. Gulick

Samuel Skinner   D: 14 Oct 1881

Richard H. Skinner   B: 1 Jan 1833   D: 30 Apr 1913

John L. Skinner   B: 10 Jul 1851   D: 17 Sep 1863

George M. Skinner   B: 27 Feb 1845   D: 9 Jun 1903
CSA: 43rd VA Cavalry, Co. A

Ella Skinner   B: 25 Sep 1839   D: 31 Mar 1927

Elizabeth Skinner   B: 20 May 1811   D: 31 Jan 1869
w/o Samuel Skinner

Sarah J. Lee   B: 19 Jun 1855   D: 12 Jan 1918

Lot: 96   1898 Owner: Wm. Francis

Susan Haxall Frost   B: 1876   D: 1965
w/o Wade Hampton Frost

Mary Daes Frost   D: 25 May 1918

William H. Francis   Age: 59 yrs   D: 20 Aug 1873

Susan Haxall Frost Parrish   B: 11 Jun 1916   D: 18 Jul 1994

Ann E. Francis   B: 16 Mar 1826   D: 20 Mar 1887
w/o William H. Francis

Wade Hampton Frost   B: 1881   D: 1938

Lot: 97   1898 Owner: Not Listed

William H. Abell   B: 14 Oct 1858   D: 8 Oct 1925
s/o Elijah & Sarah Abell

Ann Eliza Abell   B: 14 Jan 1851   D: 13 Apr 1926
d/o Thornton & Ellen Leach

Lot: 99   1898 Owner: J.W. Mitchell

Mary Jane Ball   B: 25 Sep 1829   D: 27 Feb 1914
w/o James Fenton Ball

Albert Ashby Mitchell	B: 1865	D: 1951
Carrie Pearson Mitchell	B: 1875	D: 1940
Elizabeth Mann Mitchell	B: 1840	D: 1922
Guy C. Mitchell	B: 1902	D: 1957
James W. Mitchell	B: 1868	D: 1953
Carrie Lou Risdon Hutchison	B: 8 May 1912	D: 25 Dec 1996
Rozier Jennings Mitchell	B: 1900	D: 1975

Lot: 99A   1898 Owner: H.A. Spitler

| Homer A. Spitler | B: 31 Dec 1879 | D: 15 Oct 1954 |
| Elizabeth Broun Spitler | B: 10 Feb 1885 | D: 12 Jan 1970 |

Lot: 101   1898 Owner: Jno Butler

Susan Poston	Age: 55 yrs	D: 18 Mar 1872 w/o William W. Poston
*William W. Poston	Age: 54-11-29	D: 19 Apr 1873
Sarah Butler	Age: 38 yrs	D: 29 Nov 1853 w/o John Butler

Lot: 104   1898 Owner: John Carter

George Robert Carter	B: 31 Oct 1855	D: 5 Feb 1922
Rutledge Carter	B: 1903	D: 1959
Francis Carter	B: 1880	D: 1947
William M. Carter	B: 1877	D: 1933
William Hunter Carter	B: 26 Apr 1857	D: 2 May 1921
George P. Carter	B: 1894	D: 1967
C. W. S. Turner	B: 28 Jul 1849	D: 8 Feb 1909
Elizabeth Turner	B: 1863	D: 1931

Katherine Gordon McKoy Carter   w/o George Robert Carter
                              B: 26 Apr 1873   D: 10 Aug 1920

| Carolyn Walker McCoy | B: 12 Jul 1899 | |
| William Milton McCoy | B: 8 Jul 1881 | D: 11 Aug 1971 |

Lot: 105   **1898 Owner: F.M. Carter**

M. Emily Yellot Carter   Age: 30 yrs   D: 5 Apr 1882
w/o John Carter, Jr.

Jonathan Carter   Age: 66 yrs   D: 12 Sep 1849

Sarah C. Carter   B: 11 Nov 1860   D: 27 May 1862
d/o Francis M. & M. A. Carter

Elizabeth Carter   B: 20 Jun 1785   D: 28 Oct 1862
w/o Jonathan Carter

infants Carter   B: 26 Jun 1875   D: 17 Jun 1876
c/o John & E. Carter

Francis C. Turner   B: 1893   D: 1935

Francis M. Carter   B: 25 Jan 1824   D: 17 Feb 1903

John Jr. Carter   B: 22 Mar 1852   D: 24 Jun 1887

Emily M. Carter   Age: 5 mos   D: 11 Aug 1882

Margaret A. Carter   Age: 53 yrs   D: 5 Jun 1882
w/o Francis M. Carter

Bushrod Anderson   B: 11 Apr 1802   D: 4 Jul 1859

Susan Frances Bailey Anderson   D: 12 Nov 1846
d/o B. & N. Anderso n   Age: 8 yrs

Lot: 106   **1898 Owner: Not Listed**

Frank Lewis Baer   B: 1896   D: 1981

Mabel Van Dyke Baer   B: 1900

Martha Ellen Furr   B: 1872   D: 1958

William A. Stephenson   B: 3 Jun 1801   D: 20 Nov 1881

Lot: 107   **1898 Owner: John Francis**

Independence C. Francis   B: 4 Jul 1840   D: 6 Apr 1865
s/o John & Alferna Francis   CSA: 8th VA Infantry, Co. A

Dangerfield F. Neill   B: 30 Jun 1838   D: 18 Mar 1917
CSA: 6th VA Cavalry, Co. A

Francis Marion Neill   B: 6 Aug 1880   D: 28 Oct 1895
s/o D. F. & Mary A. Neill

Mary A. Neill   B: 26 Jul 1842   D: 27 Dec 1899
w/o D. F. Neill

John Francis	B: 1 Sep 1800	D: 9 Aug 1859
		s/o Enoch & Ann Francis

Hannah Ann Francis	B: 1 Jan 1833	D: 19 May 1858
		d/o John & Alferna Francis

Alferna Francis	B: 10 Jan 1804	D: 16 Aug 1842

*Fanny Louise Neill	B: 11 May 1887	D: 28 Sep 1887
		d/o D.F. & Mary A. Neill

Lot: 108   1898 Owner: Jas L. Crain

Jane Francis Crain	Age: 22 yrs	D: 3 Aug 1834
		d/o James & Ann Crain

James Crain	B: 25 Oct 1780	D: 16 Jan 1859

Rebecca Bronaugh Crain	Age: 28 yrs	D: 14 Jun 1841
		d/o James & Ann Crain

Ann Crain	Age: 59 yrs	D: 2 Jun 1844
		w/o James Crain

Robert Alexander Crain	Age: 2 yrs	D: 27 Jan 1825
		s/o James & Ann Crain

Lot: 109   1898 Owner: Mrs. Martha Fields

Bessie Huff Hurst	B: 11 Feb 1884	D: 2 Jan 1949
		w/o Nathan Hurst

John W. Field	Age: 76 yrs	D: 11 May 1911

James L. Huff	B: 19 Jun 1856	D: 28 May 1928

Martha Field	Age: 60 yrs	D: 1860

Mary E. Huff	B: 2 Jun 1850	D: 13 Jun 1925

Lot: 110L   1898 Owner: Jas A. Cox

James A. Cox	B: 21 Jun 1833	D: 21 Oct 1917

Catharine E. Cox	Age: 35 yrs	D: 15 Jan 1875
		w/o James A. Cox

George Leachman Cox	Age: 3 yrs	D: 2 Oct 1865
		s/o James A. & Catharine E. Cox

Aletha Abner Cox	B: 19 Jul 1851	D: 3 Jan 1925
		w/o James A. Cox

Lot: 110U   1898 Owner: Wm Cole

Elizabeth Ussery Cole	B: 17 Sep 1904	D: 19 Nov 1988
Francis Marion Cole	B: 3 Aug 1902	D: 9 Mar 1977
Katherine Virginia Cole	B: 27 Sep 1874	D: 27 Jun 1951
William Samson Cole	B: 6 Nov 1867	D: 3 Aug 1952

Lot: 111   1898 Owner: B.F. Carter

Rebecca M. Carter	B: 24 Dec 1815	D: 16 Nov 1896 w/o B. F. Carter, Sr.
A. May Carter	B: 27 Sep 1855	D: 22 Apr 1939
Margarett R. Carter	B: 9 Apr 1858	D: 27 Apr 1902 w/o B. F. Carter, Jr.
B. F. Carter, Jr.	B: 1 Jul 1846	D: 14 Feb 1903 CSA: 43rd VA Cavalry, Co. H
R. G. Carter	B: 17 Dec 1841	D: 19 Feb 1940
Frank R. Carter	B: 1843	D: 1927
Fannie Carter Thomas	B: 24 Jul 1852	D: 30 Mar 1926 w/o Clarence Thomas
Richardetta R. Carter	B: 14 Jul 1848	D: 11 Dec 1936
Kate E. Carter	B: 31 Oct 1839	D: 24 Oct 1908
Maj. John W. Carter	B: 12 Dec 1843	D: 26 Jun 1911 CSA: Chew's Battery
B. F. Carter, Sr.	B: 28 Nov 1814	D: 22 Dec 1895
Clarence Thomas		D: 16 Oct 1910
Henry Arthur Carter	Age: 4 yrs	D: 17 May 1857

Lot: 112   1898 Owner: John R. Carter

Herbert R. Carter	D: 2 Apr 1918 s/o John R. & Maria E. Carter
Mary Marshal Carter	D: 23 Apr 1918 d/o John R. & Maria E. Carter

Lot: 113   1898 Owner: Davis & Iden

Ann E. Davis	B: 12 Nov 1812	D: 6 Apr 1869 w/o John W. Davis

Frank Iden	no dates s/o Lott W. & Lucy A. Iden
John W. Davis	Age: 76 yrs D: 8 May 1891
Willie A. Sinclair	B: 7 Jan 1872 D: 27 Oct 1873 s/o George S. & Annie E. Sinclair
Edwin Iden	s/o Lott W. & Lucy A. Iden
James W. Davis	Age: 12 yrs D: 2 Dec 1849 s/o John W. & Elizabeth Davis
Lucy A. Iden	Age: 53 yrs D: 15 Jun 1877 w/o Lott W. Iden
Mary Alice Iden	d/o Lott W. & Lucy A. Iden
Lott W. Iden	Age: 65 yrs D: Nov 1873

Lot: 114   1898 Owner: Thos. Davis

Catharine A. Logan Dawson	B: 3 Aug 1851 D: 21 May 1925 w/o W. F. Dawson
Samuel Logan	B: 5 May 1811 D: 10 Dec 1867
Ida Fauntleroy Dawson	B: 3 Dec 1871 D: 31 Mar 1964
Laura V. Logan	B: 22 May 1857 D: 16 Apr 1937
Thomas S. Davis	B: 28 Apr 1812 D: 16 Dec 1856
William Fauntleroy Dawson	B: 30 Nov 1837 D: 22 Mar 1906 CSA: 8th VA Infantry, Co. C
Sarah D. Logan	B: 15 Jul 1821 D: 3 Oct 1880 w/o Samuel Logan

Lot: 115   1898 Owner: Chas Byrnes

*Jennie B. Byrne	Age: 69 yrs D: 8 Mar 1857 w/o James Byrne
Charles Byrne	B: 2 Feb 1816 D: 4 Jul 1906
Frances E. Byrne	Age: 30 yrs D: 30 Jul 1853 w/o Charles Byrne

Lot: 116   1898 Owner: Jno Swain

| Elizabeth Ann Swain | Age: 14 yrs   D: 14 Jul 1857
d/o John & Maria Swain |

Lot: 117   1898 Owner: H. Lewis

| Arthur Lee Lewis | B: 6 Feb 1862 | D: 15 Aug 1884 |
| | | s/o Harrison & M. J. Lewis |

Ann C. Lewis   B: 4 Jun 1860   D: 23 Aug 1861
d/o Harrison & M. J. Lewis

Harrison Lewis   B: 7 Oct 1822   D: 5 Oct 1912

Walter T. Lewis   B: 17 Mar 1865   D: 1 Nov 1865
s/o Harrison & M. J. Lewis

Mahala J. Lewis   B: 5 Apr 1834   D: 18 Dec 1886

Burr W. Lewis   B: 28 Oct 1858   D: 2 Nov 1865
s/o Harrison & M. J. Lewis

Richard E. Lewis   B: 13 Oct 1868   D: 3 Jan 1896
s/o Harrison & M. J. Lewis

Edwin H. Lewis   B: 10 Sep 1866   D: 28 Jan 1897
s/o Harrison & M. J. Lewis

A. Virginia Lewis Benjamin   B: 19 Apr 1857   D: 19 Aug 1937

Lot: 118U   1898 Owner: Wm Gulick

Margaret I. Benton   B: 12 Sep 1818   D: 28 Jan 1888

Lot: 118L   1898 Owner: J.G. Dowdell

Dr. J. G. Dowdell   Age: 41 yrs   D: 29 Mar 1888

Lot: 119   1898 Owner: J.S. Gulick

Margaret A. Rogers   B: 29 Sep 1844   D: 29 Oct 1879

Robert Milton Gulick   B: 1848   D: 1925

Henry H. Gulick   B: 7 Nov 1857   D: 21 Nov 1873

Ann V. Gulick   B: 22 Oct 1817   D: 22 Apr 1882
w/o James H. Gulick

James H. Gulick   B: 9 Oct 1814   D: 27 Mar 1864

Lot: 120   1898 Owner: J.M. Garnett

James Mercer Garnett   B: 24 Apr 1840   D: 18 Feb 1916
s/o Theodore S. & F. I. Garnett

James Mercer Garnett Jr.   B: 1872   D: 1942

| Catherine Garnett | B: 4 Jan 1849 | D: 8 Dec 1919 |
| | | w/o James Mercer Garnett |

Lot: 123   1898 Owner: B.F. Leith

C. Irvin Leith	B: 1880	D: 1978
Estelle F. Leith	B: 1871	D: 1960
Mary L. Leith	B: 4 Sep 1843	D: 25 Oct 1924
		w/o B. F. Leith
Thomas William Leith	Age: 12 yrs	D: 21 Feb 1882
		s/o B. F. & Mary Leith
B. F. Leith	B: 30 May 1841	D: 16 Oct 1919
		CSA: 8th VA Infantry, Co. E
Sarah E. Leith	B: 20 May 1869	D: 10 Oct 1876
Olivia L. Megeath	B: 27 Oct 1872	D: 28 Dec 1936
Alfred P. Megeath	B: 25 Jun 1870	D: 28 Dec 1939

Lot: 124L   1898 Owner: Dr. Holt/Mrs. J.H. Mullen

Pamelia Tiffany Mullen	B: 1875	D: 1963
Richard H. Holt	B: 1898	D: 1933
John Henry Mullen	B: 1870	D: 1930

Lot: 124U   1898 Owner: Mason Newlon

Mason Newlon	B: 5 Dec 1817	D: 1 Mar 1904
		s/o G. W. & Sarah Newlon
Emsey Newlon	Age: 78 yrs	D: 23 Feb 1894
		w/o Mason Newlon
Sarah Newlon	Age: 81 yrs	D: 11 Aug 1881

Lot: 125L   1898 Owner: W.H. Adams

Edwin T. Adams	B: 1872	D: 1939
William Henry Adams	B: 31 Oct 1834	D: 1 Jun 1913
Eliza Haynes Adams	B: 22 Feb 1847	D: 28 Nov 1931
		w/o W. H. Adams

Lot: 125U   1898 Owner: James H. Haynes

Genevieve Haynes	B: 12 Apr 1856	D: 16 Jan 1914
Rev. J. A. Haynes	B: 13 Dec 1822	D: 30 Mar 1880
Mary Camm Haynes	B: 20 Feb 1824	D: 15 Jan 1895
Lucy Roy Mason	Age: 43 yrs	D: 16 Nov 1870 d/o John & Eliza Mason
*Robert Rupp	Age: 28 yrs	D: 9 Aug ___
Charles B. Haynes	B: 26 Oct 1851	D: 12 Nov 1901

Lot: 126   1898 Owner: S. Tillett

L. F. Skillman	Age: 53 yrs	D: 2 Jul 1892
Catherine J. Skillman	B: 14 Jul 1843	D: 20 Apr 1887 w/o L. F. Skillman
John Hawling	B: 3 Jun 1854	D: 10 Nov 1862 s/o Joseph & Martha D. Hawling
Caroline S. Tillett	Age: 81 yrs	D: 23 Jan 1892 w/o Samuel A. Tillett
Samuel A. Tillett	B: 13 Apr 1820	D: 13 Jan 1875

Lot: 127   1898 Owner: Unmarked graves

Massa M. McCarty	B: 15 Dec 1867	D: 11 Dec 1892 s/o W. M. & F.E. McCarty
Annie Sinclair	B: 1 Sep 1851	

Lot: 128   1898 Owner: A.M. Smith

A. M. Smith	B: 27 Aug 1823	D: 6 Jan 1904
Martha Byrne Smith	B: 2 Nov 1820	D: 13 Oct 1898 w/o Alex. M. Smith
Sydnor Smith	B: 25 Feb 1857	D: 19 Jun 1859 s/o Alex. & Martha Smith
Edgar M. Smith	Age: 24 yrs	D: 29 Apr 1875
Ella Smith	B: 1855	D: 1938
William Clinton Smith	B: 9 Jul 1848	D: 24 Jan 1894

Lot: 129   1898 Owner: Thos Jones

Priscilla Jones	B: 6 Oct 1810	D: 10 Jul 1875
		w/o Thomas Jones
Thomas Jones	B: 6 Sep 1806	D: 19 Mar 1859
John T. Jones	B: 27 Mar 1847	D: 27 Feb 1852
		s/o Thomas W. & P.C. Jones

Lot: 130   1898 Owner: R.W. Noland

Lucy Gilmer Noland	d/o R. W. N. & Louisa M. Noland	
R. W. N. Noland	B: 22 Feb 1822	D: 30 Nov 1886
Elizabeth M. Noland		D: 1832
Louisa Minor Noland	Age: 37 yrs	D: 30 Sep 1859
Lloyd Noland, Jr.	B: 16 Dec 1844	D: 22 Nov 1875
Kate Noland	d/o R. W. N. & Louisa M. Noland	
Ellenor Noland	Age: 65 yrs	D: 17 Feb 1819
Jane L. Love		D: 1836

Lot: 131   1898 Owner: Wm Berkley

Dorothy Allen Smith Berkeley	B: 26 Jan 1911	D: 16 Sep 1994
Cynthia Berkeley	B: 7 Aug 1859	D: 14 Apr 1916
	d/o W. N. & Cynthia W. S. Berkeley	
William Noland Berkeley	B: 28 Feb 1826	D: 25 Apr 1907
	CSA: 8th VA Infantry, Major	
Mary Edmonia Berkeley	B: 10 Jul 1861	D: 7 Aug 1916
	d /o W. N. & Cynthia W. S. Berkeley	
Francis Lewis Berkeley	B: 21 Apr 1859	D: 6 May 1942
Edmund Berkeley	B: 10 Aug 1912	D: 1 Oct 1993
Cynthia White Berkeley	B: 20 Sep 1829	D: 13 Mar 1869
Ethel Grissey Berkeley	B: 23 Feb 1877	D: 14 Jul 1957
		w/o Francis Lewis Berkeley

Lot: 132   1898 Owner: L. Berkley

Lucy Norborne Fontaine	Age: 65 yrs	D: 2 Feb 1874
Thomas Campbell Cox	B: 28 Nov 1866	D: 10 Jul 1869
		s/o R. S. & Mary L. Cox

Charles Fenton Berkeley   B: 13 Nov 1833   D: 22 Oct 1871
CSA: 8th VA Infantry, Co. D

Frances Callender Berkeley   B: 19 Apr 1797   D: 13 Sep 1855
w/o Lewis Berkeley

Lewis Berkeley   B: 27 Feb 1789   D: 13 Apr 1853

Lot: 133   1898 Owner: Wm Benton, Jr.

John Maxim Lee   B: 5 Apr 1927

Sarah W. Benton   B: 6 Jun 1829   D: 26 May 1904
w/o William H. Benton

Clarence H. Roberts   B: 6 Apr 1895   D: 2 Sep 1895
s/o W. E. & C. B. Roberts

Louise Snead Benton   B: 29 Apr 1895   D: 4 Mar 1993

Frank May Benton   B: 17 Feb 1893   D: 13 Sep 1963

Rosalie Virginia Benton Lee   B: 3 Oct 1927

William H. Benton   B: 26 Feb 1821   D: 29 Dec 1904

Lot: 134   1898 Owner: J. Gouchnauer

Harriet A. Gochnauer   B: 16 Dec 1809   D: 4 Mar 1875
w/o Joseph Gochnauer

Sarah M. Gochnauer   Age: 12 yrs   D: 21 Oct 1847
d/o Joseph & Harriet A. Gochnauer

Francis W. Gochnauer   Age: 21 yrs   D: 16 Jul 1863
s/o Joseph & Harriet A. Gochnauer   CSA: 1st VA Cavalry, Co. H

Mary E. Gochnauer   Age: 10 yrs   D: 24 Oct 1847
d/o Joseph & Harriet A. Gochnauer

Georgiana Gochnauer   Age: 15 yrs   D: 4 Oct 1862
d/o Joseph & Harriet A. Gochnauer

Joseph Gochnauer   B: 19 Apr 1805   D: 25 Aug 1890

Harriet J. Gochnauer   Age: 3 yrs   D: 25 Oct 1847
d/o Joseph & Harriet A. Gochnauer

Lot: 135   1898 Owner: F.M. Cole

Mary M. Cole   B: 11 Mar 1842   D: 9 Apr 1907
w/o Francis M. Cole

*infant Cole   Age: 6 yrs   D: 22 Aug 1867

	s/o Francis M. & Mary M. Cole	
Henry H. Rogers	B: 18 Jun 1875	D: 24 Oct 1964
Ada C. Rogers	B: 12 Jul 1877	D: 9 Jul 1969
Francis M. Cole	B: 12 Aug 1833	D: 11 Aug 1889

Lot: 135A   1898 Owner: Not Listed

| Mary Lee M. Trenary | B: 13 Jan 1927 | |
| Richard N. Trenary | B: 27 Nov 1926 | D: 21 Jun 1973 |

Lot: 136   1898 Owner: Wm Dodd

Phobe Young	Age: 84 yrs	D: 11 Jan 1895
Rachel Dodd	B: 6 Aug 1813	D: 8 Feb 1890
Bertha T. Ferguson	B: 21 Sep 1881	D: 21 Dec 1881
	d/o G. O. & M. T. Ferguson	
John William Dodd	B: 1 Feb 1814	D: 10 Feb 1890
Martha Thomas Ferguson	B: 3 Sep 1854	D: 21 Oct 1881
	w/o George O. Ferguson	

Lot: 137   1898 Owner: Jno D. Rogers

George Lee, Jr.	B: 21 Oct 1863	D: 9 Nov 1883
Ellen Lee Rogers	Age: 60 yrs	D: 1 Sep 1862
		w/o Asa Rogers
Charlotte Rust Rogers	B: 26 Sep 1836	D: 23 Mar 1923
		w/o Arthur Lee Rogers
Asa Rogers	B: 24 Jun 1802	D: 20 Sep 1887
		s/o Hugh & Mary Rogers
Laura Frances Lee	B: 29 Nov 1835	D: 29 May 1917
		w/o George Lee
William Wellford Rogers	Age: 7 mos	D: 26 Nov 1855
	s/o John D. & Parke F. Rogers	
Arthur Lee Rogers	B: 21 Oct 1831	D: 13 Sep 1871
		CSA: Loudoun Artillery
Beverly Randolph Lee		D: 12 Mar 1877
	s/o George & Laura F. Lee	

Lot: 138   1898 Owner: Asa Rogers

Rosie E. Griffith	B: 16 Jun 1878	D: 10 Dec 1935
Walter S. Griffith	B: 11 May 1875	D: 23 Mar 1950

Lot: 138A   1898 Owner: Not Listed

Samuel L. Moyer	B: 2 Nov 1899	D: 8 Oct 1955
Jane Moyer Marshall	B: 13 Oct 1930	D: 20 Jul 1982
		w/o Richard Fern Marshall
Rosalie Griffith Moyer	B: 21 Jul 1904	D: 28 Oct 1992
Peggy Anne Moyer	B: 24 Jul 1933	D: 10 Apr 1934

Lot: 139   1898 Owner: James S. Skinner

Jane Elizabeth Skinner	Age: 30 yrs	D: 5 Feb 1848
		w/o James Skinner
Jane Skinner	B: 25 Sep 1851	D: 18 May 1918
James Skinner	B: 6 Feb 1816	D: 15 Jun 1876
Lucy Skinner	w/o James Skinner	D: 28 Oct 1888
Annie Skinner	B: 28 Mar 1854	D: 28 Dec 1930
Bettie Skinner	Age: 35 yrs	D: 29 May 1854
		w/o James Skinner

Lot: 140   1898 Owner: Wm Benton, Sr.

Rosa Miller Clarke	B: 8 Jun 1862	D: 30 Jun 1935
Thomas H. Benton	Age: 55 yrs	D: 31 Oct 1888
Alice L. Benton	B: 6 Sep 1896	D: 15 Sep 1896
		d/o W. C. & Rosa M. Benton
William K. Benton	B: 11 Mar 1900	D: 8 Nov 1972
William Benton	B: 25 Dec 1788	D: 28 Jul 1881
Florence W. Benton	B: 27 Feb 1889	D: 28 Jan 1903
		d/o W. C. & Rosa M. Benton
Sarah Benton	Age: 60 yrs	D: 5 Feb 1854
		w/o William Benton
Lois M. Benton	B: 14 Jun 1898	D: 23 Aug 1999

John W. Benton	Age: 24 yrs	D: 13 Aug 1853
		s/o William & Sarah Benton
Catharine W. Benton	Age: 50 yrs	D: 9 Dec 1855
		w/o William Benton
Grace Browning Benton	B: 1890	D: 1974
William Clarke	B: 2 Mar 1858	D: 23 Nov 1936

Lot: 141   1898 Owner: W.B. Cochran

Caroline Cochran	B: 3 Sep 1841	D: 23 Feb 1919
Catherine Powell Cochran	B: 3 Nov 1814	D: 17 Feb 1895
Katherine Woodward	B: 18 May 1887	D: 8 Apr 1970
H. R. Woodward	B: 1861	D: 1934
Katherine Dudley Richards	B: 24 May 1860	D: 18 Aug 1911
Fanny Dudley Woodward	B: 23 Sep 1865	D: 30 Sep 1908
Nancy Whiting Cochran	Age: 2 yrs	D: 29 Aug 1839
		d/o William B. & Catherine Cochran
Fanny Berkeley Dudley	B: 4 Feb 1839	D: 6 Oct 1865
		w/o Thomas U. Dudley, Jr.
Lizzie	Age: 3 yrs	D: 25 Dec 1849
William B. Cochran	B: 9 Jan 1810	D: 12 Jul 1898
*Mary Aldrich Dudley		D: 5 Mar 1915

Lot: 142   1898 Owner: Lloyd Noland

Nellie Mackenzie Tabb	B: 10 Mar 1888	D: 16 Oct 1940
Ann Whiting Noland	B: 12 Mar 1830	D: 31 Mar 1831
		d/o Lloyd & Elizabeth W. Noland
Anna Lloyd Noland	B: 25 Apr 1835	D: 23 Mar 1838
		d/o Lloyd & Elizabeth W. Noland
Elizabeth Winn Noland	B: 25 Sep 1801	D: 28 Oct 1888
Nancy Whiting Noland	Age: 30 yrs	D: 21 Jun 1823
Nellie Mackenzie Tabb	B: 24 Aug 1861	D: 24 Jul 1926
Lloyd N. Tabb	B: 21 Aug 1894	D: 6 Jul 1960
Thomas Lloyd Noland	Age: 17yrs	D: 4 Jul 1834

John Proser Tabb	B: 27 Nov 1854	D: 29 Jan 1927
Lloyd Noland	B: 14 Dec 1790	D: 24 Apr 1871
John P. Tabb, Jr.	B: 1890	D: 1976
Noble B. Noland	B: 3 Mar 1838	D: 28 Nov 1858

Lot: 143   1898 Owner: N. Beveridge

Noble Beveridge	Age: 64 yrs	D: 8 Dec 1844
Nina Carter Tabb	B: 21 Nov 1883	D: 29 Jan 1950
Sarah Smith	Age: 75 yrs	D: 3 Feb 1843
John Mackenzie Tabb	B: 10 Dec 1886	D: 15 Oct 1916

Lot: 145   1898 Owner: B. Crain

Mary Crain	Age: 84 yrs	D: 27 Nov 1839
Catharine Crain	Age: 40 yrs	D: 15 Feb 1835
		w/o B. Crain

Lot: 146   1898 Owner: Jos Taylor

Joseph D. Taylor	B: 13 Sep 1803	D: 31 Jan 1884
Cornelius S. Taylor	Age: 27 yrs	D: 2 Jul 1859
	s/o Joseph D. & Frances Taylor	
Catharine A. Taylor		D: Mar 1866
Thomas M. Johnson	B: 7 Apr 1874	D: 16 Sep 1880
	s/o G. S. & Annie Johnson	
Charles M. Taylor	B: 1867	D: 1924
Annie T. Johnson	B: 28 Sep 1839	D: 2 Jul 1900
	w/o George S. Johnson	
Frances Taylor	B: 12 Aug 1809	D: 27 May 1890
	w/o Joseph D. Taylor	
George S. Johnson	B: 1839	D: 1916

Lot: 147   1898 Owner: Jno Hunter

| Lear Rose | | no dates |

Lot: 148   1898 Owner: Jno Pickett

| Willie Pickett | Age: 1 yr | D: 2 Feb 1856 |
| | s/o John & Sarah A. Pickett | |

Eloise Pickett Storey   B: 21 Apr 1858   D: 13 Nov 1913

John S. Pickett   B: 20 Jan 1820   D: 24 Nov 1876

Julia Pickett   B: 24 Aug 1860   D: 3 Nov 1865
                                          d/o J. S. & S. A. Pickett

Katie Pickett   B: 31 May 1852   D: 31 Aug 1853
                                          d/o John & Sarah A. Pickett

Robert Lee Pickett   B: 27 Aug 1862   D: 8 Nov 1943

Sarah Kerfoot Pickett   B: 27 Nov 1826   D: 19 Jul 1902

James S. Pickett   B: 6 May 1775   D: 11 Jun 1852

Lot: 149   1898 Owner: H. Smith

Henry G. Smith   B: 2 Jul 1831   D: 7 Jul 1866

Lucy Adams Smith   B: 31 Aug 1870   D: 11 Sep 1944

Mary W. Smith   B: 15 Aug 1841   D: 27 Jan 1891

Hugh Smith   B: 27 Jan 1793   D: 21 May 1864

Elizabeth Smith   B: 2 Jul 1801   D: 1 Jul 1875

Daniel K. Smith   B: 25 Mar 1859   D: 26 Apr 1938

Bettie L. Smith   B: 30 Sep 1848   D: 22 Mar 1915

Lot: 150   1898 Owner: Robt Hitaffer

R. C. Hitaffer   B: 29 Mar 1836   D: 8 Sep 1864

Lot: 151   1898 Owner: Thos Francis

Mary Leith Tyler   B: 23 May 1874   D: 18 Apr 1961

William E. Tyler   B: 19 Aug 1866   D: 13 Feb 1945

Thomas J. Francis   B: 21 Aug 1838   D: 2 Dec 1866
                                          CSA: 8th VA Infantry, Co. D

Thomas Francis   B: 12 Feb 1803   D: 15 Jan 1869

Sarah A. Francis   B: 6 Sep 1812   D: 13 Jan 1899
                                          w/o Thomas Francis

James M. Francis   B: 14 Sep 1840   D: 21 Jul 1861

                                          CSA: 1st VA Cavalry, Co. H

Catherine Francis   B: 29 Oct 1854   D: 24 May 1904

                                          d/o Thomas & Sarah Francis

J. Toliver Megeath   B: 16 May 1842   D: 16 Feb 1875
                                        CSA: Fauquier Artillery

Ella C. Francis   B: 9 May 1856   D: 6 Apr 1881
                                    d/o Thomas & Sarah Ann Francis

Lot: 152L   1898 Owner: Steve McCarty

Enoch F. McCarty   B: 15 Aug 1840   D: 21 Jul 1861
                       s/o Stephen W. & Elizabeth A. McCarty
                                    CSA: 1st VA Cavalry, Co. H

Elizabeth A. McCarty   B: 12 Dec 1816   D: 26 Jun 1862
                                        w/o Stephen W. McCarty

Stephen W. McCarty   B: 28 Nov 1809   D: 3 May 1892

Lot: 152U   1898 Owner: Jno Seaton

Norman M. Seaton   B: 5 Sep 1909   D: 11 Dec 1933

Lot: 153   1898 Owner: D.J. Weadon

Francis Weadon   Age: 19 yrs   D: 22 Mar 1855

Sarah Jane Weadon   B: 25 Mar 1843   D: 9 Dec 1851
                                    d/o John & Fanny Weadon

Fanny Weadon   B: 7 Feb 1799   D: 18 Feb 1875

Lot: 154   1898 Owner: Jno R. Crupper

John R. Crupper, Sr.   B: 29 Sep 1803   D: 9 Dec 1857

Lot: 155   1898 Owner: Thos L. Broun

Elizabeth Ellen Broun   Age: 12 yrs   D: 9 Apr 1847

Elizabeth Broun   Age: 35 yrs   D: 15 Jan 1838

Edwin C. Broun   Age: 57 yrs   D: 10 Aug 1839

Maria L. Tebbs   Age: 55 yrs   D: 4 Aug 1876
                                        w/o Rev. F. C. Tebbs

James Channel Broun   Age: 6 yrs   D: 17 May 1828

Maria Broun   Age: 31 yrs   D: 28 Aug 1818

Sally Broun   Age: 16 yrs   D: 5 Jan 1849

Rev. F. C. Tebbs   Age: 55 yrs   D: 18 Nov 1875

Lot: 156   1898 Owner: Spence Rector

Spencer Rector   Age: 77 yrs   D: 30 Mar 1885

Jane W. Rector	Age: 69 yrs	D: 5 Feb 1884
		w/o Spencer Rector
W. S. Harrison	B: 5 Feb 1844	D: 15 Oct 1922
Lella W. Rector	B: 20 Nov 1870	D: 31 Mar 1874
		d/o W. C. & M. A. Rector
Martha Ann Rector	B: 29 Mar 1847	D: 17 Mar 1932
		w/o W. C. Rector
Catherine J. Harrison	B: 17 Apr 1847	D: 12 Nov 1924
		w/o W. S. Harrison
Lucy E. Harrison	B: 10 Jan 1843	D: 17 Jul 1879
		w/o W. S. Harrison
W. C. Rector	B: 15 Mar 1844	D: 8 Mar 1926

Lot: 157   1898 Owner: J.F. Simpson

John F. Simpson	Age: 58 yrs	D: 27 Feb 1891
Catharine Simpson	B: 17 May 1796	D: 8 Jun 1855
		w/o Samuel Simpson

Lot: 158   1898 Owner: Maria McCarty

Billington McCarty	B: Oct 1816	D: Jul 1900
		Age: 84 yrs

Lot: 159   1898 Owner: Geo L. Bitzer

Alcinda Bitzer	Age: 40 yrs	D: 9 Nov 1857
		w/o G. L. Bitzer
Dorothy Bitzer	Age: 84 yrs	D: 27 Mar 1849
		w/o Harmon Bitzer
George L. Bitzer	Age: 71 yrs	D: 29 Oct 1871
Harmon Bitzer	Age: 68 yrs	D: 11 Jan 1832

Lot: 160   1898 Owner: B.P. Noland

Lavinia P. Anderson	Age: 56 yrs	D: 24 Dec 1858
Susan C. Noland	B: 27 Jun 1827	D: 17 Mar 1872
		w/o Burr P. Noland
Joseph Drexel Dabney	B: 13 Oct 1882	D: 26 May 1890
		s/o Virginius & Anna Dabney
William A. Wilson	B: 15 May 1840	D: 29 Feb 1876

| Thomas Lloyd Noland | Age: 2 yrs | D: 8 Aug 1858 |
| | | s/o Burr P. & S. C. Noland |

| Corrie Harrison Noland | B: 20 Aug 1840 | D: 13 Aug 1876 |
| | | w/o Burr P. Noland |

| Burr Powell Noland | B: 20 Oct 1818 | D: 22 Oct 1889 |

| Burr Powell Noland | B: 7 Dec 1866 | D: 14 Sep 1927 |
| | s/o Burr Powell & Susan Wilson Noland | |

Lot: 161   1898 Owner: Jos W. Taylor

| Catharine Taylor | B: 1793 | D: 14 Mar 1855 |
| | | w/o Jesse Taylor |

| *Marian Scott Scruggs | Age: 0-5-29 | no dates |
| | | d/o J. Emmett & S.C. Scruggs |

| Samuel Swart | B: 1 Mar 1821 | D: 8 Jan 1854 |

Lot: 162   1898 Owner: J.W. Waters

| Bernice Waters | no dates   d/o E. G. & Annie Waters |

| E. H. Waters | B: 24 Oct 1841 | D: 20 Nov 1846 |

| Edward Waters | B: 2 Aug 1891 | D: 20 Mar 1895 |
| | | s/o E. G. & Annie Waters |

| J. M. Waters | Age: 21 days | D: 9 Feb 1844 |

| Jonathan Waters | Age: 37 yrs | D: 13 Sep 1852 |

| Louise Waters | no dates   d/o E. G. & Annie Waters |

| Mary E. Waters | B: 18 Mar 1819 | D: 12 Sep 1904 |
| | | w/o Jonathan Waters |

| Mary Jane Waters | | D: 10 Apr 1899 |

| William Rogers Waters | B: 13 Apr 1847 | D: 6 Jun 1847 |

| B. A. Waters | B: 5 Jan 1844 | D: 5 Apr 1846 |

Lot: 163   1898 Owner: H. Rogers/R.L. Adams

| Clarence W. Hudgins | B: 10 Sep 1860 | D: 12 Jan 1936 |

| Mary Adams Hudgins | B: 18 Mar 1863 | D: 8 Nov 1945 |
| | | w/o Clarence W. Hudgins |

| Ruth Ellen Sisson | | D: 6 Feb 1889 |

Lot: 164   1898 Owner: Hugh Rogers

Hamilton Rogers	B: 1795	D: 20 Aug 1882
Mary H. Rogers	B: 14 Jun 1802	D: 21 Jul 1884
Mary Roberta Rogers	B: 20 Sep 1842	D: 8 Nov 1843
Fenton Mercer Rogers	B: 27 May 1844	D: 27 Nov 1846
		s/o Hamilton & Mary Rogers
S. Adin Rogers	B: 19 Mar 1832	D: 10 May 1864
		CSA: 1st VA Cavalry, Co. A
William H. Rogers	B: 23 Aug 1824	D: 13 Jan 1907
John Lewis Rogers	B: 10 Dec 1842	D: Jul 1880
		CSA: 1st VA Cavalry, Co. H
Jane S. Rogers	B: 17 Jun 1831	D: 13 Apr 1835
		d/o James & Martha Rogers
Mary Rogers	B: 24 Sep 1776	D: 2 Nov 1863
		w/o Hugh Rogers
Hugh Rogers	B: 19 May 1768	D: 15 Aug 1853

Lot: 164A   1898 Owner: Not Listed

Joe Mancuso	B: 10 May 1898	D: 31 Oct 1980
Charles H. Adams	B: 17 Feb 1893	D: 6 Dec 1960
Mattie H. Adams	B: 1860	D: 1950
Mattie L. Adams Mancuso	B: 20 Feb 1896	D: 19 Oct 1981
Julia E. Adams Boyden		no dates
William L. Boyden		no dates

Lot: 165   1898 Owner: Estate of S.H. Fred

Dorothy Kepler Fred	B: 11 Sep 1900	D: 16 Apr 1935
Nannie Conway Fred	B: 23 Dec 1885	D: 21 Oct 1972
S. H. Rogers Fred	B: 2 Oct 1893	D: 29 Jul 1981
Frank Lee Fred	B: 7 Jan 1892	D: 25 Oct 1894
		s/o Samuel R. & Kate C. Fred
Edwin Broun Fred	B: 22 Mar 1887	D: 16 Jan 1981
Rosa Parrott Fred	B: 29 Oct 1891	D: 1 May 1980

Lot: 166   1898 Owner: N. Skinner

Nathaniel Jackson Skinner	B: 18 Feb 1824	D: 12 Apr 1880

Elizabeth K. Brown	B: 19 Jun 1902	D: 6 Jan 1990

Sanford H. Brown	B: 7 Jun 1903	D: 30 Mar 1990

Julia Augusta Skinner   B: 7 Jul 1836   D: 18 Jan 1893
w/o Nathaniel Jackson Skinner

Henry Marshall Kendrick   B: 1858   D: 1944

Mazie Skinner Kendrick   B: 1865   D: 1938
w/o Henry Marshall Kendrick

Lot: 167L   1898 Owner: Sarah Smith

Lucy Josephine Smith   B: 6 Sep 1837   D: 19 Aug 1854
d/o J. T. & Sarah W. Smith

Sullivan Smith   B: 22 Feb 1833   D: Aug 1865
s/o J. T. & Sarah W. Smith   CSA: 7th VA Cavalry, Co. A

Lot: 167U   1898 Owner: G.W. Adams

Anne F. Carrington Montague B: 28 Mar 1883   D: 25 Jan 1943
w/o William P. Montague

William P. Montague   B: 13 Mar 1878   D: 6 Jan 1959

Laura W. Adams   B: 23 Aug 1861   D: 13 Aug 1940

Anne M. Adams   B: 20 Mar 1866   D: 26 Dec 1942

Lot: 168   1898 Owner: G.W. Adams

George W. Adams   B: 4 Jul 1818   D: 3 Mar 1885

Bettie Withers Adams   B: 20 Sep 1847   D: 29 Dec 1863
d/o George W. & Anna M. Adams

Caroline J. Adams   B: 22 Aug 1864   D: 23 Jun 1865
d/o George W. & Anna M. Adams

Francis L. Adams   B: 23 Sep 1851   D: 1 Feb 1854
s/o George W. & Anna M. Adams

Georgie B. Carrington   B: 30 Sep 1849   D: 16 Feb 1939
w/o Dr. W. F. Carrington

*A.C. Montague   B: 28 Apr 1913   D: 18 Sep 1915

Horace E. Adams   B: 20 Feb 1856   D: 15 Jul 1928

W. P. Montague, Jr.	B: 16 Oct 1910	D: 5 Aug 1911

Ann English Adams   B: 2 Dec 1821   D: 9 Jan 1902
                                               w/o George W. Adams

infant daughter Adams   no dates
                                    d/o George W. & Anna M. Adams

John H. Adams   B: 2 Oct 1857   D: 7 Aug 1860
                                    s/o George W. & Anna M. Adams

Lot: 169   1898 Owner: W. Beveridge

Anne Haxall Dudley   B: 4 Jan 1878   D: 30 Jan 1969

Thomas Underwood Dudley   B: 12 Feb 1870   D: 21 Apr 1949

Thomas Underwood Dudley, Jr.   B: 21 Apr 1902   D: 15 Apr 1948

John Rowland Dudley   B: 9 Oct 1913   D: 25 Feb 1979

Lot: 170   1898 Owner: E.J. Short

Sithey Atwell   Age: 55 yrs   D: 24 Sep 1836

J. P. H. Short   B: 27 Apr 1807   D: 5 Aug 1850

Lot: 171   1898 Owner: Geo W. Hutchison

George H. Hutchison   B: 3 Jul 1826   D: 11 Aug 1912

Minnie Hutchison   B: 21 Feb 1867   D: 15 Dec 1944

Sallie Bettie Hutchison   B: 20 Jul 1855   D: 6 Sep 1857
                                    d/o George H. & Susan B. Hutchison

Silas B. Hutchison   B: 1851   D: 1937

Fannie Hutchison   B: 1860   D: 1934

George Lucian Hutchison   Age: 28 yrs   D: 19 Sep 1897

Silas Beaty   B: 18 Jan 1785   D: 20 Jun 1844

Frances Beaty   Age: 80 yrs   D: 27 Feb 1869
                                                  w/o Silas Beaty

Susan Beaty Hutchison   B: 2 Aug 1829   D: 27 Jan 1907
                                               w/o George H. Hutchison

Lot: 172   1898 Owner: J.P. Green

S. Turner Green   B: 11 Mar 1867   D: 16 May 1869
                                    s/o J. P. H. & M. A. Green

| Francis M. Green | B: 7 Nov 1823 | D: 15 May 1864 |
| | CSA: died at Spotsylvania | |

| J. P. H. Green | B: 28 Dec 1821 | D: 12 Dec 1910 |

| Mary A. Green | B: 8 May 1847 | D: 12 Apr 1906 |

| F. M. Green | B: 20 May 1864 | D: 5 Feb 1899 |
| | s/o J. P. H. & M. A. Green | |

| Alverda Green | B: 11 Jan 1824 | D: 14 Aug 1857 |
| | w/o John P. H. Green | |

| Laura Harrison Green | B: 25 Jun 1849 | D: 30 Jul 1856 |
| | d/o John P. H. & Alverda Green | |

Lot: 173   1898 Owner: Smith Adams

| Martha L. Ball | B: 22 Jul 1845 | D: 1 Mar 1876 |
| | w/o Charles H. Ball | |

| Adelaide Adam | B: 31 Jul 1810 | D: 8 Aug 1890 |
| | w/o William Francis Adam | |

| Albert Adam | B: 4 Aug 1852 | D: 30 Nov 1862 |
| | s/o William F. & Adelaide Adam | |

| Rose A. Badger | | D: 14 Oct 1893 |
| | w/o Harry H. Badger | |

| William Francis Adam | B: 1 Jan 1807 | D: 28 Apr 1868 |
| | s/o Mathew & Susannah L. Adam | |

| Thomas Attwell Smith | Age: 10 yrs | D: 29 Dec 1855 |
| | s/o James W. & Permelia Smith | |

| William F. Adam, Jr. | B: 29 Jul 1843 | D: 5 Apr 1917 |
| | s/o W. F. & Adelaide Adam | |

| Hannah O. Smith | B: 16 Aug 1840 | D: 28 Mar 1842 |
| | d/o James W. & Permelia Smith | |

| Robert Adam | B: 26 Aug 1847 | D: 13 Apr 1912 |

| Henry Adam | Age: 9 mos | no dates |

Lot: 174   1898 Owner: Mrs. DR Oden

| Nat S. Oden | B: 26 Sep 1857 | D: 16 Aug 1884 |
| | s/o Dr. J. Beverly & Cecelia H. Oden | |

| Mary Frances Oden | B: 6 Jan 1861 | D: 29 Aug 1862 |
| | d/o Dr. J. Beverly & Cecelia H. Oden | |

J. Cecilia Oden	B: 24 Oct 1837	D: 6 Oct 1916
		w/o Dr. J. B. Oden
Hulda Oden	B: 14 Feb 1798	D: 27 Apr 1882
*Dr. J. Beverly Oden	B: 23 Feb 1829	D: 2 Jul 1864
M. C. Sowers	B: 8 Nov 1840	D: 12 Jan 1920
Henry Beverly Oden	B: 31 May 1864	D: 2 Oct 1864
	s/o Dr. J. Beverly & Cecelia H. Oden	
Frank A. Oden	B: 2 May 1859	D: 8 Nov 1885
	s/o Dr. J. Beverly & Cecelia H. Oden	

Lot: 177   1898 Owner: Jno Fishback

Martha J. Fishback	B: 15 Sep 1817	D: 11 May 1876
		w/o G. B. Fishback
John N. Fishback	B: 17 Sep 1823	D: 2 May 1871
Ann Fishback	B: 1792	D: 1882
Ann E. Jackson Fishback	B: 1 Dec 1857	D: 27 Jul 1915
		w/o John N. Fishback
George B. Fishback	B: 7 Nov 1825	D: 13 May 1868
Louisa Fishback	B: 1814	D: 1885
Josiah T. Fishback	B: 19 Nov 1819	D: 17 Mar 1913
		s/o Nelson & Ann Fishback
John Nelson Fishback	B: Aug 1871	D: Oct 1928
		s/o Anne J. & John N. Fishback

Lot: 178   1898 Owner: H.G. Dulaney

Rebecca Ann Dulany Beverley	B: 10 Nov 1859	D: 19 Mar 1948
		w/o John Hill Carter Beverley
Roberta Randolph Beverley	B: 6 May 1884	D: 31 May 1936
	d/o Rebecca Dulany & Hill Carter Beverley	
John Hill Carter Beverley	B: 6 Sep 1853	D: 27 Sep 1934
Ida Powell Dulany	B: 6 Mar 1836	D: 28 Oct 1897
		w/o Henry Grafton Dulany
Henry Grafton Dulany	B: 24 May 1834	D: 10 Oct 1888

Lot: 179L   1898 Owner: A.B. Kinsolving

Julia H. Kinsolving   B: 25 Oct 1821   D: 2 Mar 1858
                                                        w/o Rev. O. A. Kinsolving

Lucy Lee Kinsolving   B: 8 Dec 1833   D: 27 May 1862
                                                        w/o Rev. O. A. Kinsolving

Lot: 179U   1898 Owner: Mrs. M.M. Andrews

Mary Lord Minnigerode   B: 25 Jun 1896   D: 23 Jun 1918
                              d/o Eliphalet Fraser Andrews & Marietta Minnigerode

Charles Minnigerode   Age: 43 yrs   D: 25 Jan 1888

Virginia Cuthbert Powell Minnigerode   w/o Charles Minnigerode
                              B: 31 Aug 1849   D: 9 Mar 1899

Lot: 180   1898 Owner: M.F. Powell

Mary Custis Lee Carter Patchin B: 10 May 1875   D: 30 Aug 1922
                                                        w/o Robert Halsey Patchin

Katherine Powell Carter   B: 26 Jan 1839   D: 15 Sep 1903
                                                        w/o George Carter

George Carter   B: 22 Nov 1838   D: 27 Mar 1926

Marietta F. Powell   B: 24 Nov 1812   D: 9 Feb 1894
                                                        w/o George Cuthbert Powell

R. Randolph Powell   Age: 52 yrs   D: 9 Dec 1883

George Cuthbert Powell   Age: 42 yrs   D: 26 Jun 1849

Thomas Burr Powell   Age: 3 yrs   D: 8 Oct 1844
                                                        s/o G. C. & M. E. Powell

Conrad Harrison Powell   Age: 21 yrs   D: 20 Jan 1855

Lot: 181   1898 Owner: Dr. Fauntleroy

Turner F. Loughborough   B: 29 Aug 1885   D: 21 May 1975

Caroline Virginia Fauntleroy Loughborough
                              B: 15 Feb 1851   D: 1 Apr 1934
                                                        w/o Augustine Loughborough

John Fouchee Fauntleroy   B: 7 Aug 1809   D: 4 Feb 1884

Louise D. Loughborough   B: 23 Sep 1888   D: 10 Jul 1980

Lavina Beverly Turner Fauntleroy   w/o John Fouchee Fauntleroy
                              B: 5 Mar 1814   D: 30 Aug 1892

Marietta T. Fauntleroy	B: 18 Mar 1854	D: 9 Oct 1855
	d/o Dr. John & Lavinia Fauntleroy	
Edward D. Fauntleroy	B: 7 Feb 1849	D: 7 Jun 1859
	s/o Dr. John & Lavinia Fauntleroy	
Augustine Loughborough	B: 18 Nov 1852	D: 3 Jan 1931

Lot: 183   1898 Owner: E. Byrne

Ewell Byrne	Age: 48 yrs	D: 25 Jul 1862

Lot: 185   1898 Owner: R.B. McCormack

Robert B. McCormick	B: 7 Apr 1826	D: 11 Jun 1901
Thomas W. Raynolds	B: 10 Jul 1798	D: 5 Jul 1867
Katherine Seibert McCormick	B: 1873	D: 1968
	w/o Charles M. McCormick	
Katharine Raynolds McCormick	w/o Robert B. McCormick	
	B: 19 Sep 1827	D: 25 Mar 1873
Rosalie McCormick	B: 21 Nov 1858	D: 8 Aug 1879
	d/o R. B. & K. R. McCormick	
Charles Monod McCormick	B: 1862	D: 1933
Philip Withers McCormick	B: 1920	D: 1930

Lot: 186   1898 Owner: S.C. Noland

Loleta Noland Meyer	B: 9 Jan 1871	D: 19 Sep 1946
Maud R. Noland	Age: 5 yrs	D: 8 Nov 1864
	d/o William B. & Lucy Noland	
Sarah C. Noland	Age: 54 yrs	no dates
William Berkley Noland	B: 23 Apr 1827	D: 16 Oct 1901
William Claude Noland	B: 16 Feb 1867	D: 10 Jun 1911
H. B. P. Noland	B: 29 May 1837	D: 30 May 1857
	s/o Thomas J. & Sarah C. Noland	
F. Bulah Noland	Age: 2 yrs	D: 18 Oct 1864
	d/o William B. & Lucy T. Noland	
Robert A. Meyer	B: 3 Aug 1879	D: 9 Apr 1951
Lucy Chinn Noland	B: 2 Apr 1828	D: 10 Apr 1911

Coral L. Noland   B: 1851   D: 1852
                               d/o William B. & Lucy T. Noland

Lot: 187   1898 Owner: Unmarked graves

Elizabeth Tyler Moore Hoffman   B: 14 May 1906   D: 19 Jun 1982
                               d/o Mary W. Chinn & John D. Moore

Charles W. Hoffman   B: 29 May 1896   D: 8 Dec 1963
                               s/o Joseph W. & Minnie Harris Hoffman

Lot: 188   1898 Owner: W. Rawlings

William Rawlings   B: 17 Apr 1794   D: 10 Nov 1859

Virginia E. Carter Rawlings   B: 11 Jun 1838   D: 23 Jun 1905
                               d/o John D. & Elizabeth T. Rawlings

Lucinda Rawlings   B: 22 Jun 1797   D: 5 Dec 1864

John D. Rawlings   B: 1 Jun 1803   D: 14 Nov 1859

Martha Strother   B: 29 Apr 1789   D: 9 Jun 1859

Elizabeth T. Rawlings   B: 22 Apr 1813   D: 2 Dec 1893
                               w/o John D. Rawlings

Lot: 189   1898 Owner: S.E. Mathews

Squire E. Matthews   B: 18 Aug 1803   D: 28 Jun 1871

Winfield S. Matthews   B: 30 May 1848   D: 1 Aug 1848

Rosalia Elgin Matthews   B: 23 Dec 1852   D: 28 Apr 1912
                               w/o C. B. Matthews

Mary A. Matthews   B: 31 May 1842   D: 9 May 1847

Elizabeth F. Matthews   B: 17 Oct 1874   D: 27 Feb 1875
                               d/o C. B. & R. S. Matthews

Eliza F. Matthews   B: 28 Mar 1815   D: 28 Sep 1903

Charles B. Matthews   B: 6 Mar 1851   D: 12 Apr 1921

Benjamin D. Matthews   B: 3 Nov 1844   D: 20 May 1847

Lot: 190   1898 Owner: J.T. Cline

Marion Virginia Cline   B: 29 Oct 1830   D: 29 Jul 1855
                               w/o J. T. Cline

infant daughter Cline   D: 5 Jun 1869
                               d/o John T. & Mary M. Cline

| Corrie V. Cline | B: 10 Jul 1853 | D: 19 Mar 1941 |
| | | d/o John T. & Marion V. Cline |

John Thomas Cline   B: 5 Jul 1823   D: 5 Feb 1884

Minnie Bell Cline   B: 22 Nov 1867   D: 24 Oct 1868
d/o John T. & Mary M. Cline

Lot: 191   1898 Owner: Jno Nixon

Mary Nixon   B: 8 Dec 1812   D: 15 Jul 1864
w/o Jonathan W. Nixon

Hannah Isabella Nixon   Age: 2 yrs   D: 21 Oct 1846
d/o J. W. & Mary Nixon

Harriet Cromwell Nixon   Age: 6 yrs   D: 16 Oct 1846
d/o J. W. & Mary Nixon

Ida Edmonia Nixon   Age: 1 yr   D: 15 Nov 1852
d/o J. W. & Mary Nixon

Jonathan W. Nixon   B: 19 Dec 1807   D: 2 Nov 1874

Martha Ann Nixon   Age: 6 yrs   D: 4 Nov 1852
d/o J. W. & Mary Nixon

Emma C. Nixon Reamer   B: 25 Oct 1853   D: 19 Mar 1896
w/o Christian Reamer

Harry C. Reamer   B: 29 Oct 1882   D: 9 Apr 1964

Christian Reamer   B: 3 Jan 1849   D: 8 Dec 1921

*Frank Reamer   B: 31 Nov 1886   D: 15 Jan 1887
s/o C. & E.N. Reamer

*John H. Reamer   B: 29 May 1884   D: 29 Sep 1884
s/o C. & E.N. Reamer

Lot: 192   1898 Owner: R.L. Rogers

Norman McVeigh   no dates
s/o Dr. William H & H. R. McVeigh

Matilda B. McVeigh   B: 1 Aug 1827   D: 1 Dec 1910
w/o J. Milton McVeigh

J. Milton McVeigh   B: 16 Nov 1826   D: 2 Nov 1904
CSA: 35th VA Cavalry, Co. F

Dr. William Harvey McVeigh Age: 36 yrs   D: 24 Apr 1864

Harriet Rogers McCormick   B: 23 Jul 1833   D: 10 Jun 1912
                            w/o William Harvey McVeigh

Ida M. Rogers   B: 15 Sep 1850   D: 31 Mar 1851
                            d/o R. L. & N. H. Rogers

Annie Imogen Bywaters   D: 15 Jan 1887
                    d/o Mattie D. F. & Joseph Pemberton Bywaters

Ada H. Rogers   B: 28 Sep 1854   D: 18 Oct 1950
                            d/o Richard L. & Nancy H. Rogers

Jesse S. Rogers   B: 31 Aug 1837   D: 11 Nov 1924

Nancy H. Rogers   B: 16 Oct 1816   D: 10 Aug 1886
                            w/o R. L. Rogers

Richard L. Rogers   B: 5 Jun 1814   D: 5 May 1906

Lot: 193   1898 Owner: J.M. McVeigh

Keren H. McVeigh   Age: 62 yrs   D: 24 Jul 1861
                            w/o Townsend McVeigh

Elizabeth McVeigh   Age: 82 yrs   D: 8 Jul 1872
                            w/o Jesse McVeigh

Amanda M. McVeigh   Age: 85 yrs   D: 31 Jul 1907

Frances E. McVeigh   B: 29 Mar 1820   D: 5 Aug 1887

Jesse McVeigh   Age: 86 yrs   D: 4 Sep 1856

Sarah E. McVeigh   B: 1826   D: 27 Sep 1892
                            w/o Maj. B. F. McVeigh

Townsend McVeigh   B: 8 Nov 1800   D: 3 Aug 1877

Angelina McVeigh Rust   B: 2 Aug 1818   D: 19 Jun 1905
                            w/o Dr. Bushrod Rust

Lot: 194   1898 Owner: Rev. S.E. Rogers

Samuel Rogers Fred   B: 14 Jun 1860   D: 19 May 1930

Frank Lee Fred   B: 3 Mar 1823   D: 30 Oct 1916

Henry H. Fred   B: 9 Oct 1856   D: 29 Jul 1886

Frank Lee Fred   B: 24 May 1862   D: 27 Oct 1886

Thomas Walter Fred   B: 14 Jan 1853   D: 29 Oct 1890

Kate Conway Fred   B: 21 Feb 1852   D: 12 Jun 1921
                            w/o Samuel Rogers Fred

| Samuel Hamilton Rogers | Age: 28 yrs | D: 28 Sep 1859 |

| Sallie J. Rogers Fred | B: 19 Nov 1827 | D: 7 Nov 1870
w/o Frank L. Fred |

| Nannie Rogers Fred | B: 4 Oct 1865 | D: 29 May 1878
d/o F. L. & S. J. Fred |

| Thomas Walter Fred | B: 24 Nov 1890 | D: 17 Jul 1963 |

Lot: 195L   1898 Owner: Miss Sally McVeigh

| Columbia McVeigh | B: 9 Aug 1836 | D: 24 Feb 1913
d/o Townsend & H. K. McVeigh |

| Jane Eliza McVeigh | B: 8 Oct 1833 | D: 13 Feb 1918 |

| Sarah Ann McVeigh | B: 18 Sep 1826 | D: 12 Nov 1899
d/o Townsend & H. K. McVeigh |

Lot: 196   1898 Owner: Burr Fred

| Henry T. Rogers | B: 10 Feb 1849 | D: 5 Apr 1906 |

| Mollie M. Willis | B: 3 Feb 1840 | D: 29 Mar 1883
w/o Rev. E. J. Willis |

| Ida Herndon Rogers | B: 1851 | D: 1910 |

| Rebecca J. Rogers Fred | B: 29 Apr 1839 | D: 14 Jan 1882
w/o Burr P. Fred |

| Burr P. Fred | B: 21 Aug 1824 | D: 6 Jul 1892 |

Lot: 197   1898 Owner: Sam Rector

| Samuel Rector | B: 22 Sep 1804 | D: 19 Jun 1890 |

| Anna Rector | B: 16 May 1814 | D: 11 Jan 1892
w/o Samuel Rector |

| Howard N. Rector | B: 7 Oct 1834 | D: 23 Jan 1901 |

| Mary Leith Rector | B: 1844 | D: 1928
w/o Howard N. Rector |

| Welby Rector
s/o Samuel & Anna Rector | Age: 24 yrs | D: 13 Aug 1864
CSA: 43rd VA Cavalry, Co. A |

| Amanda V. Rector | B: 29 Oct 1833 | D: 7 Nov 1908 |

Lot: 198   1898 Owner: B. Rogers

Sanford Rogers	Age: 81 yrs	D: 25 Jan 1866
Margaret Rogers	Age: 78 yrs	D: 27 Apr 1864 w/o Sanford Rogers
Margaret Isabel Rogers	B: 12 Jul 1866	D: 29 May 1939
Annie W. Rogers	Age: 79 yrs	D: 14 Oct 1917 w/o C. B. Rogers
Lizzie M. Hutchison	B: 28 Apr 1839	D: 17 Mar 1903 w/o John Hutchison
C. B. Rogers	Age: 85 yrs	D: 2 Mar 1914
John Hutchison	B: 20 Nov 1840	D: 14 Sep 1919 CSA: 8th VA Infantry, Co. D
R. Beverly Rogers	Age: 20 yrs	D: 12 Mar 1896 s/o Cuthbert B. & Annie Rogers

Lot: 199   1898 Owner: Wm Swart

William R. Swart	B: 24 Dec 1787	D: 10 Apr 1861
Little Sue Chamberlayne	B: 1 Jan 1888	D: 13 Jun 1888 d/o O. E. & B. R. Chamberlayne
Fannie F. Swart	B: 29 Jul 1860	D: 4 Jan 1862 d/o H. T. & M. E. Swart
Mary C. Swart	B: 24 Jan 1832	D: 3 Aug 1910
Nellie R. Swart	B: 24 Dec 1862	D: 10 Jan 1926
H. T. Swart	B: 7 Nov 1830	D: 10 Jul 1894
Elizabeth Rogers Swart	B: 21 Mar 1794	D: 24 Feb 1881 w/o William R. Swart

Lot: 200   1898 Owner: Ludwell Lake

Clarence D. Lake	s/o Ludwell & H. Lake	D: 2 Jan 1883
Hubert Lake	B: 26 Aug 1878	D: 23 Aug 1879 s/o Ludwell & H. Lake
Charles Linwood Lake	B: 6 Nov 1871	D: 6 Feb 1904
Landonia Lake Skinner	B: 8 Mar 1835	D: 9 Jul 1912 w/o Benjamin F. Skinner

Rosa Lee Lake	B: 21 Jan 1871	D: 23 Mar 1873
		d/o Ludwell & H. Lake
Samuel Owen Skinner		no dates
Mary Agnes Skinner	Age: 12 yrs	D: 7 Feb 1875
		d/o B. F & Dona Skinner
infant Skinner	no dates	c/o B. F. & Dona Skinner
Benjamin F. Skinner	B: 15 Nov 1827	D: 23 Apr 1893

Lot: 201   1898 Owner: Ludwell Lake

Bladen D. Lake	B: 18 Jun 1839	D: 1 Oct 1862
		CSA: 7th VA Cavalry, Co. A
Harry B. Lake	B: 30 Aug 1886	D: 5 Sep 1889
		s/o D. & C. H. Lake
Agnes Lake	Age: 51 yrs	D: 14 Oct 1858
		w/o Ludwell Lake
Minnie I. Smith	B: 28 Dec 1869	D: 30 Mar 1892
		d/o Henry & Sarah Smith
Margaret E. Lake	B: 19 Mar 1842	D: 24 Sep 1863
		d/o Ludwell & Agnes Lake
Mary M. Lake	B: 9 Sep 1810	D: 20 Jun 1895
		w/o Ludwell Lake
Sarah E. Smith	B: 12 Oct 1832	D: 23 Aug 1915
		w/o Dr. Henry Smith
Sophia W. Lake	B: 28 Jul 1814	D: 7 Sep 1863
		w/o Ludwell Lake
Mary A. Lake Barber	B: 21 Apr 1848	D: 24 Mar 1867
		d/o Ludwell & Agnes Lake
Ludwell L. Smith	B: 24 Sep 1867	D: 26 Oct 1899
		s/o Henry & Sarah Smith
Henry H. Smith	B: 23 Nov 1830	D: 21 Feb 1883
		s/o W. G. & Betsy B. Smith
Mary Blair Smith	B: 8 Sep 1874	D: 20 Jan 1950
		d/o Henry H. & Sarah Lake Smith
Ludwell Lake	B: 8 Feb 1805	D: 17 Jul 1876

Lot: 202   1898 Owner: Marshall Lake

Helen Lake   B: 1843   D: 1899
                                                        w/o Marshall Lake

Marshall Lake   B: 1828   D: 1888

Nellie Lake   Age: 3 yrs   D: 15 Nov 1861
                                              d/o Thomas M. & Almina H. Lake

Minnie Smith Gott   B: 26 Sep 1896   D: 28 Oct 1971
                                              d/o John & Helen Glascock

Lot: 203   1898 Owner: Joseph Fry

Christena Frey   B: 27 Dec 1816   D: 8 Apr 1877

Joseph Frey   B: 29 Nov 1805   D: 2 Jul 1876

J. W. Lawson   Age: 73 yrs   D: 21 Jun 1888

Ernest E. Smith   B: 14 Mar 1859   D: 7 May 1916
                                              s/o Stephen P. & Mildred G. Smith

Kate Daily Smith   w/o Ernest E. Smith   D: 9 Jul 1917

Elizabeth Frey   Age: 68 yrs   D: 7 Sep 1866
                                              d/o John P. & Ann C. Frey

Lot: 204   1898 Owner: Charles Turner

Richard H. Turner   B: 30 Dec 1835   D: 28 Feb 1875

Lot: 205   1898 Owner: Sam Seaton

Samuel L. Seaton   Age: 66 yrs   D: 26 Aug 1930

Henry M. Seaton   Age: 28 yrs   D: 2 Dec 1899
                                              s/o S. R. & E. C. Seaton

Charlotte C. Seaton   B: 9 Jan 1870   D: 16 Mar 1951

Cornelius G. Seaton   Age: 29 yrs   D: 9 Apr 1891

Edna Ellen Seaton   B: 16 Mar 1883   D: 16 Apr 1946

Emma C. Seaton   Age: 51 yrs   D: 29 Oct 1899
                                                        w/o S. R. Seaton

Encelia E. Seaton   Age: 35 yrs   D: 1 Oct 1866
                                                        w/o S. R. Seaton

Mary A. Seaton   B: 16 May 1881   D: 5 Aug 1922
                                              d/o S. R. & E. C. Seaton

Marion Dice Seaton	B: 14 Oct 1888	D: 9 Mar 1969
Samuel R. Seaton	B: 9 Aug 1836	D: 8 May 1917

Lot: 206   1898 Owner: Henry Whitlock

Ruth Bruin	Age: 24 yrs	D: 21 Dec 1897
Martha E. Bruin	B: 10 May 1850	D: 28 Feb 1929 w/o Delaney Bruin
Delaney Bruin	B: 16 Mar 1842	D: 28 Feb 1923
Amanda B. Whitlock	B: 5 Feb 1823	D: 28 Jul 1883 w/o Henry Whitlock
Clarence Whitlock	B: 7 Jan 1859	D: 29 May 1860
Sarah Whitlock	B: 3 Feb 1824	D: 18 Sep 1869 w/o Henry Whitlock
Henry Whitlock	Age: 77 yrs	D: 19 Feb 1897
Robert H. Bruin	B: 10 May 1884	D: 30 Jun 1884
Robert T. Whitlock	B: 24 Oct 1852	D: 9 Dec 1882

Lot: 208   1898 Owner: S.J. Martin

Sophia W. Martin	Age: 30 yrs	D: 3 Apr 1868

Lot: 209   1898 Owner: A.J. Chamblin

A. Rush Chamblin	B: 18 May 1850	D: 23 Dec 1876
Carroll Cooke Chamblin	B: 1899	D: 1926
Ida Russ Chamblin	B: 1883	D: 1931 d/o A. Brooke & Mary A. Chamblin
Dr. John Chamblin	Age: 31 yrs	D: 2 Aug 1869 s/o A. G. & E. B. Chamblin
Rush Chamblin	B: 6 Dec 1880	D: 21 Apr 1884 s/o A. B. & Annie Chamblin
Brooke Bartlett Chamblin, Sr.	B: 1890	D: 1971
Evelina B. Chamblin	B: 26 Jan 1806	D: 27 Apr 1888 w/o A. G. Chamblin
Billie M. Chamblin	B: 1 Nov 1902	D: 10 Feb 1904 s/o A. B. & Mary Chamblin
A. G. Chamblin	Age: 63 yrs	D: 3 Sep 1870

Hamill Chamblin   B: 27 May 1895   D: 11 Feb 1900
                                   s/o A. B. & Mary Chamblin

Virginia Hall Chamblin   D: 1962

Lot: 210   1898 Owner: J.H. Bradfield

Annie E. Bradfield   B: 1 Feb 1842   D: 5 Sep 1913

W. H. Bradfield   B: 6 Jul 1874   D: 31 Mar 1957

Sallie A. Bradfield   B: 29 Sep 1886   D: 9 Nov 1952
                                   w/o W. H. Bradfield

Cornelius H. Bradfield   B: 7 Mar 1830   D: 14 Oct 1886
                                   CSA: 17th VA Infantry, Co. C

Carrie Estelle Bradfield   B: 17 Apr 1869   D: 20 Mar 1870

Lot: 211   1898 Owner: Bushrod Garrison

Mary E. Jones Garrison   B: 1832   D: 6 Jan 1881
                                   w/o Bushrod T. Garrison

Bushrod T. Garrison   B: 1831   D: 1900

Lot: 212   1898 Owner: Wm Morse

Marian T. Moss   D: 8 May 1914
                                   d/o W. V. & B. K. Moss

Blanche K. Moss   B: 8 Jan 1842   D: 4 Apr 1912
                                   d/o Townsend & K. H. McVeigh

Georgianna Johnson   B: 27 Nov 1837   D: 29 Apr 1896
                                   d/o Townsend & K. H. McVeigh

Emma Ross Johnson   Age: 4 mos   D: 2 Nov 1881
                                   d/o V. M. & G. M. Johnson

*infant McVeigh   no dates

Lot: 213   1898 Owner: Jas Downs

James B. Downs   B: 13 Jan 1822   D: 1 Mar 1893

Mary A. Downs   B: 28 Dec 1820   D: 20 Dec 1876
                                   w/o James B. Downs

*Brady Randolph Downs   Age: 44-5-0   D: 23 Feb 1946

Lot: 216   **1898 Owner: Sam Cox**

Mary Carol Elgin	B: 25 Jul 1955	D: 23 Mar 1996
Samuel Cox	B: 1799	D: 1873
Sarah Chamblin Cox	B: 1796	D: 1893

Lot: 217   **1898 Owner: Wilford Redman**

Robert L. Redman	B: 18 Dec 1865	D: 6 Feb 1904
Sherman L. Redman	B: 5 Sep 1854	D: 3 May 1875
Wilford Redman	B: 20 Apr 1832	D: 8 Mar 1919
	CSA: 6th VA Cavalry, Co. A	
Martha E. Redman	B: 12 Jun 1837	D: 21 Nov 1875
William Redman	B: 11 Mar 1863	D: 3 Jul 1903

Lot: 218L   **1898 Owner: Robt Bowman**

Robert C. Bowman	B: 1809	D: 1874
Ellen Skinner Storey	B: 4 Apr 1896	D: 5 Oct 1961
infant daughter Storey		D: 21 Sep 1928
	d/o R. P. & E. S. Storey	

Lot: 218U   **1898 Owner: L.R. Skinner**

| Ludwell J. Skinner | B: 1861 | D: 1919 |
| Janie Smith Skinner | B: 1869 | D: 1936 |

Lot: 219   **1898 Owner: Mrs. B. Batts**

Charles A. Bodmer	B: 16 Apr 1871	D: 20 Jul 1894
	s/o George & Margaret Bodmer	
Margaret Bodmer	B: 1 Dec 1837	D: 28 Feb 1917
	w/o George Bodmer	
George Bodmer	B: 14 Jul 1831	D: 12 Apr 1910
Lewis H. Bodmer	B: 22 May 1878	D: 29 Sep 1905
	s/o George & Margaret Bodmer	
*Miss Mary Bodmer	Age: 26-1-11	D: 10 May 1943
Catherine Bodmer	B: 13 Jan 1879	D: 9 Sep 1922
	d/o George & Margaret Bodmer	

Lot: 220   1898 Owner: Romulus Ferguson

Mary C. Ferguson	B: 10 Jun 1825	D: 21 Dec 1914
Mary C. Ferguson	B: 9 Jun 1856	D: 9 Jan 1878
		d/o Romulus & Mary C. Ferguson
Walter R. Ferguson	B: 4 May 1865	D: 24 Sep 1874
		s/o R. & C. Ferguson
Romulus Ferguson	B: 20 Dec 1825	D: 13 Mar 1895
Walter R. Ferguson	B: 25 Jan 1885	D: 11 Aug 1947
J. W. Ferguson	B: 19 Jul 1851	D: 14 Feb 1923
Flora M. Ferguson	B: 6 Feb 1860	D: 19 Jul 1940

Lot: 221   1898 Owner: Samuel Barker

Rebecca Ann Barker	Age: 63 yrs	D: 5 Sep 1876
		w/o Samuel Brison Barker
Samuel Brison Barker	Age: 66 yrs	D: 10 Jul 1872

Lot: 223   1898 Owner: Mrs. Rosa Dodd

Mason B. Dodd	B: 1 Sep 1803	D: 3 Jun 1884
Mariah F. Dodd	B: 30 Jun 1828	D: 6 Jan 1896
		w/o Mason B. Dodd

Lot: 223A   1898 Owner: Not Listed

Ricard R. Ohrstrom	B: 1922	D: 1995
Monique Von Mudra Ohrstrom	B: 15 Oct 1932	D: 19 Dec 1967
Elizabeth J. Ohrstrom	B: 1907	D: 1968
George L. Ohrstrom	B: 1894	D: 1955

Lot: 224   1898 Owner: Mrs. Alex G. Smith

Mary S. Smith	B: 14 Dec 1840	D: 19 Mar 1916
Alexander G. Smith	B: 31 Aug 1803	D: 25 Feb 1884
Margaret Smith	B: 16 Apr 1805	D: 11 Jul 1872
		w/o A. G. Smith
Lottie R. Smith Burton	B: 26 Mar 1844	D: 12 Jul 1921
		w/o J. H. Burton
Henrietta Schaffner	Age: 78 yrs	D: 23 Feb 1876

Edward A. Smith	B: 24 Aug 1831	D: 2 Feb 1882

Lot: 225L   1898 Owner: J.R. Clarke

John R. Clark	Age: 43 yrs	D: 19 Aug 1871
Kate E. Clark	Age: 66 yrs	D: 25 Apr 1901 w/o John R. Clark

Lot: 225U   1898 Owner: Wm Clarke

Sarah J. Clark	B: 28 Feb 1839	D: 7 Mar 1922
Wade N. Clarke	Age: 50 yrs	D: 3 Sep 1874
Wayland D. Altman	B: 26 Aug 1901	D: 24 Oct 1908
Hattie Martin Altman	B: 10 May 1868	D: 27 Jan 1956

Lot: 226   1898 Owner: Rev. L. Mardus

Catherine Isabella Marders		D: 20 Apr 1866 w/o Elder Lovell Marders
Elder Lovell Marders	Age: 72 yrs	D: 16 Nov 1869

Lot: 227   1898 Owner: O.A. Scanland

Joel A. Clark	B: 22 Feb 1816	D: 10 Mar 1890
Amanda D. Clark	B: 11 Dec 1822	D: 21 Sep 1876 w/o Joel A. Clark
John S. Scanland	Age: 86 yrs	D: 30 Dec 1875
Sophronia Scanland	Age: 77 yrs	D: 7 Dec 1873

Lot: 228   1898 Owner: Silcott Moffett

Emma D. Burgess	B: 7 Jun 1849	D: 30 Mar 1916 w/o H. P. Burgess
Laura E. Moffett	B: 9 Jan 1860	D: 16 Oct 1943
Maria Jones	Age: 79 yrs	D: 7 Jan 1887
John T. Moffett	B: 17 Jul 1832	D: 24 Nov 1923
Landon C. Silcott	B: 21 Jan 1829	D: 7 Apr 1883
Jane M. Moffett	B: 13 Jun 1827	D: 10 Sep 1900 w/o J. T. Moffett

Lot: 230U   1898 Owner: Mrs. E.B. Lipps

Elbert B. Lipps   B: 8 Mar 1891   D: 21 Jul 1965

Cicero Lipps   B: 1926   D: 1926
                                                    s/o E. B. & S. M. Lipps

Jonathan Lipps   B: 1922   D: 1931
                                                    s/o E. B. & S. M. Lipps

Sue Kirk Lipps   B: 5 Mar 1896   D: 21 Jun 1975

Lot: 232   1898 Owner: Unmarked graves

F. Patricia Hummer   D: 17 Nov 1932
                                                    d/o H. S. & H. G. Hummer

Edna Downs Ball   B: 26 Sep 1882   D: 18 Aug 1954

Ernest Ball   B: 22 Jun 1877   D: 18 Jun 1922

*Vernon Ball   D: 14 Mar 1922
                                                    s/o Ernest & Edna Ball

Bernard 'Bill Zandy' Zandeciacoma
                           B: 27 Apr 1881   D: 13 Jun 1921

*Howard Norman Carty   D: 3 May 1928

Lot: 233   1898 Owner: Hulfish

Garrett Ewin Hulfish   B: 27 Aug 1873   D: 28 Mar 1892

G. D. Hulfish   B: 16 Aug 1846   D: 7 Feb 1895

Clinton C. Hulfish   B: 28 Oct 1888   D: 24 Aug 1957

Herbert Hulfish   B: 8 Mar 1870   D: 13 Nov 1889

S. M. Hulfish   B: 4 Sep 1844   D: 9 May 1922
                                                    w/o G. D. Hulfish

Lot: 234   1898 Owner: H.M. Smith

H. M. Smith   B: 10 Jul 1839   D: 5 Sep 1910

Elizabeth Smith   B: 24 Oct 1843   D: 4 Jul 1908
                                                    w/o H. M. Smith

Dean Beverly James   B: 16 Apr 1861   D: 8 Apr 1921

Annie Smith James   B: 31 Oct 1866   D: 11 Mar 1929

Martha S. Smith   B: 31 Jan 1870   D: 13 Dec 1881
                                                    d/o H. M. & Elizabeth Smith

William H. Smith	B: 8 Nov 1879	D: 25 Jan 1958

Lot: 235   **1898 Owner: Wallace Tiffany**

Wallace N. Tiffany	B: 31 May 1885	D: 1 Sep 1885
		s/o W. N. & M. G. Tiffany
Hugh Adair Tiffany	B: 8 Jan 1878	D: 1 Nov 1880
		s/o W. N. & M. G. Tiffany
infant son Tiffany	c/o W. N. & M. G. Tiffany	no dates
Hugh Tiffany	Age: 73 yrs	D: 10 May 1875
Tacie J. Elgin	B: 6 Nov 1849	D: 29 Dec 1915
Wallace Newton Tiffany	B: 3 Apr 1850	D: 4 Mar 1920
infant son Tiffany	c/o W. N. & M. G. Tiffany	no dates
Effie Tiffany	B: 29 Aug 1880	D: 18 Jun 1881
		d/o W. N. & M. G. Tiffany
Mary Gertrude Tiffany	B: 9 Jan 1848	D: 4 Jan 1897
Sarah Hamilton Tiffany	B: 13 Aug 1822	D: 6 Jun 1908
		w/o Hugh Tiffany

Lot: 236   **1898 Owner: Chas A. Smith**

John Henry Smith	B: 1 Dec 1839	D: 15 Apr 1921
Randolph Clay Smith	B: 20 Jul 1845	D: 17 Jan 1924
Seldon M. Gibson	B: 4 Jul 1807	D: 13 Feb 1889
Edward S. Duffey	B: 25 Jul 1841	D: 23 Dec 1926
Amanda M. Duffey	B: 11 Feb 1842	D: 24 Jan 1926
Charles Augustus Smith	Age: 9 mos	no dates
		s/o Charles A. & Olive P. Smith
Charles A. Smith	Age: 72 yrs	no dates
Augustus G. Smith	Age: 72 yrs	D: 15 Feb 1879
Anna M. Smith	Age: 77 yrs	D: 17 Dec 1887
		w/o Augustus G. Smith
Olive Peterman Smith	Age: 36 yrs	no dates
		w/o Charles A. Smith

Lot: 237   1898 Owner: B. Underwood

Joseph M. Davis   B: 1 Jul 1847   D: 21 Feb 1908

Susan H. Underwood   B: 1842   D: 1922
                                        w/o Bushrod Underwood

Laura L. Underwood   B: 9 Nov 1874   D: 19 Oct 1876
                                        d/o B. & S. H. Underwood

Bushrod Underwood   B: 16 Jan 1844   D: 25 Dec 1899
                                        CSA: 43rd VA Cavalry, Co. A

Lot: 238   1898 Owner: Jas Gregg

Catha J. Gregg   B: 14 Jan 1793   D: 27 May 1875

Clarence B. Sinclair   B: 27 Feb 1898   D: 19 Mar 1901

Mary L. C. Gregg   B: 20 Feb 1849   D: 30 May 1918
                                        w/o J. W. Gregg

Elizabeth A. Gregg   B: 11 Mar 1825   D: 27 Sep 1901

James W. Gregg   B: 3 Dec 1829   D: 22 Sep 1900
                                        CSA: 8th VA Infantry, Co. C

Susan P. Gregg   Age: 75 yrs   D: 30 Nov 1907

Allen Gregg   B: 20 Mar 1801   D: 30 Jan 1878

Rebecca Gregg   B: 15 Nov 1788   D: 5 Mar 1878

Lot: 239L   1898 Owner: Chas W. Hoffman

Frederick Samuel Warren   B: 1969   D: 1988

Pauline P. Warren   B: 24 Jul 1909   D: 21 Jan 1991

Nelson P. Warren   B: 3 May 1907   D: 30 Dec 1995

Geraldine M. Warren   B: 27 Nov 1916

Charles Weston Warren, Sr.   B: 15 Nov 1909   D: 3 Aug 1981

Lot: 239U   1898 Owner: H.B. Linkins

Carrie Elizabeth Linkins   B: 17 Nov 1871   D: 18 Jul 1955

James Dallas Linkins   B: 22 Nov 1884   D: 24 Jun 1944

Caroline C. Linkins   B: 7 Sep 1840   D: 28 Jan 1921

Mary E. Linkins   B: 1879   D: 1880

Lot: 240   1898 Owner: S. Craig

Samuel Craig	B: 16 Mar 1819	D: 3 Jun 1894
Ann M. Craig	B: 25 Feb 1818	D: 14 Jun 1899
Ann Craig	B: 4 Jul 1844	D: 3 Dec 1914
Francis T. Craig	B: 2 Aug 1846	D: 17 May 1910
James S. Craig	B: 31 Jul 1879	D: 3 May 1880

Lot: 241   1898 Owner: C.M. Woolf

Carroll D. Woolf	B: 1883	D: 1963
Robert D. Woolf	B: 1850	D: 1926
Kate A. Woolf	B: 1877	D: 1884
		d/o R. D. & K. A. Woolf
Pattie W. Tate	B: 1913	D: 1971
Hunter Woolf	B: 1874	D: 1875
		s/o R. D. & K. A. Woolf
Sophy Bowie	w/o Carroll D. Bowie	no dates
Kate Ayre Woolf	B: 1844	D: 1877
		w/o Robert D. Woolf

Lot: 242   1898 Owner: Horace Smith

S. Ellen Smith	B: 1843	D: 1901
		w/o Horace Smith
James Priest	B: 1812	D: 1892
A. Landon Moffett	B: 1873	D: 1931
Horace Smith	B: 1845	D: 1919
James Priest Smith	B: 1873	D: 1883
		s/o H. & S. E. Smith
E. Mattie Moffett	B: 1875	D: 1964
Horace S. Moffett	B: 14 Oct 1905	D: 30 Nov 1970

Lot: 243   1898 Owner: J.H. Priest

Susan Ellen Priest Hough	B: 1 Jul 1877	D: 31 Dec 1958
Mary Furr Priest	B: 12 Oct 1871	D: 30 May 1895
Walter T. Priest	B: 1868	D: 1961

J. H. Priest   no dates

Lot: 244   1898 Owner: J.T. Cochran

Laura V. Cochran Elgin	B: 2 Mar 1859	D: 4 Jan 1932
John Thomas Cochran	B: 4 Sep 1826	D: 11 Aug 1905
John T. E. Cochran	B: 27 Jun 1854	D: 12 Aug 1928
Elizabeth Lodge Cochran	B: 5 May 1825	D: 14 Apr 1886
		w/o John T. Cochran
Richard Fleet Cochran	Age: 1day	D: 9 Nov 1867
		s/o John T. & E. Cochran
Robert Elgin	B: 11 Apr 1854	D: 11 Oct 1912
*Dwight L. Nevitt	Age: 59 yrs	D: 16 Oct 1943
*Mollie C. Nevitt	Age: 75-1-13	D: 25 Dec 1944
William Nathan Cochran	B: 23 Oct 1860	D: 14 May 1880
		s/o John T. & E. Cochran

Lot: 245   1898 Owner: Robt Turner

Edward S Turner	B: 28 Jun 1879	D: 16 Feb 1926
E. Shirley Turner	B: 10 Mar 1917	D: 22 Feb 1987
Sarah Louise Sanford Turner	B: 18 Aug 1887	D: 8 Dec 1917
		w/o Edward S. Turner
Mary West Turner	B: 26 Feb 1854	D: 9 Feb 1881
		w/o Robert F. Turner
Margaretta F. Turner	B: 2 Sep 1877	D: 18 Feb 1960

Lot: 246   1898 Owner: J.S. Redd

Matilda D. Moore	B: 5 Mar 1893	D: 14 May 1924
Mildred N. Moore	B: 28 Sep 1900	D: 4 Aug 1924
Martha E. Redd	B: 23 Apr 1829	D: 8 Jul 1925
Mary Louise Moore	Age: 10 mos	D: 3 Jul 1898
William Moore	B: 4 Oct 1844	D: 11 Jun 1913
		CSA: 8th VA Infantry, Co. E
Joseph W. Moore	B: 6 Apr 1896	D: 18 Jul 1925
Ettie Redd	B: 17 Jul 1860	D: 18 Nov 1885
		d/o Joseph S. & Martha E. Redd

Joseph S. Redd	B: 22 Feb 1824	D: 5 Mar 1887
Josephine Redd Moore	B: 10 Jul 1857	D: 3 Dec 1942
A. J. Redd	Age: 62 yrs	D: 24 Aug 1881

Lot: 247U   1898 Owner: Robert Costello

infant son Costello	B: 5 Mar 1891	D: 7 Mar 1891
		s/o Robert & A. Costello
Mary E. Costello	B: 10 Feb 1879	D: 30 Oct 1882
Robert Costello	B: 19 Dec 1849	D: 1 Jul 1917
Aramantha Costello	B: 10 May 1851	D: 6 Mar 1929
		w/o Robert Costello

Lot: 248   1898 Owner: James Dishman

Mary V. Dishman	B: 7 Oct 1878	D: 23 Dec 1893
		d/o J. W. & E. V. Dishman
Margaret B. Dishman	Age: 2 yrs	D: 23 Oct 1882
		d/o J. W. & E. V. Dishman
Beulah B. Dishman	B: 12 Oct 1882	D: 11 May 1957
W. A. Dishman	B: 20 Jun 1884	D: 11 Sep 1935
J. W. Dishman	B: 24 Jul 1839	D: 10 Nov 1913
Emma V. Dishman	B: 28 Mar 1853	D: 26 Nov 1935
		w/o J. W. Dishman

Lot: 249L   1898 Owner: Mrs. W. Clemens

Nannie Clemons Huff	B: 1875	D: 1954
W. Herbert Huff	B: 1892	D: 1967
Billy Clemons	B: 1865	D: 1929

Lot: 249U   1898 Owner: E.M. Redmon

| Martha E. Redman | B: 16 Feb 1880 | D: 3 Feb 1890 |
| | | d/o E. M. & Kate Redman |

Lot: 250   1898 Owner: D.G. Mead

Annie Bolton Meade	B: 23 Nov 1831	D: 24 Mar 1899
		w/o Drayton Meade
Drayton G. Meade		D: 10 Dec 1911
John Henry Hill Sands		D: 18 Mar 1910

Catherine Jane Sands   D: 16 Dec 1911

Josephine Meade   B: 13 Apr 1866   D: 27 Feb 1883
                                                   d/o D. G. & A. B. Meade

Drayton Hill Meade   B: 1871   D: 1955

Courtenay M. Meade   B: 1856   D: 1945

Champe Eubank Meade   B: 1878   D: 1956

Lot: 251   1898 Owner: J.M. Martin

Lizzie A. Rutter Martin   B: 30 Sep 1847   D: 11 Feb 1919
                                                   w/o Joseph M. Martin

Rev. J. D. Martin   B: 21 Jan 1859   D: 2 Sep 1899

Joseph M. Martin   B: 20 Feb 1853   D: 21 Apr 1925

John W. Martin   B: 4 Mar 1824   D: 15 Feb 1901
                                                   CSA: 8th VA Infantry, Co. C

Jane W. Martin   B: 17 Mar 1825   D: 10 Aug 1906

Thomas A. Martin   B: 15 Mar 1847   D: 6 Nov 1893
                                                   s/o J. W. & Jane W. Martin

Lot: 252   1898 Owner: J.H. Skinner

James H. Skinner   B: 15 Jan 1848   D: 8 Jun 1923

Rebecca Ellen Skinner   B: 21 Jan 1856   D: 18 Mar 1927
                                                   w/o James H. Skinner

infant Skinner   B: 1 Aug 1900   D: 4 Aug 1900
                                                   c/o C. L. & E. E. Skinner

Robert Cochran   B: 11 Jul 1882   D: 11 Sep 1882
                                                   s/o S. L. & A. A. Cochran

H. A. Garrell Skinner   Age: 1 yr   D: 6 Jul 1911
                                                   d/o J. J. & E. J. Skinner

*infant Skinner   s/o J.J. & E.J. Skinner D: AT BIRTH

Robert Emmett Skinner   B: 27 Jan 1892   D: 21 Oct 1918

Mary Tiffany Skinner   B: 17 Mar 1892   D: 14 Feb 1967

William Cochran Skinner   B: 17 May 1880   D: 15 Nov 1931

Lot: 253   1898 Owner: J.S. Palmer

| Ann Elizabeth Palmer | B: 28 Sep 1822 | D: 23 Apr 1881 |
| | | w/o J. S. Palmer |

| William F. Whaley | B: 12 Nov 1855 | D: 27 Dec 1945 |
| | | h/o Orra V. Whaley |

| Mary Francis Palmer | B: 6 Oct 1857 | D: 2 Nov 1917 |

| Webster C. Palmer | B: 15 Apr 1852 | D: 23 Jun 1891 |

| Harry H. Palmer | B: 23 Sep 1882 | D: 5 Dec 1941 |

| Orra V. Palmer Whaley | B: 28 Mar 1855 | D: 22 Feb 1936 |
| | | w/o W. F. Whaley |

Lot: 254   1898 Owner: J.A. Hutchison

| Mary A. Rutter | B: 29 Jun 1826 | D: 10 Oct 1910 |

| Annie Hutchison | Age: 28 yrs | D: 23 Sep 1881 |
| | d/o Joseph A. & Margaret Hutchison | |

| Mary Nelson Thomas | B: 20 Oct 1863 | D: 25 Feb 1901 |
| | | w/o Tarlton B. Thomas |

| Ann S. Hutchison | B: 4 Feb 1818 | D: 15 Jun 1898 |

| Joseph A. Hutchison | B: 26 May 1822 | D: 7 Jun 1909 |

| Lucile Catherine Thomas | B: 18 Feb 1895 | D: 12 Mar 1897 |
| | d/o T. B. & M. N. Thomas | |

| J. Gilbert Thomas | B: 31 Aug 1886 | D: 13 May 1906 |

| Sarah E. Hutchison | B: 29 Feb 1829 | D: 27 Mar 1904 |
| | | w/o Joseph A. Hutchison |

Lot: 255   1898 Owner: John Gains

| Mary E. Gaines | Age: 6 yrs | D: 20 May 1911 |
| | | d/o J. J. & M. E. Gaines |

| John J. Gaines | Age: 55 yrs | D: 30 Jul 1907 |

Lot:256   1898 Owner: George Bodmer

| George W. Bodmer | B: 30 Apr 1854 | D: 13 Dec 1916 |

| Jacob Leslie Bodmer | B: 4 Oct 1891 | D: 27 Aug 1924 |

| Elouise Virginia Bodmer | B: 22 Feb 1862 | D: 30 May 1931 |
| | | w/o G. W. Bodmer |

*George Sidney	B: 30 Aug 1893	D: 25 Jun 1894
Mary M. Bodmer	Age: 35 yrs	D: 29 Oct 1884
		w/o George W. Bodmer

Lot: 258   1898 Owner: John Thompson

Mary Belle Fleming	B: 24 Sep 1862	D: 7 Mar 1939
William C. Fleming	B: 9 Mar 1857	D: 27 Aug 1938
Milvin Fleming	B: 22 Sep 1888	D: 13 Oct 1888
		s/o W. C. & M. B. Fleming
Margaret E. Thompson	B: 29 Dec 1830	D: 13 Aug 1921
		w/o John F. Thompson
John F. Thompson	Age: 79 yrs	D: 20 Aug 1912
Emma Marion Fleming	B: 24 Feb 1890	D: 19 Aug 1898
		d/o W. C. & M. B. Fleming
Emily Jane Trussell	Age: 27 yrs	D: 4 Jan 1886
		w/o Charles R. Trussell
Lola A. Fleming	Age: 1 yr	D: 29 Nov 1900
		d/o W. C. & M. B. Fleming

Lot: 258A   1898 Owner: Not Listed

Karen Juanita Fout	B: 1954	D: 1957

Lot: 259   1898 Owner: Wm Bodmer

Noland M. Downs	B: 1893	D: 1972
Pauline Downs	B: 1898	D: 1961
Ann M. Bodmer	B: 10 Apr 1825	D: 2 Feb 1902
Charles H. Downs	B: 1867	D: 1902
William Bodmer	B: 4 Mar 1863	D: 6 Apr 1947
Minnie Downs Heyl	B: 1869	D: 1944
Jacob Bodmer	B: 16 Jun 1822	D: 26 Dec 1888

Lot: 260   1898 Owner: H.M. Woolf

Henry M. Woolf	B: 22 Dec 1817	D: 24 May 1898
Julia A. Dowell	B: 22 Oct 1832	D: 17 Mar 1882
Hardwick E. Woolf	B: 6 Sep 1857	D: 11 Aug 1886

Nannie Woolf Saunders	B: 24 Feb 1866	D: 14 May 1910
Agnes Shenck	B: 31 Dec 1812	D: 25 Jul 1835
Charles M. Woolf	B: 1863	D: 1912
		h/o Mary E. Woolf
Katherine E. Woolf	B: 4 Mar 1831	D: 30 Aug 1907

Lot: 261   1898 Owner: L.A. Woolf

John A. Woolf	Age: 27 yrs	D: 29 Sep 1888
Samuel A. Woolf	B: 14 Feb 1833	D: 14 Jan 1910
Warren M. Woolf	B: 24 Jan 1900	D: 23 Jan 1980
Alverda M. Woolf	B: 27 Nov 1906	
Sarah E. Woolf	Age: 68 yrs	D: 4 Dec 1900

Lot: 262   1898 Owner: Wm Grimes

Baylous P. Grimes	B: 5 Mar 1890	D: 10 Apr 1959
Lucy Ann Grimes	B: 10 Apr 1850	D: 20 Mar 1922
		w/o William Grimes
Wesley Francis Grimes	B: 10 Feb 1893	D: 2 Aug 1966
William Grimes	B: 5 Aug 1848	D: 10 Sep 1929

Lot: 263   1898 Owner: J.S. Welch

J. Selden Welsh	B: 1832	D: 1926
Rev. John J. Welsh	Age: 21 yrs	D: 14 May 1890
		s/o J. Selden & Mary L. Welsh
Mary Martin Welsh	B: 1848	D: 1904
Minnie McDonald	B: 1884	D: 1952

Lot: 264   1898 Owner: W.P. Hatcher

William P. Hatcher	B: 28 Dec 1842	D: 21 Nov 1902
William Grafton Hatcher	B: 1 Sep 1882	D: 20 Oct 1918
Catherine C. Hatcher	B: 22 Dec 1855	D: 21 Feb 1934
Richard W. Hatcher	B: 20 May 1893	D: 25 Jul 1942
Bertha Kelly Allison	B: 6 Jun 1889	D: 4 Aug 1971

Lot: 265U   1898 Owner: J. Squires

| John Squires | B: 20 Sep 1819 | D: 13 Apr 1890 |

| Margaret Ramey Squires | B: 9 Aug 1841 | D: 28 Jan 1913
w/o John Squires |

| Ada C. Leonard | B: 20 Sep 1863 | D: 3 Mar 1900 |

Lot: 266   1898 Owner: J.F. Harringdon

| Mary J. Hinson Herringdon | B: 5 Jul 1834 | D: 11 Apr 1907
w/o James F. Herringdon |

| James F. Herringdon | B: 9 Apr 1830 | D: 10 Nov 1908 |

| *Annie L. Herringdon | Age: 79-4-4 | D: 9 Nov 1947 |

Lot: 267   1898 Owner: W. Elgin

| W. T. Rogers | Age: 79 yrs | D: 29 Jun 1912 |

| Mary Brady Elgin | B: 29 Oct 1920 | D: 10 Feb 1921
d/o Roger & Virginia Elgin |

| Mary T. Elgin | B: 5 Jul 1865 | D: 8 Jan 1922
w/o W. L. Elgin |

| Roger L. Elgin | B: 1891 | D: 1990 |

| Roger Lee Elgin, Jr. | B: 18 Sep 1919 | D: 7 Aug 1964 |

| Virginia Sanders Elgin | B: 1892 | D: 1956 |

| Wallace G. Elgin | B: 5 Jul 1865 | D: 8 Jan 1922
s/o W. L. & Mary T. Elgin |

| Willie Lee Elgin | B: 3 Feb 1863 | D: 20 Feb 1943 |

| Jean Norman Elgin | B: 8 May 1924 | D: 10 Aug 1993 |

Lot: 268   1898 Owner: H.S. Tiffany

| Hugh S. Tiffany | B: 29 Sep 1861 | D: 4 Dec 1940 |

| Walter J. Tiffany | B: 20 Dec 1886 | D: 5 Dec 1910 |

| Elizabeth Jane Cochran Tiffany | B: 23 Jun 1857 | D: 13 Aug 1928 |

Lot: 269   1898 Owner: Spencer Hall

| Catherine T. Hall | B: 20 May 1873 | D: 10 May 1955 |

| Raymond S. Hall | B: 1892 | D: 1976 |

| Pauline E. Hall | B: 2 May 1893 | D: 14 Mar.1955 |

Mary Elizabeth Hall	d/o J. S. & Mary E. Hall	no dates
Florence E. Hall	B: 9 Sep 1897	D: 1 Mar 1981
Clyde Oral Hall	B: 23 Mar 1894	D: 13 Oct 1954
Amos T. Hall	B: 29 Jun 1904	D: 29 Aug 1955
Gladys Beatrice Hall Elliott	B: 7 Sep 1899	D: 11 Nov 1956
J. Spencer Hall	Age: 74 yrs	D: 3 Dec 1917

Lot: 270   1898 Owner: W & A.P. Smith

Frank H. Smith	B: 21 Mar 1883	D: 14 Feb 1970
Alfred E. Smith	B: 21 Apr 1878	D: 31 Oct 1899
	s/o Silvester & Henrietta Smith	
Amanda S. Wells	B: 20 Aug 1876	D: 28 Oct 1907
*Henrietta S. Smith	B: 8 Oct 1854	D: 25 Sep 1916
Sarah Ellen Smith	B: 24 Nov 1848	D: 3 May 1937
		w/o Peter Smith
Peter Smith	B: 28 Mar 1848	D: 5 Jan 1892

Lot: 271   1898 Owner: R.E. Russell

Emma Lee Russell	B: 7 Nov 1866	D: 3 Aug 1946
Cosmelia Virginia Russell	B: 16 May 1868	D: 22 Apr 1965
Bessie Russell	B: 1 Apr 1872	D: 25 Dec 1914
Anthony Brewis 'Bud' Russell	B: 1907	D: 1980
William H. Russell	Age: 75 yrs	D: 17 Feb 1915
William Calhoun Furr	B: 1869	D: 1939
U. Ellen Furr Russell	B: 11 Nov 1835	D: 1 Jun 1917
		w/o Robert E. Russell
Robert E. Russell	B: 14 Dec 1834	D: 4 Sep 1891

Lot: 272   1898 Owner: Z.T. Flynn

Z. T. Flynn	B: 15 Feb 1849	D: 7 Feb 1907
Rola H. Flynn	B: 7 Feb 1879	D: 3 Dec 1905
	s/o Z. T. & R. L. Flynn	

Lot: 273U   1898 Owner: Mrs. V.M. Smith

J. W. Smith	B: 21 Dec 1824	D: 17 Dec 1906

Lot: 274L   1898 Owner: D.W. Swart

Hugh T. Swart   B: 2 Sep 1894   D: 11 Feb 1972

Roberta H. Swart   B: 27 Jan 1852   D: 18 Jan 1941

William A. Swart   B: 23 Sep 1853   D: 8 Nov 1941

Lot: 274U   1898 Owner: R.H. Legard

R. H. Legard   B: 20 Oct 1893   D: 13 Jul 1982

Mamie S. Legard   B: 5 Jan 1889   D: 29 Nov 1973

Lot: 275   1898 Owner: Mrs. Rosalie Noland

Lloyd Noland   B: 25 Jul 1880   D: 27 Nov 1949

Martha Woods Noland   B: 30 Sep 1886   D: 22 Apr 1959
                                                         w/o Philip H. Noland

Margaret Gillick Noland   B: 5 Jan 1880   D: 4 Feb 1953
                                                         w/o Lloyd Noland

Philip Haxall Noland   B: 4 Feb 1886   D: 25 Feb 1969

Lot: 276   1898 Owner: Miss C.S. Noland

Rosalie Haxall Noland   B: 21 Jan 1852   D: 29 Jan 1935
                                                         d/o R. Barton Haxall

Barton Haxall Noland   B: 8 Oct 1881   D: 3 Mar 1955

Cuthbert Powell Noland   B: 25 May 1850   D: 12 Nov 1912
                                                         s/o Maj. Burr Powell Noland

Lot: 277   1898 Owner: J.E. Francis

Naomi Yates Francis   B: 2 Jan 1868   D: 5 Feb 1955

Emily Cranberry Francis   B: 26 Jul 1849   D: 12 Jul 1929

J. E. Francis   B: 11 Feb 1834   D: 4 Feb 1908

Nannie M. Francis   B: 26 Oct 1882   D: 23 Nov 1968

Albert E. Francis   B: 20 Feb 1892   D: 30 Jan 1972

Thomas Edward Francis   B: 25 Jun 1867   D: 15 Nov 1937

Lot: 278   1898 Owner: Mrs. E.P. Turner

Edward P. Turner   B: 14 Jul 1849   D: 13 Jan 1891

Llwyn Turner   B: 1881   D: 1961

Frances Turner Knox   B: 1883   D: 1967

Philip Marion Knox	B: 1879	D: 1959
Mary Beverly Turner	B: 10 Feb 1856	D: 16 Mar 1918
		w/o Edward Palmer Turner

Lot: 279   1898 Owner: J.E. Mount

James M. Mount	B: 2 Mar 1837	D: 6 Apr 1920
		CSA: 8th VA Infantry, Co. E
Jane Downing Smith	B: 8 May 1843	D: 18 Mar 1920
Ann W. Mount	B: 19 Jan 1838	D: 9 Mar 1931
Maria Louise Mount	B: 28 Apr 1836	D: 24 Feb 1901
		w/o C. E. Mount
Maria E. Burks	B: 6 Nov 1820	D: 22 Feb 1912
Fitzhugh Mount		D: 30 Aug 1857
		s/o Dr. J. E. & M. J. Mount
Charles E. Mount	B: 2 Mar 1828	D: 2 Mar 1890
Dr. John E. Mount	Age: 80 yrs	D: 3 Oct 1897

Lot: 280   1898 Owner: Rufus Downs

Maggie Kinsel Downs	B: 15 Jun 1866	D: 31 May 1957
Rufus B. Downs	B: 20 Apr 1859	D: 5 Nov 1945
Robert C. Downs	B: 17 Oct 1884	D: 10 May 1976
Myrtle Caton Downs	B: 16 Dec 1890	D: 14 Nov 1972

Lot: 281L   1898 Owner: A.L. O'Bannon

Lila H. O'Bannon	B: 1867	D: 1950
Albert L. O'Bannon	B: 1860	D: 1939
Tabitha Hull	B: 20 Jun 1831	D: 16 Aug 1904

Lot: 281U   1898 Owner: W.J. Rhodes

Randolph C. Rhodes	B: 28 Jan 1899	D: 9 Mar 1974
John William Rhodes	B: 1874	D: 1962
Doris A. Rhodes	B: 20 Feb 1914	D: 1 Oct 1953
Katherine Rhodes	B: 12 Jul 1903	D: 26 Aug 1905
		d/o J. W. & M. E. Rhodes

Mary Elizabeth Rhodes   B: 1867   D: 1916
                                                 w/o John W. Rhodes

Lot: 282L   1898 Owner: J.B. Hutchison

T. Benton Hutchison   B: 31 Jan 1835   D: 6 Jul 1890
                                            CSA: 8th VA Infantry, Co. B

Lot: 282U   1898 Owner: J.R. Hutchison

John R. Hutchison   B: 24 Oct 1829   D: 3 May 1895
                                            CSA: 8th VA Infantry, Co. D

Lot: 283   1898 Owner: Chas Minnegerode

Charles Minnigerode   B: 1 Apr 1873   D: 20 Jan 1949
                                  s/o Charles & Virginia P. Minnigerode

Dorothy Loane Minnigerode   B: 12 Apr 1903   D: 23 Aug 1944
                                             w/o John H. Minnigerode

Jodie Ann Minnigerode   B: 20 Sep 1956   D: 18 Oct 1956
                                        d/o Bryan & Joan Minnigerode

Mary Shepard Bryan Minnigerode
                               B: 8 Oct 1892   D: 4 Mar 1966
                                  d/o Dr. John H. & Susan Turner Bryan

Susan Turner Minnigerode   B: 1 Jul 1867   D: 27 Feb 1913
                                           w/o Charles Minnigerode

Julia Hunt Bryan Minnigerode B: 2 Aug 1891   D: 22 Nov 1969
                                  d/o Dr. John H. & Susan Turner Bryan

Lot: 284L   1898 Owner: Geo Y. Dodd

Emma Dodd   B: 10 Mar 1886   D: 21 Nov 1917

G. Y. Dodd   B: 2 Dec 1844   D: 2 Oct 1918

George W. Dodd   Age: 4 mos   D: 8 May 1878
                                             s/o G. Y. & M. O. Dodd

M. O. Dodd   B: 2 Apr 1850   D: 14 Apr 1931

infant son Dodd   D: 1 Sep 1884
                                             s/o G. Y. & M. O. Dodd

Lot: 284U   1898 Owner: Miscellaneous

J. Marvin Leith   B: 15 Jun 1878   D: 10 Jun 1957

T. Gabriella Leith   B: 1 Dec 1866   D: 8 Jul 1933

Lot: 285L   1898 Owner: Marguerite Montgomery

Margaret H. G. Montgomery	B: 25 Aug 1834	
George C. Montgomery	B: 15 Dec 1868	D: 10 Sep 1914
George R. Montgomery	B: 24 Oct 1833	D: 15 Jun 1898
John H. Montgomery	B: 7 Oct 1866	D: 24 Aug 1896
Elizabeth Sidebottom	B: 13 Mar 1795	D: 31 Jan 1885
S. Merton Sidebottom	B: 30 Oct 1827	D: 3 Feb 1887

Lot: 286   1898 Owner: Sanford Gulick

G. William Gulick	B: 3 Jul 1866	D: 24 Dec 1901
		s/o Sanford & Nancy Gulick
Nancy R. Gulick	B: 3 Mar 1828	D: 10 Apr 1919
		w/o Sanford Gulick
Mary J. Gulick	B: 1858	D: 8 Dec 1941
Jessie G. Gulick	B: 2 Sep 1876	D: 1 Jan 1959
		w/o G. William Gulick
Ellen Gulick	B: 1856	D: 1940
Alice Amelia Gulick	B: 30 Jul 1863	D: 16 Nov 1926
		d/o Sanford & Nancy R. Gulick
Sanford Gulick	B: 10 Nov 1813	D: 14 Nov 1878

Lot: 288L   1898 Owner: Mrs. L.E. Winston

Annie E. Winston	B: 20 Sep 1861	D: 3 Sep 1896
		w/o William H. Winston
Hamilton B. Winston	B: 24 Sep 1818	D: 15 Nov 1884
Jay T. Winston	B: 5 Mar 1873	D: 19 Mar 1889

Lot: 288U   1898 Owner: Miscellaneous

Elizabeth H. Carter	B: 1843	D: 1917
		w/o James W. Carter
James W. Carter	B: 1838	D: 1922

Lot: 289   1898 Owner: F.M. Kerrick

Sidney Jane Kerrick	B: 19 Jan 1844	D: 19 Apr 1909
		w/o F. M. Kerrick

F. M. Kerrick	B: 23 Mar 1840	D: 31 Jul 1907
		CSA: Fauquier Artillery
Julian U. Davis	B: 4 Apr 1908	D: 5 Jul 1909
		s/o J. H. & E. Davis
Mary C. Kerrick	B: 8 Mar 1883	D: 14 Apr 1966
John Neal Kerrick	B: 6 Oct 1871	D: 25 Nov 1936
Annie L. Kerrick	Age: 25 yrs	D: 8 Jan 1900
		d/o F. M. & S. J. Kerrick
Francis M. Kerrick, Jr.	B: 7 Mar 1880	D: 6 Mar 1959
Hugh Edwin Kerrick	B: 27 May 1884	D: 27 May 1955

Lot: 290   1898 Owner: Nelson Hixon

Florence H. Davis	B: 1882	D: 1943
Lavinia H. Wright	B: 17 Mar 1824	D: 9 Mar 1901
		w/o Charles W. Wright
William N. Hixson	B: 14 Nov 1855	D: 10 Aug 1933
Martha E. Hixson	Age: 36 yrs	D: 10 Mar 1892
		w/o William N. Hixson
*I.W. Hixson		no dates
Howard R. Davis	B: 1885	D: 1947
*infant Hixson		no dates

Lot: 291L   1898 Owner: Irving Furr

Catherine O. Furr	B: 1931	D: 1932
Olivia Ross Furr	B: 1899	D: 1931
Irving M. Furr	B: 1889	D: 1947

Lot: 291U   1898 Owner: James M. Benton

James M. Benton	B: 18 Sep 1819	D: 13 Jul 1895
Margaret A. Benton	B: 17 Jul 1823	D: 4 Jul 1894
		w/o J. M. Benton
S. Elizabeth Baldwin	B: 1 Jan 1850	D: 7 Nov 1943
John W. Baldwin	B: 4 Oct 1853	D: 17 Aug 1932

Lot: 292   **1898 Owner: Mrs. S.P. Smith**

Mildred Gardner Smith   B: 17 Mar 1841   D: 21 Nov 1908
                                                  w/o Stephen Pritchard Smith

Minnie Pritchard Smith   B: 31 Oct 1863   D: 10 Aug 1942

Nellie Smith   B: 11 Nov 1869   D: 18 Jul 1929

E. Conway Smith   B: 7 Apr 1860   D: 28 Dec 1941

Carroll N. Smith   B: 22 Aug 1874   D: 23 Nov 1930

Tennessee Smith   B: 12 Apr 1867   D: 5 Apr 1932

W. F. Carpenter   B: 3 Nov 1873   D: 23 Nov 1959

Olive Gardner Smith Carpenter B: 22 Nov 1877   D: 2 Aug 1956

Stephen Pritchard Smith   B: 29 Feb 1828   D: 24 Apr 1908

Lot: 293L   **1898 Owner: J.R. Lawrence**

Elizabeth Ann Lawrence   B: 1862   D: 1904

Lot: 293U   **1898 Owner: Miscellaneous**

Walter S. Hitt   Age: 59 yrs   D: 17 Apr 1909

Sarah A. Hitt   Age: 61 yrs   D: 17 Jun 1910
                                                  w/o W. S. Hitt

Lot: 294   **1898 Owner: Dallas Furr**

Dallas Furr   B: 18 Apr 1845   D: 6 Aug 1903
                                                  CSA: 43rd VA Cavalry, Co. A

Johnson R. Furr   B: 27 Dec 1846   D: 7 Jan 1916
                                                  s/o William & Emsey Furr

Blanche Megeath Furr   B: 19 Mar 1854

Harry Elton Furr   B: 19 Mar 1883   D: 10 Aug 1947

Susan R. Furr   B: 19 Mar 1845   D: 18 Nov 1899
                                                  w/o Dallas Furr

Leola Furr   Age: 6 mos   D: 4 Jun 1892
                                                  d/o Johnson & Blanche Furr

Lot: 295   **1898 Owner: Mrs. H.F. Grant**

Charles Adrian Grant   B: 22 May 1857   D: 12 Apr 1908

Edward Mayne Grant   Age: 5 mos   D: 20 Oct 1893
                                                  s/o H. F. & H. E. F. Grant

| Henry Grant | B: 15 Sep 1809 | D: 15 Nov 1892 |
| Henry Falconer Grant | B: 6 Mar 1851 | D: 30 Jun 1913 |

Lot: 296L   1898 Owner: Miscellaneous

James F. Crupper	B: 19 Feb 1846	D: 7 Sep 1908
		CSA: 35th VA Cavalry, Co. A
John Urire Mitchell	Age: 66 yrs	D: 2 Oct 1902
		CSA: 7th VA Cavalry, Co. A
Annie D. Mitchell	B: 15 Sep 1840	D: 26 Dec 1925
		w/o John U. Mitchell

Lot: 296U   1898 Owner: Marshall Finch

Martha J. Finch	B: 23 Aug 1830	D: 23 Jan 1904
		w/o Marshall B. Finch
Marshall B. Finch	B: 14 Dec 1833	D: 16 Jun 1913
Margaret C. Finch	B: 13 Jul 1860	D: 15 Apr 1913
Susie Marshall Monroe	B: 19 Nov 1896	D: 13 Aug 1983
M. J. Finch Mitchell	B: 19 Sep 1871	D: 15 Jun 1924

Lot: 297L   1898 Owner: Mrs. E.R. Potts

Eduard Potz		D: 6 Feb 1901
Robert Henry Downs, Jr.	B: 1 Nov 1917	D: 12 Jul 1992
L. Estelle Downs	B: 10 Nov 1890	D: 29 Apr 1971
Sarah D. Chappelle	B: 1897	D: 1992
L. Francis Chappelle	B: 1904	D: 1964

Lot: 297U   1898 Owner: W.F. Cloud

Minnie Relle Cloud	B: 15 May 1866	D: 18 Mar 1901
		w/o William F. Cloud
Ruby P. Downs	B: 16 Jul 1899	D: 11 May 1997
Charles M. Downs	B: 22 Jan 1895	D: 24 Dec 1973
*infant Downs		D: 29 Mar 1902
		s/o C.M. & L.T. Downs

Lot: 298   1898 Owner: Geo Pickett

| George K. Pickett | B: 11 Mar 1851 | D: 11 Jul 1930 |

Margaret Moore Pickett	B: 24 Jan 1875	D: 1 Jun 1959 w/o H. H. Pickett
Mary Lewis Pickett	B: 28 Aug 1846	D: 12 Jan 1926 w/o George Pickett
Nannie Turner Pickett	B: 18 Oct 1879	D: 7 Dec 1893 d/o G. K. & M. L. Pickett
Henry Hampton Pickett	B: 17 Dec 1871	D: 5 Mar 1934

Lot: 299   1898 Owner: Henry Davis

Frances Eleanor Davis	Age: 8 mos	D: 20 Jun 1897
Julia E. Davis	B: 12 Apr 1868	D: 3 Sep 1947
John Morgan Davis	B: 11 Jun 1898	D: 30 Jun 1912 s/o Henry & Julia E. Davis
Henry Davis	B: 15 Jul 1866	D: 25 Feb 1942
J. H. Moffett	B: 30 Jul 1827	D: 17 Aug 1901

Lot: 300L   1898 Owner: Eugene Downs

Eugene M. Downs	B: 1880	D: 1970
Louise Katherine Downs	B: 20 Mar 1906	D: 19 Dec 1912 d/o Eugene & Lovie Downs
Lucy R. Downs	B: 1886	D: 1940

Lot: 300U   1898 Owner: Chas M. Downs

Charles Mason Downs	B: 24 Aug 1853	D: 13 May 1915
Sara Foster	B: 15 May 1822	D: 15 Jan 1899
Lucy Foster Downs	B: 6 Jan 1858	D: 25 Jul 1954
Eugene D. Rutter	B: 21 Aug 1907	D: 24 Dec 1908
Pierce Downs	B: 13 May 1847	D: 5 Jun 1904

Lot: 302   1898 Owner: Mrs. M.M. Andrews

Margarita M. Thomas	B: 5 May 1905	D: 27 Dec 1973
Arthur G. Thomas	B: 7 Sep 1882	D: 22 Apr 1973

Lot: 303   1898 Owner: Mrs. M.M. Andrews

**Mary Lord Andrews

Marietta Minnegerode Andrews	B: 11 Dec 1869	D: 7 Aug 1931

Mary-Lord Andrews Coppedge B: 29 Dec 1921   D: 22 Jun 1996
d/o E. F. & Helen C. Tucker Andrews

**Marietta Fauntleroy Turner Powell   no dates

**Virginia Cuthbert Powell Minnegerode   no dates

Eliphalet Fraser Andrews   B: 24 Oct 1898   D: 31 May 1932

Helen Tucker Andrews Hixson B: 15 Dec 1923   D: 10 Aug 1995
d/o E. F. & Helen C. Tucker Andrews

Lucy Minnegerode   B: 8 Feb 1871   D: 24 Mar 1935
**not buried in this lot, but name appears on marker

Lot: 304L   1898 Owner: J.P. & C.C. Middleton

M. Jacksie Moffett Middleton B: 9 Apr 1863   D: 20 Nov 1946

Clarence C. Middleton   B: 30 Mar 1867   D: 13 Sep 1936

Lot: 304U   1898 Owner: Raymond Mercer

Evangeline P. Mercer   B: 17 Jun 1895   D: 31 Mar 1974

Raymond D. Mercer   B: 9 Dec 1895   D: 10 Apr 1963

Lot: 306   1898 Owner: Chas Dawson

*Guy C. Dawson   Age: 36-5-17   D: 5 Jan 1937

Franklin Leslie Dawson   B: 14 May 1892   D: 11 Oct 1918
s/o Charles W. & H. B. Dawson

Eliza H. Dawson   B: 4 Jun 1877   D: 23 Sep 1903
w/o William H. Dawson

Lot: 307   1898 Owner: Mrs. K. Gibson

Kate H. Gibson   B: 1832   D: 1920
w/o Howard J. Gibson

Kate A. Gibson   B: 1873   D: 1956

George W. Staples   B: 1881   D: 1947

Howard J. Gibson   B: 1835   D: 1902

Maude Gibson Staples   B: 1884   D: 1937

Lot: 308   1898 Owner: Elton/Flynn

Carrie Elton Chinn   B: 7 Dec 1873   D: 30 Jun 1954

infant daughter Chinn   D: 1933
d/o Marion W. & M. Louise Chinn

William Luck Chinn	B: 22 Oct 1899	D: 3 May 1918
	s/o J. Stretchley & C. Elton Chinn	
J. Stretchley Chinn	B: 11 Sep 1855	D: 15 Feb 1906
Louise M. Chinn	B: 13 Jan 1903	
Marion W. Chinn	B: 9 May 1902	D: 12 May 1986

Lot: 309   1898 Owner: Mrs. Agnes Heflin

Lemuel William Heflin	B: 9 Feb 1890	D: 26 Sep 1963
Agnes A. Heflin	B: 23 Sep 1864	D: 16 Apr 1941
James M. Heflin	B: 22 Jan 1862	D: 30 Jan 1912
Alfred M. Keys	B: 21 Oct 1922	D: 13 Jul 1923
	s/o J. C. & Ora N. Keys	

Lot: 310   1898 Owner: W.F. Harris

Maggie O. Shackelford	B: 11 Nov 1871	D: 30 Dec 1901
	d/o J. N. & M. E. Shackelford	
F. C. Harriss	B: 4 Jul 1844	D: 9 May 1937
Mary L. Harriss	B: 20 Aug 1844	D: 6 Oct 1929
		w/o F. C. Harriss

Lot: 311L   1898 Owner: J.W. Soper

John Wheeler Soper	B: 17 Apr 1863	D: 20 Feb 1926
Ella Gertrude Soper	B: 12 Jun 1882	D: 1 Feb 1918
Edna Soper Turner	B: 3 Jun 1907	D: 31 Mar 1989
Milton C. Condon	B: 26 Nov 1904	D: 25 Aug 1950

Lot: 311U   1898 Owner: C. McIntyre

Gertrude M. Barmore	B: 12 Dec 1881	D: 15 Apr 1935

Lot: 312   1898 Owner: Estate of R.H. Leith

Joseph L. Leith	B: 28 Nov 1860	D: 26 Jan 1938
R. Howard Leith	B: 19 Jun 1828	D: 25 Dec 1902
Mary Frances Leith	B: 20 Jul 1867	D: 5 Dec 1940
Martha C. Leith	B: 21 Sep 1830	D: 18 Feb 1903
Julian H. Leith	B: 23 Apr 1905	D: 27 Apr 1958
Arthur F. Leith	B: 8 Aug 1862	D: 13 Aug 1942

Lot: 313L   1898 Owner: L. Wilkerson

Sallie Elizabeth Wilkerson	Age: 89 yrs	D: 29 Jun 1948
Kirkwood Wilkerson	B: 27 Jun 1859	D: 6 Jan 1929
Amanda Louise Wilkerson	B: 8 May 1900	D: 31 Jan 1901
		d/o Lycurgus & Sallie Wilkerson

Lot: 313U   1898 Owner: F. Flynn

Frances Carter Flynn	B: 15 Sep 1915	D: 6 Jun 1933
Fleetwood Flynn	B: 1870	D: 1915
Fannie L. Flynn	B: 1871	D: 1938

Lot: 314   1898 Owner: Mrs. J.W. Skinner

Maud Skinner Webster	B: 1875	D: 1952
Ollie T. Skinner	B: 1878	D: 1965
W. J. Skinner	B: 23 Oct 1838	D: 13 Nov 1901
		CSA: 7th VA Cavalry, Co. A
Mary Skinner Seaton	B: 14 Mar 1872	D: 22 Nov 1936
Annie E. Skinner	B: 1865	D: 1942
W. F. Triplett	B: 15 Apr 1854	D: 5 Dec 1919
Sarah H. Skinner	B: 22 Nov 1837	D: 7 Aug 1924
J. W. Skinner	B: 1879	D: 1956

Lot: 314A   1898 Owner: Not Listed

Kemp B. Jr. Furr	B: 12 Jan 1899	D: 11 Jan 1951
Kemp B. Furr	B: 2 Jul 1825	D: 11 Sep 1912
Walter L. Furr	B: 1 Oct 1886	D: 12 Jul 1973
Margaret M. Furr	B: 25 Jul 1861	D: 3 Jul 1949
		w/o Kemp B. Furr
Carl H. Furr	B: 21 Aug 1888	D: 2 Feb 1981
Violet F. Hines	B: 1895	D: 1976

Lot: 315   1898 Owner: J.W. Leith

| Richard Henry Leith | Age: 19 yrs | D: 18 Dec 1900 |

Lot: 316   1898 Owner: E.M. Jeffries

Braxton B. Jeffries	B: 1812	D: 1900
Catherine Jeffries	B: 1832	D: 1900

Lot: 317   1898 Owner: W.W. Holton

W. W. Holton	B: 20 Mar 1866	D: 5 Oct 1952
Marietta V. Holton	B: 14 Nov 1834	D: 7 Feb 1909
Edward U. Holton	B: 27 Jun 1863	D: 15 Mar 1927
Edward T. Holton	B: 28 Jul 1826	D: 15 Jul 1900
Beulah Dowdell Holton	B: 1870	D: 1915
Ann S. Wade	B: 1829	D: 1907

Lot: 318   1898 Owner: H.R. Rogers

Robert L. Rogers	B: 1862	D: 1943
Armstead Carter Rogers	B: 1864	D: 1925
Clara Bowen Rogers	B: 1867	D: 1931
		w/o Powell Rogers
Hugh Rogers	B: 1828	D: 1899
		CSA: 8th VA Infantry, Co. F
Hamilton Rogers	B: 1860	D: 1935
Powell Rogers	B: 1858	D: 1938
Rosalie Dalrymple Powell Rogers		w/o Hugh Rogers
	B: 1830	D: 1903
John Leven Rogers	B: 1869	D: 1913
Henry Wyer Rogers	B: 1854	D: 1888

Lot: 319   1898 Owner: H.R. Dulaney

Anne Willing Carter	B: 4 Mar 1863	D: 11 Dec 1949
		w/o Henry Rozier Dulany
Anne Dulany Hayne	B: 25 May 1900	D: 26 Nov 1933
		w/o Frank Brevard Hayne
Thomas Carter Dulany	B: 18 Nov 1902	D: 2 Nov 1924
	s/o Henry R. Dulany & Anne W. Carter	
Jane Thompson Dulany	B: 1 Feb 1922	D: 9 Jan 1996
		w/o Benjamin Weems Dulany

Henry Rozier III Dulany   B: 29 Aug 1946   D: 5 Nov 1978
s/o Benjamin W. & Jane T. Dulany

Henry Rozier Dulany   B: 17 Sep 1857   D: 8 Apr 1940
s/o Henry Grafton & Mary Eliza Dulany

Lot: 320L   1898 Owner: Mrs. G.A. Troth

Mary W. Hulfish Troth   B: 28 Oct 1887   D: 18 Dec 1932
w/o George A. Troth

George A. Troth   B: 11 Dec 1885   D: 30 Sep 1918

Lot: 321   1898 Owner: B.T. Pearson

Otis E. Sullivan   B: 8 Apr 1911   D: 15 Mar 1975

Gladys Campbell Pearson   B: 11 Aug 1890   D: 21 Jan 1898
d/o B. C. & R. A. Pearson

Ruth A. Pearson   B: 9 Aug 1860   D: 9 Feb 1936
w/o B. C. Pearson

Ann E. Griffith   B: 11 Feb 1849   D: 5 Sep 1905
w/o W. M. Griffith

Ollie M. Sullivan   B: 4 Jul 1904   D: 14 Mar 1988

B. C. Pearson   B: 22 Mar 1858   D: 19 May 1940

Lot: 322   1898 Owner: Mrs. J.S. Ferguson

John S. Ferguson   B: 7 Sep 1852   D: 1 Aug 1917

Lelia A. Ferguson   B: 20 Nov 1857   D: 19 Sep 1938

Lot: 323   1898 Owner: Chas Ellison

Frederick C. Ellison   B: 6 Apr 1855   D: 6 Sep 1891
s/o Charles E. & Emma C. Ellison

Emma Collett Ellison   B: 9 Jun 1829   D: 8 Apr 1916
w/o Charles Edwin Ellison

Elizabeth A. Ellison   B: 22 Mar 1866   D: 7 Dec 1951

Charles Edwin Ellison   B: 30 May 1824   D: 4 Jun 1890

Alice Maude Ellison   B: 24 Sep 1871   D: 1 Jun 1944

*Mary Elizabeth Ellison   Age: 66 yrs   D: 6 Apr 1934

Lot: 324   1898 Owner: V.M. Johnson

Robert Andrew Edmondson Johnson   s/o V. M. & K. J. E. Johnson
                              B: 24 Jun 1899   D: 12 Sep 1899

Valentine Mason Johnson   B: 1837   D: 1909

Lewis Johnson   B: 1866   D: 1952

Eliza B. Johnson   B: 1838   D: 1879

Katherine E. Johnson   B: 1855   D: 1947

Lot: 325   1898 Owner: E.C. Pearson

Walter A. Pearson   B: 6 Sep 1869   D: 4 Mar 1899

Emily C. Grimes Pearson   B: 12 Nov 1870   D: 30 Jun 1935
                                              w/o Walter A. Pearson

Lucie P. Goettling   B: 31 Dec 1896   D: 1 Mar 1983
                                          w/o Dr. Charles A. Goettling

Lot: 326   1898 Owner: J. Brittlebank

Nannie Simpson Brittlebank   B: 18 Sep 1856   D: 29 Mar 1936

Frank Brittlebank   B: 5 Oct 1893   D: 26 Nov 1966

Frank Brittlebank   B: 11 Jul 1852   D: 19 Nov 1894

Ruth Keeler Brittlebank   B: 16 Sep 1895   D: 7 Jan 1986

Julius Brittlebank   B: 11 Apr 1859   D: 25 Jul 1937

Lot: 327   1898 Owner: J.T. Bodmer

Margaret Bodmer Albaugh   B: 16 Nov 1901   D: 4 Sep 1986

John P. Bodmer   B: 14 May 1905   D: 21 Aug 1977

infant son Bodmer   B: 15 Nov 1911   D: 19 Nov 1911
                                              s/o J. W. & E. L. Bodmer

Helen R. Goswellen   B: 14 Aug 1903   D: 20 Mar 1992

Elsie Joyce Jones   B: 7 Nov 1925   D: 7 Oct 1961

Virginia M. Myers   B: 20 Nov 1909   D: 30 Mar 1980

Ella L. Bodmer   B: 16 Aug 1874   D: 10 Jun 1952

John W. Bodmer   B: 30 Aug 1868   D: 1 Feb 1944

Eva G. Bodmer   B: 14 May 1908   D: 3 Apr 1982

Lot: 329   1898 Owner: E.T. Waddell

R. L. Waddell		no dates
Alice Virginia Downs	B: 29 Dec 1848	D: 21 Feb 1922
		w/o George W. Downs
George W. Downs	B: 13 Mar 1820	D: 5 Oct 1902
M. E. Waddell		no dates
Beulah Waddell	Age: 24 yrs	no dates
		w/o E. T. Waddell
Maggie M. Darnell	B: 17 Mar 1900	D: 12 Feb 1973
E. T. Waddell		no dates

Lot: 330   1898 Owner: H. Downs

Henry Downs	B: 21 Aug 1844	D: 16 Jun 1893
Virginia Allison	Age: 4 mos	no dates
		d/o John R. & Novilla M. Allison
Laura C. Downs	B: 31 May 1848	D: 15 Feb 1926
		w/o Henry Downs

Lot: 331   1898 Owner: Edw. Wine

Edward Wine	B: 1879	D: 1966
James M. Wine	B: 10 Aug 1911	D: 1 Feb 1957
Irene E. Davis Wine	B: 1884	D: 1937
		w/o Edward Wine
infant daughter Hall	d/o H. G. & M. E. Hall	no dates
Mary E. Wickham Wine	B: 8 Sep 1883	D: 19 Jul 1965
Richard L. Wine	B: 4 Aug 1922	D: 7 Aug 1928

Lot: 332   1898 Owner: Mrs. M.M. Waddell

James W. Waddell	B: 1864	D: 1938
James W. Waddell	Age: 68 yrs	D: 6 Sep 1911
		CSA: 6th VA Cavalry, Co. F
Lucille Paugh Forness	B: 1886	D: 1932
Myrtle Elizabeth Paugh	Age: 5 days	D: 1 May 1907
Marcus H. Forness	B: 1884	D: 1926

Alice V. Waddell	B: 1853	D: 1939
Walter Stewart Paugh	B: 6 Jun 1876	D: 17 Mar 1920
Mary C. Kearnes		D: 6 Nov 1898

Lot: 333L   1898 Owner: Paul Alexander

S. Paul Alexander	B: 15 Aug 1897	D: 28 Apr 1983
Richard M. Alexander	B: 1853	D: 1934
Judith L. Alexander	B: 1869	D: 1929
Maxine A. Alexander	B: 4 May 1908	D: 21 Jul 1991

Lot: 333U   1898 Owner: Mrs.John, Talbot, Sr.

Dr John Allan Talbot	B: 27 May 1882	D: 27 Apr 1967
Roberta Lackland Talbot	B: 12 Oct 1882	D: 11 Oct 1963
Barnett Thomas Talbot	B: 11 Jul 1895	D: 12 Jun 1973
John Allan III Talbot	B: 28 Aug 1920	

Lot: 334   1898 Owner: J.E. Woolf

Zella Seaton Woolf	B: 22 Apr 1891	D: 27 Aug 1933
Virginia M. Woolf	B: 29 Aug 1869	D: 7 Jun 1898
Willie Lewis Woolf	Age: 5 mos	D: 16 Jul 1892
J. Edgar Woolf	B: 28 Sep 1860	D: 25 Feb 1933
Ernest M. Woolf	B: 5 Nov 1895	D: 27 Aug 1933

Lot: 335   1898 Owner: J.W. Rawlings

William Lusby Rawlings	B: 3 Mar 1910	D: 6 Feb 1994
William S. Rawlings	B: 25 Aug 1873	D: 19 Feb 1937
Scott Kenner Rawlings	B: 11 Oct 1903	D: 31 Jan 1909
	s/o William S. & Lela Scott Rawlings	
Mary Frances Rawlings	B: 14 May 1835	D: 21 Feb 1892
	w/o J. Wesley Rawlings	
Lela S. Rawlings	B: 15 Jul 1879	D: 6 May 1967
	w/o William S. Rawlings	
J. Wesley Rawlings	B: 27 Nov 1835	D: 23 Mar 1918
	CSA: 8th VA Infantry, Co. B	
T. Harvey Rawlings	B: 6 Apr 1871	D: 29 Apr 1940

Lot: 336L   1898 Owner: Mrs. Fred Lake

Henry H. Hoppe	B: 1914	D: 1950
Daisy W. Payne	B: 20 Jul 1891	D: 10 Feb 1963
Henry D. Hoppe	B: 1890	D: 1942
Golder D. Payne	B: 6 Mar 1880	D: 14 Jul 1941
Mattie C. Hoppe	B: 1889	

Lot: 336U   1898 Owner: L.D. Means

Lewis D. Means	B: 28 Dec 1819	D: 30 Jun 1902
Alcinda A. Means	B: 8 Jun 1819	D: 9 Aug 1893 w/o Lewis D. Means
Mary E. Paxson	B: 12 Aug 1832	D: 23 Sep 1893

Lot: 337   1898 Owner: John Hawlings

Joseph William Adams	B: 23 Nov 1906	D: 1 Jun 1946
John W. Rawlings	B: 4 Sep 1852	D: 28 Dec 1943
Mary E. Adams	B: 4 Aug 1875	D: 16 Dec 1934
Elvira F. Rawlings	B: 19 Jul 1853	D: 8 Nov 1909 w/o John W. Rawlings

Lot: 338   1898 Owner: H.J. Sutphin

Emily Sutphin	B: 1828	D: 1911
Mary E. Sutphin	B: 22 May 1869	D: 24 Dec 1948
Leon M. Sutphin	Age: 1 mo	D: 21 Jun 1892 s/o M. B. & H. J. Sutphin
Martha T. Sutphin	B: 24 May 1887	D: 10 Aug 1887 d/o H. & M. Sutphin
Flora Sutphin	B: 5 Jun 1888	D: 31 Jul 1889 d/o H. & M. Sutphin
Alfred B. Sutphin	B: 1 Apr 1871	
Philip L. Sutphin	Age: 27 yrs	D: 25 Sep 1892 s/o William M. & Emily Sutphin
John W. Sutphin	Age: 36 yrs	D: 6 Nov 1892

Lot: 339   1898 Owner: Brook Rector

E. Brooke Rector	B: 7 Apr 1854	D: 22 Nov 1937
Ina Jackson Rector	B: 5 Apr 1886	D: 12 Aug 1886
		d/o E. B. & Eva Rector
Ira Brooke Rector	B: 18 Sep 1898	D: 8 Aug 1899
		s/o E. B. & Eva Rector
Sallie Whitley Rector	B: 5 Sep 1897	D: 22 Jan 1898
		d/o E. B. & Eva Rector
Jannie E. Thomas	B: 10 Jun 1883	D: 24 Feb 1915
		w/o Charles W. Thomas
Eva R. Rector	B: 1 Sep 1858	D: 29 Oct 1940

Lot: 340   1898 Owner: P.S. Gains

Lewis F. Bradshaw	B: 21 Apr 1854	D: 24 Apr 1933
Thomas W. Gaines	B: 1872	D: 1953
Martha Elizabeth Gaines	B: 23 Nov 1846	D: 19 Jan 1901
		w/o Pembrook S. Gaines
Rector Gaines	B: 25 Mar 1904	D: 21 Apr 1904
		s/o T. W. & L. V. Gaines
L. P. Gaines	Age: 24 yrs	D: 11 Oct 1897
		s/o P. S. & Martha E. Gaines
Pembrook S. Gaines	B: 5 Apr 1839	D: 13 May 1921
Laura V. Gaines	B: 1875	D: 1962
Eva Gaines Bradshaw	B: 27 Oct 1867	D: 11 Nov 1940

Lot: 341   1898 Owner: Fannie Davis

William F. Davis	B: 1847	D: 1889
Annie Lee Davis	B: 1864	D: 1936
Jack Waddell	B: 1912	D: 1968
*Miss Rose Tinsman	Age: 59-6-21	D: 30 Oct 1941
Pauline Waddell Lawrence	B: 1904	D: 1981

Lot: 342   1898 Owner: H.W. Skinner

Katie Smith Skinner	B: 15 Jun 1859	D: 16 Jan 1924
		w/o E. W. Skinner

Henry W. Skinner	B: 11 Oct 1829	D: 15 May 1885
E. W. Skinner	Age: 77 yrs	D: 28 Jun 1933
C. L. Skinner	B: 27 Dec 1859	D: 2 Jan 1916
Mary V. Skinner	B: 10 Dec 1831	D: 15 Apr 1893 w/o H. W. Skinner

Lot: 343   1898 Owner: John G. & Ashton Dodd

Charlotte D. Greenlease	B: 1855	D: 1936
Edmonia V. Dodd	B: 1852	D: 1925
Lena Foster Downs Allison	B: 3 Aug 1885	D: 16 May 1961 w/o J. D. Allison
Jane E. Hurst Dodd	B: 25 Jun 1812	D: 10 Jan 1885 w/o George A. Dodd
Mary Strobel Downs	B: 8 Feb 1881	D: 25 Jun 1957
Erman Carroll Downs	B: 25 Nov 1888	D: 19 Sep 1980
George A. Dodd	B: 1814	D: 1908

Lot: 344L   1898 Owner: Curtis Cole

| W. Curtis Cole | B: 15 Mar 1912 | D: 29 Mar 1989 |

Lot: 344U   1898 Owner: J.E. Douglass

Mary Virginia Douglass	B: 30 Aug 1884	D: 23 May 1967
Katherine Fleming Douglass	B: 9 Jan 1887	D: 17 Feb 1955
Marion Douglass	B: 10 Jan 1858	D: 30 Mar 1893 w/o J. E. Douglass
James Edward Douglass	B: 26 Jan 1858	D: 8 Jan 1937
Mary Castell Douglass	B: 23 Nov 1869	D: 26 Jul 1920 w/o J. E. Douglass

Lot: 345   1898 Owner: J.F. Laws

John Thornly Laws	B: 18 Apr 1826	D: 24 Mar 1896
John William Decker	B: 1890	D: 1982
Margaret Laws Decker	B: 1896	D: 1976
Laura Jane Laws	B: 5 Mar 1843	D: 29 Jun 1916 w/o John Thornly Laws

Lot: 346   1898 Owner: Miss Va. Yates

Virginia A. Yates   B: 1848   D: 1905

William W. Yates   B: 1842   D: 1899
                                         CSA: 8th VA Infantry, Co. K

Lot: 347   1898 Owner: James S. Carter

Susan E. Carter   B: 1832   D: 1893

James S. Carter   B: 1794   D: 1882

Fannie V. Cockrell   B: 1845   D: 1922

Mabel Nelson Carter   B: 1884   D: 1959

Robert C. Carter   B: 1840   D: 1873
                                         CSA: 6th VA Cavalry, Co. A

Robert Champ Carter   B: 1873   D: 1937

Robert Nelson Carter   B: 1908   D: 1972

Lot: 348L   1898 Owner: H. Byrne

James S. Byrne   B: 18 May 1818   D: 19 Nov 1900

Julia A. Byrne   B: 18 Jan 1816   D: 19 May 1898
                                         w/o James S. Byrne

Gladys Anderson Tyler   B: 27 Mar 1903   D: 21 May 1977

Thomas Francis Tyler   B: 4 Sep 1904   D: 10 May 1980

Lot: 348U   1898 Owner: W.F. Carter

Anne Leith Randolph   B: 1916   D: 1982

Eva V. Leith   B: 3 May 1883   D: 24 Dec 1950

Louis C. Leith   B: 28 Mar 1875   D: 19 Feb 1942

Emma M. Carter   B: 19 Apr 1828   D: 2 Jun 1910

William F. Carter   B: 24 Apr 1824   D: 10 Mar 1894

Ann Elizabeth Rawlings   B: 1 Jan 1857   D: 16 Sep 1928
                                         w/o J. M. Rawlings

Mary F. Morehead   B: 25 Jun 1858   D: 9 Aug 1913

J. M. Rawlings   B: 5 Jan 1855   D: 29 Jul 1884

John Preston Rawlings   s/o J. M. & E. Rawlings   no dates

Lot: 350   1898 Owner: W.P. Presgraves

| Lucy Ellen Presgraves | B: 28 Jan 1846 | D: 2 Jan 1922 |

Lawrence V. Watkins   B: 26 Apr 1902   D: 2 Sep 1903
                                              s/o Rev. J. H. & E. B. Watkins

Albert J. Presgraves   B: 21 Apr 1887   D: 1 May 1894

Ann Presgraves Lighliter   B: 16 Nov 1832   D: 18 Aug 1909

William R. Presgraves   Age: 85 yrs   D: 30 Apr 1889

Mary A. Presgraves   Age: 64 yrs   D: 13 Jul 1869

John R. Presgraves   Age: 27 yrs   D: 20 Jul 1863
                                              CSA: 8th VA Infantry, Co. I

James R. Presgraves   B: 21 Feb 1838   D: 15 Feb 1902
                                              CSA: 8th VA Infantry, Co. I

Lot: 351   1898 Owner: Jno McQuinn

Charles Robert McGinn   Age: 6 mos   D: 9 Jul 1858
                                              s/o John H. & Charlotte M. McGinn

Lot: 352   1898 Owner: S.C. Presgraves

Rachael White   B: 20 Apr 1774   D: 28 May 1862

Annie M. Presgraves   B: 23 Mar 1850   D: 15 Oct 1909
                                              w/o Samuel C. Presgraves

Samuel C. Presgraves   Age: 80 yrs   D: 21 Jul 1924

Lot: 353   1898 Owner: Rufus Smith

H. Hammond Smith   Age: 14 days   D: 18 Jul 1847
                                              s/o Rufus & Mary A. Smith

Robert Erle Jr. 'Robin' Ross   B: 7 Aug 1937   D: 11 Sep 1974
                                              s/o Robert E. & Dorothy Cannon Ross

P. Pembroke Smith   Age: 17 days   D: 21 Nov 1852
                                              s/o Rufus & Mary A. Smith

Jennie Smith   Age: 18 days   D: 9 Aug 1855
                                              d/o Rufus & Mary A. Smith

*Clarence Woodward   Age: 62-1-16   D: 27 Sep 1938

*Elizabeth Woodward   Age: 58-0-25   D: 14 Jun 1937

Lot: 354   1898 Owner: T.B. Leith

Theodoric B. Leith	B: 7 Jul 1833	D: 15 May 1896
		CSA: 6th Va Cavalry, Co. A
Helen Elizabeth Leith Ross	B: 3 Aug 1876	D: 4 Mar 1961
		w/o Richard Raymond Ross
Eva Carter Leith Baldwin	B: 14 Mar 1878	D: 8 Jul 1936
		w/o David H. Baldwin
Ann Gregg Leith	B: 27 Jan 1837	D: 21 Nov 1921
		w/o Theodoric B. Leith
*David H. Baldwin	B: 1873	D: 19?
*Ida L. Baldwin	B: 1878	D: 1936
*William F. Garrett	Age: 70-7-7	D: 25 Jul 1936

Lot: 356   1898 Owner: J.H. Stover

Edwin A. Stover	B: 21 Jan 1798	D: 30 Jul 1854
Richard A. Stover	Age: 11 yrs	D: 25 Dec 1851
		s/o Edwin A. & Ann Stover

Lot: 357   1898 Owner: Jacob Gochnauer

Spencer Jacob Gochnauer	B: 7 Oct 1857	D: 3 Mar 1858
		s/o William L. & Sallie M. Gochnauer
Fannie Jennie Gochnauer	B: 5 Mar 1859	D: 20 Mar 1860
		d/o William L. & Sallie M. Gochnauer
Kemp G. Furr	B: 2 Feb 1876	D: 5 Nov 1878
		s/o K. B. & A. A. Furr
Elizabeth Gochnauer	B: 14 Feb 1798	D: 19 Mar 1875
		w/o Jacob Gochnauer
Amanda Furr	B: 18 Apr 1837	D: 11 Nov 1877
		w/o Kemp B. Furr
W. L. Gochnauer	B: 29 Oct 1829	D: 21 Apr 1906
Virginia D. Gochnauer	Age: 23 yrs	D: 11 Feb 1858
		d/o J. & E. Gochnauer
Sallie M. Gochnauer	B: 3 Apr 1839	D: 1 Sep 1889
		w/o W. L. Gochnauer
Jacob Gochnauer	Age: 52 yrs	D: 17 Apr 1844

Lucie B. Gochnauer   B: 18 Apr 1862   D: 3 Jan 1863
                                  d/o William L. & Sallie M. Gochnauer

Lot: 360   1898 Owner: D. Gochnauer

Elizabeth Bleakly Gochnauer   B: 22 Aug 1818   D: 19 Nov 1858
                                              w/o David Gochnauer

William A. Gochnauer   B: 4 Sep 1870   D: 9 Dec 1870
                              s/o William L. & Sallie M. Gochnauer

Elizabeth A. Gochnauer   B: 24 Jun 1808   D: 24 Mar 1869

Preston B. Gochnauer   B: 17 Feb 1849   D: 4 Mar 1938
                                    CSA: 8th VA Infantry, Co. F

Mary A. Gochnauer   B: 3 Mar 1844   D: 28 Jan 1858
                                    d/o David & Elizabeth Gochnauer

David Gochnauer   B: 14 Sep 1811   D: 2 Jul 1859

Lot: 361   1898 Owner: E.M. Baker

Charlie E. Baker   B: 15 Nov 1838   D: 19 Mar 1893
                                    s/o Edward M. & Elizabeth R. Baker

Sally Baker   Age: 2 yrs   D: 15 Oct 1845
                                    d/o Edward M. & Elizabeth R. Baker

Elizabeth R. Baker   B: 5 Feb 1804   D: 24 Jan 1878

Silas H. Baker   Age: 19 yrs   D: 23 Jul 1861
                                    CSA: 8th VA Infantry, Co. D

*Edward M. Baker   No dates

Lot: 362   1898 Owner: Jas Graham

Catherine J. Crain   B: 23 Apr 1814   D: 8 Dec 1884
                                              w/o Philo R. Crain

Philo R. Crain   B: 19 Dec 1811   D: 27 Apr 1888

Lot: 364   1898 Owner: Betsy Fouch

Ann Fouch   B: 17 Apr 1771   D: 8 Jun 1846

Isaac Fouch   B: 15 Feb 1760   D: 28 Feb 1795

Lot: 365   1898 Owner: E.C. Broun

Catherine Barbara Broun   B: 1820   D: 1903
                                              w/o Edwin C. Broun

Edwin Conway Broun   Age: 61yrs   D: 29 Aug 1879

Edwin Leroy Broun	B: 7 Mar 1854	D: 20 Apr 1918
Philip H. Broun	Age: 29 yrs	D: 19 Feb 1885
Louisa Thruston Broun	B: 28 Sep 1856	D: 19 Aug 1932
Katherine B. H. Broun	B: 24 Sep 1893	D: 14 Dec 1896
	d/o Edwin L. & Louisa A. Broun	

Lot: 366   1898 Owner: H.J. Duffey

John P. Duffey	B: 14 Jan 1904	D: 1 Aug 1972
Virginia B. Duffey	B: 11 Jun 1907	D: 14 Sep 1990
Randolph G. Duffey	B: 8 Apr 1905	D: 20 Dec 1988
Louis Edward Duffey	B: 1902	D: 1981
Harry Johnston Duffey	B: 17 Feb 1871	D: 26 Jan 1964
Eleanor Duffey Sabin	B: 14 Feb 1907	D: 9 Aug 1991
Alice Hawkins Duffey	B: 14 Jun 1880	D: 6 May 1965

Lot: 368   1898 Owner: D.H. Sowers

Philip H. Chamblin	B: 14 Jul 1879	D: 31 Jul 1881
Joanna Hunton Hopkins	Age: 63 yrs	D: 12 Jun 1868
		w/o Philip Hopkins
Alberta Hopkins	B: 1846	D: 1926
Philip Hopkins	Age: 82 yrs	D: 15 Jun 1873
Hebe Grayson Chamblin	B: 1844	D: 2 Jan 1873
Henry H. Chamblin	B: 15 Oct 1884	D: 26 Jul 1898
Nannie H. Chamblin	B: 18 Jan 1881	D: 24 Jul 1898
William Hopkins Chamblin	B: 15 Jun 1882	D: 1 Nov 1940
Frances Hopkins Chamblin	B: 26 Aug 1842	D: 28 Jul 1898
Grayson M. Chamblin	B: 21 Aug 1870	D: 17 Mar 1905
Virginia S. M. Sowers	B: 12 Apr 1827	D: 24 Sep 1858
		w/o Daniel H. Sowers
Mattie C. Chamblin	B: 9 Nov 1878	D: 19 Jun 1898
Henry William Chamblin	B: 21 Jul 1836	D: 26 Jan 1908
	CSA: 8th VA Infantry, Co. F	

Lot: 369   1898 Owner: C.B. Adams

| Charles Douglass Adams | B: 3 Aug 1856 | D: 10 Jul 1874 |
| | | s/o Charles B. & J. A. Adams |

| C. Douglass Adams | B: 1897 | D: 1962 |

| Caroline A. Adams | B: 14 Mar 1827 | D: 20 Jan 1893 |

| C. B. Adams | B: 28 Dec 1820 | D: 12 Jan 1908 |

| E. Franklin Adams | B: 20 Feb 1896 | D: 6 Nov 1896 |
| | | s/o Robert L. & Mattie Adams |

| Margaret Megeath Adams | B: 1899 | D: 1986 |

| Julia A. Adams | B: 20 Sep 1825 | D: 6 Apr 1905 |
| | | w/o C. B. Adams |

| Thomas W. Adams | B: 1 Mar 1836 | D: 24 Feb 1883 |
| | | CSA: 8th VA Infantry, Co. D |

| Georgianna R. Adams | B: 7 Nov 1866 | D: 21 Dec 1867 |
| | | d/o C. B. & J. A. Adams |

| R. L. Adams | B: 5 Jun 1861 | D: 24 Apr 1947 |

Lot: 372   1898 Owner: Wm Rogers

| James H. Rogers | | no dates |

| Frank Slaughter | B: 1 Aug 1870 | D: 13 Nov 1893 |

| Milton M. Rogers | | no dates |

| Mollie W. Rogers | | no dates |

| Elizabeth H. Rogers | Age: 42 yrs | D: 8 Mar 1841 |
| | | w/o William Rogers |

| Ruth White Rogers | B: 13 Jan 1808 | D: 8 Dec 1874 |
| | | w/o William Rogers |

| William Rogers | | no dates |

Lot: 373   1898 Owner: J.M. Smith

| James M. Smith | B: 30 Jun 1849 | D: 15 Nov 1918 |

| Sallie J. Smith | B: 12 Oct 1856 | D: 21 Feb 1917 |

| Selina M. Smith | B: 28 Aug 1820 | D: 6 Feb 1895 |

| Elias A. Smith | B: 7 May 1816 | D: 18 Mar 1905 |

| Annie F. Smith | B: 1891 | D: 1977 |

Walter L. Smith	B: 1885	D: 1938
Edward H. Smith	Age: 14 yrs	D: 2 Dec 1880
		s/o J. M. & Sallie J. Smith

Lot: 374   1898 Owner: Jos Lowe

Raymond T. Lowe	B: 19 Dec 1899	D: 23 Sep 1913
		s/o F. T. & Maggie E. Lowe
infant Lowe		D: 26 Oct 1895
		d/o F. T. & M. H. Lowe
Catharine Russell	Age: 75 yrs	D: 20 Dec 1875
infant daughter Lowe		D: 12 Feb 1891
		d/o F. T. & M. H. Lowe

Lot: 376   1898 Owner: Wm Leith

Frances Eaty Leith	B: Mar 1807	D: 26 Nov 1862
		w/o W. G. Leith
Louisa O. Leith		no dates
William Goram Leith	B: 20 Aug 1803	D: 26 Jul 1873
Clara Leith Ross	B: 1872	D: 1965

Lot: 377L   1898 Owner: R.C. Leith

Robert L. Leith	B: 1878	D: 1931
Pauline P. Leith	B: 1897	D: 1953

Lot: 377U   1898 Owner: J.B. Cooke

Thomas Cooke	Age: 36 yrs	D: 15 Sep 1862

Lot: 378   1898 Owner: F.M. Lake

Mary E. Lake	B: 6 Jun 1854	D: 9 Oct 1925
		w/o Francis M. Lake
M. E. Lake	B: 22 Jul 1889	D: 8 Jul 1890
		d/o Francis & Mary Lake
Francis M. Lake	B: 18 Apr 1851	D: 16 Mar 1909
Dixie Lodge Lake	B: 2 Nov 1896	D: 1997
S. Rodgers Lake	B: 9 Mar 1887	D: 11 Jun 1963
Richard Joshua Lake	B: 22 May 1892	D: 27 Nov 1979
Mary Virginia Van Sickler	B: 22 Jul 1905	D: 30 Jan 1991

Ella Lake Van Sickler   B: 9 Oct 1883   D: 8 Jul 1969

Lot: 379   1898 Owner: W.H. Smith

William H. Smith   B: 7 Sep 1858   D: 31 Jul 1928

Melvin D. Smith   B: 1908   D: 1972

Serepta Belle Smith   B: 26 Oct 1871   D: 27 Oct 1953
d/o Jeremiah & Maria House Johnson

Lot: 381L   1898 Owner: Jerman Smith

Ernest S. Jerman   B: 23 Sep 1886   D: 3 Oct 1967

Smith Jerman   B: 7 Jun 1859   D: 2 Mar 1938

Edith S. Jerman   B: 16 May 1892   D: 28 Jul 1963

Annie Jerman   B: 24 Jul 1856   D: 8 May 1924
w/o Smith Jerman

Lot: 381U   1898 Owner: J.H. Pangle

Harry W. Pangle   B: 9 Mar 1893   D: 17 Jul 1935

Mary J. Pangle   B: 10 Dec 1892   D: 19 Mar 1971

Lot: 382   1898 Owner: Thomas Atkinson

William Clinton Holter   B: 14 Sep 1920   D: 28 May 1996
h/o Neville Atkinson Holter

Thomas Atkinson, Jr.   B: 31 Aug 1887   D: 11 May 74
s/o Thomas Atkinson & E. L.

Hanewinckel

Neville L. Atkinson   B: 16 Jan 1888   D: 29 Apr 1988
w/o Thomas Atkinson, Jr.

Lot: 383   1898 Owner: Edgar Ish

Edgar Ish   B: 3 Dec 1846   D: 2 Jul 1923

Pamelia C. Ish   B: 2 Jul 1846   D: 31 Aug 1938
w/o Edgar Ish

Lavinia Gertrude Ish   B: 29 May 1880   D: 4 Nov 1960
d/o Edgar & Pamelia Ish

Edna Earl Ish   B: 17 Apr 1886   D: 27 Aug 1963

Lot: 384   1898 Owner: E.J. Hall

Lettie Ball   B: 1837   D: 15 Feb 1923

Richard Dunn	B: 1873	D: 1948
Herman Edward Hall	B: 19 Oct 1904	D: 14 Jun 1931
Catherine Agnes Hall	B: 29 Dec 1875	D: 9 Sep 1935
Edward J. Hall	B: 15 Jan 1862	D: 16 Jun 1940
Mary Elizabeth Daniel	B: 30 Jun 1900	D: 5 Jan 1932

Lot: 385A   1898 Owner: Not Listed

E. Hunter Sutphin	B: 1887	D: 1976
Alfred Hunter Sutphin	B: 21 Jun 1913	D: 13 Nov 1937
Mary Eleanor Sutphin	B: 1886	D: 1951

Lot: 385L   1898 Owner: Carroll Flynn

Carroll L. Flynn	B: 1898	D: 1961
Edward Flynn	B: 23 Jan 1926	D: 17 Jul 1928
		s/o C. L. & E. M. Flynn
Eva M. Flynn	B: 1900	D: 1992

Lot: 385U   1898 Owner: Henry Moore

| *Nannie Dixon Moore | Age: 60 yrs | D: 23 Sep 1944 |

Lot: 386   1898 Owner: E. Dunn

| T. Eppa Dunn | B: 23 Sep 1890 | D: 30 Jun 1981 |
| Bessie M. Dunn | B: 18 Aug 1892 | D: 1 Dec 1969 |

Lot: 386A   1898 Owner: Not Listed

Harry Abell	B: 1884	D: 1939
William P. Abell	B: 3 Feb 1922	D: 5 Mar 1982
Rosa Ella Abell	B: 1929	D: 1987
Maggie Abell	B: 1900	D: 1987
Elmer Abell	B: 1927	
Milton E. Abell	B: 10 Dec 1923	D: 5 Aug 1975

Lot: 387L   1898 Owner: Mrs. Pierce Butler

Mary V. Butler	B: 1886	
Pierce Butler	B: 1882	D: 1943
Henry Hugh Powell	B: 1890	D: 1983

Emma D. Powell   D: 1939

Lot: 387U   1898 Owner: Kestner

Ruby J. Kestner   B: 1905   D: 1978

Lot: 388L   1898 Owner: Jas Wilson

John F. Wilson   B: 1901   D: 1937

Rosy M. Wilson   B: 1904   D: 1944
                                                    d/o James & Katie Wilson

Katie Wilson   B: 1874   D: 1958
                                                    w/o James Wilson

James Wilson   B: 1860   D: 1944

Lot: 388U   1898 Owner: Carroll Dawson

Rachel Powell Dawson   B: 18 May 1888   D: 5 Mar 1937

Frederick J. Dawson   B: 8 Jan 1907   D: 18 Feb 1996

Margery V. Dawson   B: 29 Jan 1906   D: 11 Nov 1982

George Freeman Dawson   B: 30 Aug 1920   D: 4 Dec 1982

Carroll D. Dawson   B: 1885   D: 1965

Lot: 390U   1898 Owner: Rozier Altman

Rozier B. Altman   B: 26 Oct 1900   D: 20 Aug 1971

Marie Holt Altman   B: 12 May 1932   D: 30 Aug 1936
                                           d/o Rosier B. & Sarah T. Altman

Sarah T. Altman   B: 15 Jul 1898   D: 16 Feb 1991

Lot: 391L   1898 Owner: J.M. Byrne

Ernest C. Byrne   B: 20 Mar 1886   D: 3 Dec 1950

John Moran Byrne   B: 5 Feb 1852   D: 17 Jan 1941

Frances Catherine Byrne   B: 1 Mar 1857   D: 15 Feb 1936

Lot: 391U   1898 Owner: C. & Mrs. M.M. Middleton

H. A. Middleton   B: 16 Apr 1847   D: 25 Jun 1929

M. M. Middleton   B: 25 Dec 1857   D: 30 Mar 1935

Humphrey MIddleton   B: Nov 1845   D: 19 May 1930
                                           CSA: 7th VA Cavalry, Co. H

Julia A. Middleton   B: 10 Apr 1848   D: 1 Apr 1925

Lot: 392   **1898 Owner: Estate of Mrs. K. Anderson**

John Alfred Anderson	B: 15 Feb 1851	D: 2 May 1943
Harry Otis Anderson	B: 31 Aug 1898	D: 15 Jul 1984
Katharine Anderson	B: 24 Nov 1858	D: 21 May 1925
		w/o John A. Anderson
Alice G. Anderson	B: 20 Jan 1914	D: 12 Oct 1991
John R. Anderson	B: 19 Jun 1900	D: 7 Jan 1984
Catherine E. Anderson	B: 18 Jun 1947	D: 19 Dec 1994
		d/o John R. & Alice G. Anderson
Annie Anderson	B: 12 Feb 1889	D: 18 Jun 1981
Robert F. Tilghman	B: 16 Jan 1873	D: 12 Sep 1949
Essie M. Tilghman	B: 23 Oct 1886	D: 15 Nov 1966

Lot: 393   **1898 Owner: J.R. Allison**

Novilla M. Allison	B: 1885	D: 1925
John R. Allison	B: 1877	D: 1944
Gaizelle Allison	B: 22 Jul 1912	D: 22 Apr 1933
		d/o J. R. & Novilla M. Allison
Ouida Allison	B: 25 Mar 1920	D: 24 Oct 1920
		d/o J. R. & Novilla M. Allison

Lot: 394   **1898 Owner: G.M. Pearson**

Thomas S. Owens	B: 27 Aug 1916	D: 9 Sep 1973
Eleanor P. Owens	B: 8 Apr 1905	D: 1 Apr 1988
George Marshall Pearson	B: 15 Jan 1860	D: 30 Apr 1936
Josephine Hall Pearson	B: 12 Jun 1867	D: 22 Dec 1935

Lot: 395L   **1898 Owner: Earl Alexander**

Emmett A. Roberts	B: 11 Nov 1911	D: 15 Jul 1974
Nancy Iva Roberts	B: 12 Dec 1918	D: 1 Jul 1974

Lot: 395U   **1898 Owner: Geo Canard**

Chester Keith Canard	B: 31 May 1925	D: 17 Dec 1959
Harriett A. Canard	B: 1900	D: 1966

Lot: 396   1898 Owner: Andrew Waddell

George C. Carter	B: 6 Oct 1912	D: 18 Nov 1972
Andrew L. Waddell	B: 20 Oct 1886	D: 2 Apr 1938
Mary Helen Waddell	Age: 33 yrs	D: 22 Nov 1930
Carrie Virginia Waddell	B: 6 Jul 1873	D: 18 Dec 1921 w/o A. L. Waddell
T. Waddell Carter	B: 17 Jan 1933	D: 14 Aug 1945
Elizabeth Carter Waddell	B: 31 Dec 1913	D: 25 May 1981
Fred A. Waddell	B: 28 Apr 1917	D: 10 Dec 1979

Lot: 397   1898 Owner: Carter

Betsy Carter	B: 1925	D: 1946
Ira C. Carter	B: 1890	D: 1966
Lucien A. Carter	B: 17 Nov 1859	D: 9 Nov 1920
Mattie M. Carter	B: 31 Oct 1897	D: 28 Sep 1973
William Thomas Carter	B: 2 Mar 1888	D: 9 Sep 1935
Ethel Louise Carter	B: 21 Mar 1920	D: 30 Aug 1920 d/o I. C. & A. M. Carter

Lot: 398   1898 Owner: G.M. Pearson

Josephine Pearson	B: 1 Dec 1918	D: 17 Jan 1921 d/o L. H. & M. F. Pearson
Albert L. Swart	B: 26 Jan 1888	D: 18 Aug 1968
Laurence H. Pearson	B: 28 Aug 1887	D: 13 May 1923 h/o Marie F. Pearson
Marie Pearson Swart	B: 17 Jun 1889	D: 9 May 1952
Mary Alice Pearson Bell	B: 11 Oct 1913	D: 21 Jan 1963
Elva Pearson Licklider	B: 1 May 1916	D: 17 Mar 1989

Lot: 400   1898 Owner: J.H. Lanahan

James Lacey Lanham	B: 22 Aug 1867	D: 18 Dec 1921
Grace Lanham Hutchison	B: 11 Apr 1900	D: 8 Sep 1946
Mary Reid Lanham	B: 4 Jun 1872	D: 2 Jun 1962 w/o Thomas Henry Lanham

Shirley Richard Lanham	B: 20 Dec 1898	D: 2 Mar 1960
T. Henry Lanham	B: 1869	D: 1944
Robert A. Hutchison	B: 14 Jul 1924	D: 9 Jul 1965
Ancel L. Lanham	B: 15 Feb 1897	D: 4 Aug 1960

Lot: 401   1898 Owner: Mrs. Claud Wren

Lena M. Neill	B: 19 Jan 1877	D: 1 Apr 1953
Robert E. Neill	B: 20 Nov 1873	D: 29 Jun 1951
William Roger Lambdon	B: 15 Jun 1895	D: 6 Feb 1985
Frances Carter Lambdon	B: 5 Aug 1900	D: 29 Jul 1990
Claude Wrenn	B: 1869	D: 1925
Albert Middleton Wrenn	B: 1900	D: 1920

Lot: 402   1898 Owner: Chas Cornel

Samuel Preston Jr. Luck	B: 2 Apr 1910	D: 2 Mar 1978
Oscar R. Sutphin	B: 2 Feb 1862	D: 22 Mar 1930
Nancy Swain Luck	B: 27 Dec 1937	
Martha E. Farmer Sutphin	B: 16 Feb 1860	D: 17 Mar 1934 w/o Oscar R. Sutphin
Hubert Nelson Cornell	B: 1910	D: 1937
	s/o Charles W. & Dorothy A. S. Cornell	
Dorothy A. Cornell	B: 1889	D: 1970
Charles W. Cornell	B: 1876	D: 1962

Lot: 403   1898 Owner: C.E. Harris

Viola C. Waltman	B: 29 Jan 1880	D: 19 Jul 1933
Anna C. Harris	B: 4 Jan 1854	D: 21 Sep 1948 w/o Charles E. Harris
Charles H. Harris	B: 23 Aug 1844	D: 6 Apr 1928
Elizabeth E. Mathews	B: 8 Sep 1878	D: 14 Jul 1936
Gertrude Harris	B: 28 Aug 1885	D: 4 Aug 1958
Ralph Waldo Mathews	B: 12 Oct 1890	D: 12 Feb 1953
Grace M. Benjamin	B: 1 Sep 1882	D: 14 Oct 1965

Pearl J. Harris Waltman   B: 17 Mar 1889   D: 5 May 1920

Lot: 404   1898 Owner: J.W. Hoffman

Carlton Leroy Hoffman   B: 6 Oct 1900   D: 18 Jul 1937

Joseph W. Hoffman   B: 23 Jun 1870   D: 8 Mar 1944

Lucy Sinclair Hoffman   B: 18 Nov 1895   D: 4 Dec 1953
w/o Carlton L. Hoffman

Minnie Harris Hoffman   B: 4 Jan 1872   D: 29 Jul 1950
w/o Joseph W. Hoffman

Lot: 405   1898 Owner: Hill & Herbert Rector

F. Hill Rector   B: 19 Oct 1879   D: 28 Mar 1964

Herbert B. Rector   B: 1877   D: 1953

Irene C. Rector   B: 1882   D: 1952

Annie S. Rector   B: 10 Oct 1885   D: 22 Aug 1959

Lot: 406   1898 Owner: Sam & Carroll Downs

Samuel Theodore Downs   B: 28 Jul 1902   D: 31 Jan 1925
s/o S. T. & M. J. Downs

Carroll R. Downs   B: 20 Feb 1886   D: 10 Feb 1965

Mazie A. Downs   B: 9 Feb 1897   D: 25 Jan 1973

Mary Jeanette Downs   B: 4 Dec 1865   D: 4 Jun 1928
w/o S. T. Downs

Samuel T. Downs   B: 14 Feb 1859   D: 2 Jul 1942

Robert N. Downs   B: 21 Oct 1923   D: 22 Oct 1923
s/o C. R. & M. A. Downs

Lot: 407   1898 Owner: A.S. Duffey

Augustus S. Duffey   B: 19 Nov 1869   D: 22 May 1942

Augustus S. Jr. Duffey   B: 13 May 1900   D: 5 Jul 1919

May Pegram Duffey   B: 16 Sep 1877   D: 5 Jan 1935

Lot: 408   1898 Owner: H.R. Duffey

Anna L. Duffey   B: 1874   D: 1966

Harriet Duffey Nelson   B: 9 Nov 1904   D: 12 Jul 1987

Edward R. Duffey   B: 1883   D: 1955

Ellen Pagaud Hawkins   B: 12 Jan 1844   D: 31 Dec 1921
                                                      w/o Rev. J. T. Hawkins

Lot: 409   1898 Owner: W.B. Dawson

Lillie Holliday Rosenberger   B: 1885   D: 1957

William B. Dawson   B: 26 Aug 1882   D: 30 Jul 1970

Roberta C. Dawson   B: 9 Dec 1879   D: 27 Sep 1959

Pauline Hazel Dawson   B: 11 Jan 1910   D: 26 Aug 1919
                                                      d/o W. B. & Roberta C. Dawson

Elkon L. Holliday   B: 3 Mar 1898   D: 7 Feb 1936

Lot: 410   1898 Owner: T.B. Winter

T. B. Winter   B: 1855   D: 1941

Fannie B. Winter   B: 1879   D: 1960

Belle Winter   B: 28 Jul 1877   D: 1 Jan 1953

Mary C. Winter   B: 1854   D: 1931
                                                      w/o T. B. Winter

Lot: 411   1898 Owner: Mrs. R.R. Turner

Lavinia Beverley Turner   B: 27 Feb 1871   D: 8 Oct 1954

infant daughters Cox   B: 8 Apr 1946   D: 11 Apr 1946
                                                      d/o Daniel T. & Elizabeth R. Cox

Margaret Elise Price Turner   B: 30 Jan 1883   D: 8 Nov 1969
                                                      w/o Robert Randolph Turner

Elizabeth Randolph Turner Cox
                               B: 19 Apr 1916   D: 2 Sep 1990

Robert Randolph Jr. Turner   B: 24 Aug 1909   D: 28 Feb 1948

Daniel Townsend Cox   B: 17 May 1906   D: 18 Jan 1990

Robert Randolph Turner   B: 22 Dec 1873   D: 29 Mar 1926

Lot: 412   1898 Owner: Col. F.W. Harris

Martha Harris   B: 8 Apr 1904   D: 28 Oct 1969

Floyd Morrison Harris   B: 25 Jun 1905   D: 15 Mar 1956

Eleanor Truax Harris   B: 12 Jan 1868   D: 4 Aug 1937

Eleanor Harris   B: 19 Apr 1901   D: 15 May 1942

Caro Bayard Hall		D: 24 May 1962
		w/o Grayson Mason Hall
Duval Holladay Tyler	B: 7 Jan 1900	D: 29 Mar 1970
Mary V. Harris Tyler	B: 31 Dec 1902	D: 12 Jan 1977
		w/o Duval Tyler
Floyd W. Harris	B: 26 Jun 1861	D: 8 Feb 1955

Lot: 414   1898 Owner: E.B. Goode & Mrs. W. Goode

William E. Goode	B: 1893	D: 1932
E. Virginia Goode		no dates
Edward B. Goode	B: 1861	D: 1934
Eliza G. Goode	B: 1860	D: 1935
Robert E. L. Goode	B: 1899	D: 1959

Lot: 415   1898 Owner: Hulbert

Arthur John White	B: 6 Dec 1888	D: 15 Nov 1963
Michael Ridgely White	B: 26 Nov 1950	D: 2 May 1986
Carolyn Hulbert White	B: 3 Oct 1892	D: 27 May 1970
Bettina Belmont Ward	B: 14 Jan 1919	D: 20 Oct 1993
Newell J. Jr. Ward	B: 30 Oct 1917	D: 22 Oct 1982
Daniel Sands Ward	B: 11 May 1949	D: 30 Oct 1984
Elizabeth Chalfont Johnstone Hulbert		
	B: 11 Dec 1863	D: 13 Dec 1921

Lot: 416   1898 Owner: Hulbert

Camilla Livingston Erwin	B: 27 Mar 1902	D: 30 Apr 1978
William P. Hulbert	B: 1885	D: 1981
Marie Louise Hulbert Dupont	B: 14 Aug 1912	D: 3 Jul 1991
Silvie Livingston Hulbert	B: 21 Jul 1905	D: 21 Sep 1985
Mary Chittenden Hulbert	B: 25 Apr 1866	D: 14 Jul 1939

Lot: 417   1898 Owner: K. Cromer

| Zelma W. Cromer | B: 27 Dec 1902 | D: 12 Apr 1976 |
| Thomas K. Cromer | B: 1863 | D: 1927 |

R. Russell Cromer	B: 10 Nov 1899	D: 7 Jul 1957
Jeremiah Keith Cromer Cromer	B: 7 Mar 1903	D: 7 Mar 1984
Katherine A. Cromer	B: 1865	D: 1933
Mary Ellen Cromer	B: 1910	D: 1916
Kenneth Vincent Cromer	B: 1901	D: 1958

Lot: 418   1898 Owner: Mrs. Helen Herrington

Percy E. Herringdon	B: 18 Apr 1896	D: 1 Jan 1932
Thomas E. Herringdon	B: 1859	D: 1937
Maggie D. Herringdon	B: 1874	D: 1965
Janie Lee Herringdon	B: 1898	D: 1997
Susie H. Carder	B: 1901	D: 1984

Lot: 419   1898 Owner: Dr. V. Johnson Russell

Geraldine M. Russell	B: 1906	D: 1982
William Ormond Russell	B: 1918	D: 1990
Robert A. Russell	B: 1911	D: 1971
Matilda Tompkins Russell	B: 26 Aug 1872	D: 24 Nov 1947
Johnston Russell	B: 1906	D: 1970
Anthony Brewis Russell	B: 29 Apr 1870	D: 17 Jul 1927
Florence Humphrey Russell	B: 11 Aug 1881	D: 2 Jan 1921 w/o Johnson Russell
Johnson Russell	B: 1 Apr 1876	D: 28 Jun 1937

Lot: 420   1898 Owner: Estate of J.A. Marshall

Madge L. Marshall	B: 20 Jul 1909	D: 23 Jan 1996
Eliza Randolph Marshall	B: 1858	D: 1928
Julia McIlvaine Marshall	B: 1884	D: 1956 w/o Charles T. Marshall
Charles Turner Marshall	B: 1883	D: 1953
Jaquelin Ambler Marshall	B: 1858	D: 1923
Charles S. Marshall	B: 12 Dec 1912	D: 24 Jul 1988

Lot: 421   **1898 Owner: E.H. Tiffany**

| Earle Hamilton Tiffany | B: 10 Jun 1894 | D: 9 Apr 1967 |
| Marie Skinner Tiffany | B: 11 Mar 1898 | D: 16 Oct 1989 |

Lot: 422   **1898 Owner: J.B. Hall**

Virginia Gordon Holliday	B: 28 Jan 1897	D: 2 Jul 1974
Ada Catherine Holliday Hall	B: 16 Mar 1877	D: 12 Jun 1921 w/o John B. Hall
Margaret Holliday	B: 23 Apr 1857	D: 17 Mar 1929 w/o Joseph H. Holliday
Lewis C. Holliday, Jr.	B: 11 Mar 1925	D: 6 Jan 1960
Ethel May Holliday Hall	B: 2 Mar 1889	D: 24 Feb 1957
Lewis C. Holliday	B: 18 Jun 1894	D: 15 Sep 1966
Joseph H. Holliday	B: 16 Oct 1845	D: 28 Feb 1927
John Barnes Hall	B: 4 Mar 1880	D: 29 Jun 1955

Lot: 423   **1898 Owner: J.W. Cochran**

| *Mollie J. Williams | Age: 70-5-9 | D: 27 Sep 1938 |
| Joseph Walter Cochran | B: 9 Apr 1865 | D: 13 Oct 1936 |

Lot: 424   **1898 Owner: R.E. Fletcher & Estate of E.W. Fletcher**

H. Elizabeth Fletcher	B: 1871	D: 1940
Mary V. Fletcher	B: 1840	D: 1926
Katie L. Fletcher	B: 1868	D: 1949
R. Ernest Fletcher	B: 1875	D: 1955

Lot: 425U   **1898 Owner: Miscellaneous**

John Turner Dawson	B: 9 Mar 1891	D: 19 Dec 1982
Margaret Foster Dawson	B: 16 Oct 1900	D: 3 Jul 1983
Alice E. Seaton	B: 1860	D: 1931

Lot: 426L   **1898 Owner: Mrs. E.M. Ferguson**

| James Sydnor Ferguson | B: 5 Nov 1878 | D: 6 Jun 1956 |
| Sue Mount Ferguson | B: 15 Mar 1882 | D: 28 Dec 1956 |

| Nellie Underwood | B: 5 Jun 1850 | D: 25 Feb 1923 |

Lot: 426U   1898 Owner: Laura Mitchell

| Laura E. Mitchell | Age: 67 yrs | D: 3 Jan 1931 |
| *Richard Henry Mitchell | Age: 76 yrs | D: 15 Jan 1946 |

Lot: 427L   1898 Owner: L. White

Luther L. White	B: 21 Oct 1900	D: 1 Mar 1971
E. Gertrude White	B: 13 Sep 1900	D: 10 Apr 1971
Preston G. White	B: 28 Jun 1929	D: 3 Oct 1981
Luther Lee White, Jr.	B: 7 Sep 1921	D: 23 Feb 1922

s/o L. L. & G. S. White

Lot: 427U   1898 Owner: Not Listed

| Walter A. Bridge | B: 8 Apr 1895 | D: 2 Dec 1920 |
| Thodore Bridge | B: 26 Apr 1936 | D: 26 Apr 1936 |

Lot: 428   1898 Owner: Hewitt

Ellen Altmanspacker	B: 5 Jul 1865	D: 20 Feb 1931
Eloise May	B: 13 Jun 1897	D: 28 Dec 1955
M. Emily Chown Hewitt	B: 11 Feb 1905	D: 4 Nov 1923

d/o H. T. & A. T. Hewitt

| Amy Ridgeway | B: 1893 | D: 1967 |
| Alice Tierney Hewitt | B: 26 Jan 1877 | D: 26 Feb 1928 |

w/o Henry Thomas Hewitt

Henry Thomas Hewitt	B: 8 Nov 1849	D: 25 Jan 1927
Nellie A. Smallwood	B: 18 May 1891	D: 29 May 1984
Claude R. Smallwood	B: 2 Sep 1890	D: 8 Feb 1966

Lot: 429L   1898 Owner: Ashby Bridge

Lillian Bridge

Lot: 429U   1898 Owner: Mrs. John Sullivan

| John T. Sinclair | B: 14 May 1852 | D: 2 Apr 1922 |
| James William Sinclair | B: 1905 | D: 1971 |

Lot: 430   1898 Owner: Paul L. Smith/Claude Smallwood

| Pierre E. Abadie | B: 1918 | D: 1989 |

| B. May Abadie | B: 1923 | |

Lot: 431L   1898 Owner: T.B. Davis

Mildred Greble Davis   B: 25 Apr 1889   D: 30 Apr 1955

Thomas Bealle Davis   B: 13 Dec 1875   D: 3 Jul 1948

Lot: 431U   1898 Owner: D.C. Sands

Daniel Cox Sands   B: 22 Nov 1875   D: 10 May 1963

Edith Kennedy Sands   B: 4 Jul 1875   D: 14 Jul 1948

Lot: 432   1898 Owner: C. Oliver Iselin

Elizabeth B. Iselin   B: 9 Apr 1897   D: 29 Sep 1977

Charles Oliver Iselin, Jr.   B: 25 Aug 1890   D: 4 Feb 1979

Lot: 434   1898 Owner: P. Leach

Norman F. Leach   B: 9 May 1904   D: 2 Sep 1994

Charlotte Ann Leach   B: 26 May 1905   D: 18 May 1936
                                          w/o Norman F. Leach

Delia Lee Leach   B: 30 Mar 1933   D: 26 Jun 1933
                                          d/o N. F. & C. A. Leach

Tessie R. Leach   B: 7 Jan 1901   D: 25 Oct 1918
                                          d/o Peter & Theresa Leach

Lot: 434A   1898 Owner: Not Listed

Fern Loraine Legge Adams   B: 27 Oct 1927   D: 27 May 1994
                                          w/o Carl Douglas Adams

Lot: 435L   1898 Owner: Nannie Sutphin

Minnie S. Tarpy   B: 1906   D: 1983

Nannie K. Sutphin   B: 1873   D: 1950

A. Webster Sutphin   B: 16 Sep 1900   D: 24 Oct 1918
                                          s/o E. & E. N. Sutphin

Lot: 435U   1898 Owner: Costello

Mary E. Costello   B: 1896   D: 1979

James H. Costello   B: 1892   D: 1934

Lot: 436L   1898 Owner: B.F. Gray

Robert H. McCauley	B: 21 Jan 1910	D: 3 Jun 1925
		s/o H. D. & E. B. McCauley
Lucy H. Gray	B: 22 Mar 1866	D: 11 Dec 1953
B. Frank Gray	B: 10 Jun 1866	D: 1 Jan 1942
Henry M. Hollman	B: 9 Sep 1911	D: 31 Jul 1912
Elizabeth B. McCauley	B: 1870	D: 1954
John O. McCauley	B: 18 Nov 1901	D: 18 Aug 1925
		s/o H. D. & E. B. McCauley
Eva M. Sowers	B: 1907	D: 1963
Furlong Carter Legge	B: 22 Oct 1912	D: 22 Jul 1913
Henry D. McCauley	B: 21 Jan 1866	D: 30 Jun 1939
Aneliza Grey Edmonds	B: 13 Jan 1888	D: 30 Nov 1954
		w/o Carroll Edmonds
Mary A. Sowers	B: 1928	D: 1995
Delbert F. Sowers	B: 16 Jan 1949	D: 1 Jan 1997
David F. Sowers	B: 21 Sep 1949	D: 23 Jul 1998

Lot: 436U   1898 Owner: B.F. Gray

Ernest Reid Altman	B: 8 Sep 1911	D: 11 Mar 1942
Henry E. Altman	B: 9 Aug 1850	D: 1 Dec 1935
Lillian Reid Altman	B: 30 Jan 1886	D: 19 Feb 1916
		w/o J. G. Altman
Julian G. Altman	B: 29 May 1890	D: 4 Nov 1963
Eliza E. Petty	B: 24 Aug 1856	D: 15 May 1920

Lot: 437   1898 Owner: Mrs. W.R. Keeler

Laura Cole Keeler	B: 7 Jul 1868	D: 17 Sep 1955
Edwin Castell Reamer	B: 24 Aug 1891	D: 8 Sep 1966
Mary Keeler Reamer	B: 4 Mar 1900	D: 23 Nov 1984
William Ryan Keeler	B: 21 Oct 1861	D: 18 Sep 1912

Lot: 439   1898 Owner: Mrs. E.V. Craig

E. Burns Seaton	B: 19 Aug 1886	D: 13 Dec 1954
Emma V. Craig	B: 27 Jun 1847	D: 8 Jul 1933
George F. Craig	B: 15 Dec 1872	D: 19 Jul 1912
George W. Craig	B: 20 Nov 1841	D: 19 Jan 1919
		CSA: 35th VA Cavalry, Co. A
Nena Craig Seaton	B: 25 Jun 1877	D: 22 Jul 1971

Lot: 440U   1898 Owner: J.T. Dawson

Clarence Thomas Dawson	B: 9 Dec 1885	D: 13 Aug 1967
Sara C. Dawson	B: 21 Jun 1851	D: 7 Oct 1920
		w/o J. Turner Dawson
Mary Anna Dawson	B: 13 Feb 1876	D: 18 Mar 1884
		d/o J. T. & S. C. Dawson
Roland Harris Dawson	B: 15 Mar 1888	D: 14 Feb 1969
J. Turner Dawson	B: 22 Jun 1845	D: 14 Sep 1924

Lot: 441   1898 Owner: J.E. Riley

Amelia Ann Edmonds	B: 6 Aug 1852	D: 13 Jun 1935
Frances Moma Moore	B: 8 Apr 1927	D: 20 Jun 1984
Rosa Lee Riley	B: 15 Dec 1869	D: 21 Sep 1912
Lena M. Riley	B: 15 Jan 1892	D: 27 Dec 1975
Joe Riley		no dates
Henry A. Riley	B: 14 Feb 1922	D: 1 Oct 1958
		h/o Dorothy M. Riley

Lot: 442   1898 Owner: W.S. Payne

Clyde H. Payne	B: 14 Sep 1908	D: 5 Apr 1909
		s/o W. S. & A. B. Payne
Virginia L. Payne	B: 5 Feb 1906	D: 16 Jun 1910
		d/o W. S. & A. B. Payne
Annie B. Payne	B: 24 Sep 1887	D: 8 Jul 1923
		w/o William S. Payne

Lot: 443   1898 Owner: Estate of Mrs. T.W. Seaton

Effie Frances Weakley   B: 2 Mar 1921   D: 13 Mar 1921

Floyd Seaton Weakley   B: 13 Jul 1926   D: 15 Jul 1926

Wilburn B. Seaton   B: 1878   D: 1961

Ann Catherine Seaton   B: 25 Oct 1843   D: 20 Jan 1917

Preston T. Seaton   B: 8 Jun 1874   D: 11 Mar 1927

Thomas W. Seaton   B: 9 Feb 1842   D: 22 May 1905

Lot: 444   1898 Owner: J.T. Potts

Charles E. Johnston   B: 12 Oct 1896   D: 4 Mar 1967

James T. Potts, Jr.   B: 9 Jan 1902   D: 10 Oct 1907
                                                s/o J. T. & H. A. Potts

infant son Potts   B: 1898   D: 1898

Helen Schumann Potts   B: 1869   D: 1960
                                                w/o James T. Potts

Ethel Potts Johnston   B: 28 Aug 1895   D: 28 Sep 87
                                                w/o Charles E. Johnston

James Thompson Potts   B: 1867   D: 23 Oct 1935

Lot: 445L   1898 Owner: Frank Ball

Alice R. Ball   B: 6 Oct 1905   D: 6 Dec 1914
                                                d/o Frank & Jane Ball

Frank Ball   B: Oct 1870   D: Jun 1933

Jane Ball   B: Mar 1877   D: Dec 1962

Lot: 445U   1898 Owner: Z.T. Flynn

Molly R. Flinn   B: 1883   D: 1955

James H. Flinn   B: 1928   D: 1995

Z. Taylor Flinn   B: 1885   D: 1961

Joseph P. Flinn   B: 1912   D: 1954

Lot: 446L   1898 Owner: C.B. Dawson

Ella Dawson   B: 8 May 1857   D: 29 Sep 1910
                                                w/o G. B. Dawson

George Bradford Dawson   B: 23 Apr 1847   D: 1 Jun 1928

Lot: 446U   1898 Owner: Mrs. Hilda Furr

Edward K. Furr	B: 1864	D: 1911
Hilda D. Furr	B: 1880	D: 1958

Lot: 447   1898 Owner: J.E. Bodmer

Alice W. Bodmer	B: 1877	D: 1959
James Franklin Bodmer	B: 1874	D: 8 May 1947
James Franklin Bodmer, Jr.	B: 5 Sep 1898	D: 5 Jun 1943

Lot: 448   1898 Owner: Miscellaneous

Martha F. Kimes	B: 28 Mar 1840	D: 6 Apr 1914 w/o G. W. Kimes
Lyman B. Kirkpatrick	B: 15 Jul 1916	D: 3 Mar 1995
George W. Kimes	B: 18 May 1829	D: 22 Nov 1916

Lot: 451   1898 Owner: Estate of W.C. Crouch

Margaret A. Crouch	B: 1 Jul 1854	D: 12 Oct 1928 w/o Thomas W. Crouch
Pauline P. Crouch	B: 1898	D: 1992
William S. Crouch	B: 1886	D: 1946
Thomas Walter Crouch	B: 20 Sep 1880	D: 19 Mar 1959
H. Marvin Crouch	B: 10 Apr 1891	D: 28 Apr 1961
Thomas W. Crouch	B: 2 Sep 1855	D: 12 Jan 1916
Jessie S. Crouch	B: 1891	D: 1977
Clarence H. Crouch	B: 1889	D: 1974
Abner O. Crouch	B: 27 Sep 1895	D: 12 Sep 1925 s/o T. W. & M. A. Crouch

Lot: 452L   1898 Owner: Mrs. Lorema Hall

Rosier W. Hall	B: 1 Aug 1883	D: 27 Aug 1918

Lot: 452U   1898 Owner: Mrs. E.M. Fletcher

Elijah M. Fletcher	B: 1864	D: 1925
*Mrs. Kate Fletcher		D: 15 Dec 1947

Lot: 453   1898 Owner: Edgar Henry

Edgar F. Henry	B: 7 Mar 1877	D: 24 Dec 1926
Harry H. Henry	B: 1903	D: 1961
Samuel J. Woodward	B: 1856	D: 1948
Mary C. Woodward	B: 1859	D: 1955
James F. Henry	B: 1911	D: 1969
Mollie B. Henry	Age: 37 yrs	D: 7 Sep 1917 w/o Edgar F. Henry

Lot: 454   1898 Owner: George Powell

George F. Downs	B: 8 Oct 1872	D: 29 Nov 1936
Annabelle R. Downs	B: 26 Jul 1916	D: 30 Jun 1919
Ruth P. Downs	B: 24 Dec 1891	D: 3 Sep 1980
Alma A. Powell	B: 25 Aug 1865	D: 27 Mar 1915 w/o George W. Powell
*Pfc. Claude G. Powell	Age: 21-11-26	D: 16 Dec 1943

Lot: 455   1898 Owner: C.D. Furr

Hazel E. Burkley	B: 27 Sep 1910	D: 16 Oct 1940

Lot: 456   1898 Owner: T.C. Gregg

Lucy C. Ella Gregg	B: 30 May 1887	D: 28 Jun 1919 w/o Thomas C. Gregg

Lot: 457L   1898 Owner: Alec Furr

Mary Furr	B: 12 Aug 1872	D: 2 Nov 1918

Lot: 457U   1898 Owner: Mrs. F. Squires

Arizona O. Squires	B: 20 Dec 1897	D: 3 Jan 1916 d/o W. H. & F. E. Squires
William H. Squires	B: 15 Jan 1861	D: 24 Oct 1903
Tennessee E. Squires	B: 15 Aug 1892	D: 15 Jun 1909 d/o W. H. & F. E. Squires
Fatha E. Squires		D: 18 Mar 1928

Lot: 458   1898 Owner: M.S. Reed

Rosemary A. Sweeney	B: 19 Sep 1940	D: 5 Nov 1943
Sadie B. Reed	B: 11 Jun 1893	D: 19 Jun 1990
Samuel T. Reed	B: 9 Jan 1923	D: 9 Jan 1923
Mary Ann Sweeney	B: 9 Aug 1952	D: 11 Aug 1952
Matthew Scott Reed	B: 29 Jan 1887	D: 5 Sep 1960

Lot: 458A   1898 Owner: Not Listed

William Lynwood Silvious	B: 1 Jun 1948	D: 24 Feb 1993
Eugenia Callahan Hale	B: 12 Oct 1916	D: 25 Apr 1995
Mary Ellen Runion Silvious	B: 1 Jul 1924	
Samuel Franklin Silvious, Sr.	B: 28 Mar 1921	D: 29 Sep 1993

Lot: 459L   1898 Owner: C. Payne

| Carroll Lee Payne | B: 22 Sep 1900 | D: 3 Jan 1935 |
| Thomas D. Payne | B: 31 Aug 1928 | D: 26 Jul 1982 |

Lot: 459U   1898 Owner: C. Costello

Lottie Virginia Costello   B: 26 Oct 1910   D: 26 Apr 1927
d/o Charles E. & Lillie Costello

*Charles Costello   Age: 70-11-21   D: 11 Sep 1947

Lot: 461A   1898 Owner: Not Listed

William Beveridge	B: Feb 1772	D: 26 Aug 1853
Lucy Beveridge	B: 1 Apr 1781	D: 8 Jun 1847
John W. Cavano	Age: 28 yrs	D: 8 Aug 1854
Mary Rennoe	B: 10 Mar 1812	D: 17 Jan 1888

Lot:C-2   1898 Owner: H.E. Jackson

| Dorothy Patterson Jackson | B: 27 Oct 1897 | D: 11 Oct 1986 |
| Howell Edmunds Jackson | B: 14 Sep 1896 | D: 17 Feb 1973 |

Lot:C-3   1898 Owner: B. Drue Hutchison

Milton Benjamin Hutchison   B: 30 May 1869   D: 10 Feb 1910
h/o Alice Taylor Hutchison

Goldie Grimes Hutchison   B: 27 Oct 1898   D: 26 Jun 1959

Frances Ann Hutchison Turner B: 23 Jan 1906   D: 4 Jun 1970
                                    w/o Francis Adams Turner

Francis Adams Turner   B: 29 Sep 1895   D: 25 Oct 1963

Benjamin Drurah Hutchison   B: 21 Jan 1899   D: 25 Oct 1979

Alice Cornelia Taylor Hutchison   w/o Milton B. Hutchison
                              B: 30 Jan 1871   D: 30 Nov 1962

Lot:C-4   1898 Owner: I.H. Dawson

Thomas Hazard Gardiner   B: 26 May 1895   D: 25 Dec 1953

Saidy Lawrence Gardiner   B: 24 Nov 1898   D: 7 May 1996

Earl Howard Dawson   B: 26 Jan 1899   D: 5 Jun 1972

Ruth Lawrence Dawson   B: 16 Jan 1907   D: 29 Sep 1963

CSA   Confederate Circle

D. Duffey   CSA: 2nd LA

J. R. Watkins

E. A. Deats   CSA: 4th VA Cavalry

Lt. J. R. Deckrow   CSA: 42nd VA

D. J. Wallis   CSA: 38th GA

Deupree   CSA: LA

J. Dudley   CSA: VA

P. E. Teal   CSA: GA

Grand Turk   CSA: LA

Wm Adam

Lt. John Tiffany   Age: 21 yrs   D: 23 Jul 1863
                                    CSA: Co. D, 27th VA

J. W. Morrison

B. F. Teys   CSA: GA

Thomas Watson   CSA: 9th VA

Mr. Brent   CSA: VA

John Underwood

A. Brewett   CSA: LA

Capt. Arnett	
Lewis T. Atwood	CSA: GA
Lt. Bishop	CSA: 4th GA
A. J. L. Black	CSA: 37th NC
Martin Boots	
Serg. E. Calvert	CSA: GA
Lt. Edmonds	CSA: Stuart's Cavalry
Lt. White	CSA: NC
John T. Taylor	CSA: NC
A. D. Cook	
Lt. J. A. Deal	CSA: Co. K, 13th Vol.
Sergt. George D	
P. B. Willis	CSA: 42nd VA
L. Whitefield	CSA: 9th VA
F. H. G. Breathed	CSA: Stuart Horse Artillery
C. W. Reiley	CSA: NC
Robert Pew	CSA: AL
Nicholas Roach	CSA: 7th LA
L. T. Emmerson	CSA: AL
W. Tucker	
Elijah Linville	CSA: 21st NC
Mr. Morgan	
Lt. George Means	CSA: 6th VA Cavalry
Pat Logan	CSA: 7th LA
J. A. Lynch	CSA: NC
M. L. Kimball	CSA: 9th LA
M. Maroney	
John H. Russell	CSA: Mont. Co., Md.
John Isaac Phillips	B: 17 Apr 1840 D: 3 Nov 1862
	CSA: Stuart Horse Artillery

T. B. Maroney	
Wm. McCoy	CSA: 37th NC
Charles McDonough	CSA: Mosby's Batt.
Serg. J. M. Morton	CSA: LA
G. E. Owen	CSA: NC
W. Parker	CSA: Stuart Horse Artillery
Lt. H. Phelps	CSA: GA
S. F. McGee	CSA: 15th AL Cavalry
John E. McKee	
George Mannings	CSA: GA
Mr. Johnson	
William Farnby	CSA: GA
Lt. Fontee	CSA: LA
Charles Godsey	CSA: VA
George Godsey	
James Sylvester	CSA: LA
Lt. Henry Hailey	CSA: 7th LA
Dr. R. F. Harland	
H. H. Hendricks	
A. S. Horgoff	
Capt. Houston	CSA: Fayetteville, NC
D. H. Lawrence	CSA: 7th NC
Mr. Hudson	
C. F. Schaffer	CSA: Co. I, 15th VA
Jas. T. Johnston	CSA: 60th GA
J. Jones	CSA: NC
Mathias Jones	CSA: 33rd NC
Patrick Kern	CSA: VA
John Kesner	

Jas. Keys	CSA: GA
E. Ryney	
S. Morgan	CSA: 59th NC
John Keys	CSA: GA
A. Strong	CSA: 4th VA

Solon Cemetery

The Cemetery association organized in 1883. In March of that year Elias A. & Selina M. Smith sold two acres to the association for $250 opposite the old Shiloh Church. Many of the early graves were unmarked since few of the former slaves could read, and oral tradition passed on the location of family graves. – *Eugene M. Scheel*

West   West   East

1	W 1-1	W 2-1	W 3-1	W 4-1	W 5-1	W 6-1		E 1-1	E 2-1	E 3-1
	W 1-2	W 2-2	W 3-2	W 4-2	W 5-2	W 6-2		E 1-2	E 2-2	E 3-2
	W 1-3	W 2-3	W 3-3	W 4-3	W 5-3	W 6-3		E 1-3	E 2-3	E 3-3
	W 1-4	W 2-4	W 3-4	W 4-4	W 5-4	W 6-4		E 1-4	E 2-4	E 3-4
	W 1-5	W 2-5	W 3-5	W 4-5	W 5-5	W 6-5		E 1-5	E 2-5	E 3-5
	W 1-6	W 2-6	W 3-6	W 4-6	W 5-6	W 6-6		E 1-6	E 2-6	E 3-6
	W 1-7	W 2-7	W 3-7	W 4-7	W 5-7	W 6-7		E 1-7	E 2-7	E 3-7
	W 1-8	W 2-8	W 3-8	W 4-8	W 5-8	W 6-8		E 1-8	E 2-8	E 3-8
	W 1-9	W 2-9	W 3-9	W 4-9	W 5-9	W 6-9			E 2-9	E 3-9
	W 1-10	W 2-10	W 3-10	W 4-10	W 5-10	W 6-10				E 3-10
	W 1-11	W 2-11	W 3-11	W 4-11	W 5-11	W 6-11		E 1-9		E 3-11
	W 1-12	W 2-12	W 3-12	W 4-12	W 5-12	W 6-12		E 1-10		
	W 1-13	W 2-13	W 3-13	W 4-13	W 5-13	W 6-13				E 3-12
	W 1-14	W 2-14	W 3-14	W 4-14	W 5-14	W 6-14	E 0-14	E 1-13	E 2-13	E 3-13
	W 1-15	W 2-15	W 3-15	W 4-15	W 5-15	W 6-15	E 0-15	E 1-14	E 2-14	E 3-14
80	W 1-16	W 2-16	W 3-16	W 4-16	W 5-16	W 6-16	E 0-16	E 1-15	E 2-15	E 3-15

west single graves 1-80

West   West   East

SOLON CEMETERY

East   **East**   **N**

E 4-1	E 5-1	E 6-1	E 7-1	E 8-1
E 4-2	E 5-2	E 6-2	E 7-2	E 8-2
E 4-3	E 5-3	E 6-3	E 7-3	E 8-3
E 4-4	E 5-4	E 6-4	E 7-4	E 8-4
E 4-5	E 5-5	E 6-5	E 7-5	E 8-5
E 4-6	E 5-6	E 6-6	E 7-6	E 8-6
E 4-7	E 5-7	E 6-7	E 7-7	E 8-7
E 4-8	E 5-8	E 6-8	E 7-8	E 8-8
E 4-9	E 5-9	E 6-9	E 7-9	E 8-9

E 4-10	E 5-10	E 6-10	E 7-10	E 8-10
E 4-11	E 5-11	E 6-11	E 7-11	E 8-11

E 4-12	E 5-12	E 6-12	E 7-12	E 8-12
E 4-13	E 5-13	E 6-13	E 7-13	E 8-13
E 4-14	E 5-14	E 6-14	E 7-14	E 8-14
E 4-15	E 5-15	E 6-15	E 7-15	E 8-15

East

E-1	E-17	E-33	1
E-2	E-18	E-34	
E-3	E-19	E-35	
E-4	E-20	E-36	
E-5	E-21	E-37	
E-6	E-22	E-38	
E-7	E-23	E-39	
E-8	E-24	E-40	east single graves 1-68
E-9	E-25	E-41	
E-10	E-26	E-42	
E-11	E-27	E-43	
E-12	E-28	E-44	
E-13	E-29	E-45	
E-14	E-30	E-46	
E-15	E-31	E-47	
E-16	E-32	E-48	68

East

New Lots

N-1	N-8	N-19
N-2	N-9	N-20
N-3	N-10	N-21
N-4	N-11	N-22
N-5	1-12	N-23
N-6	N-13	N-24
N-7	N-14	N-25
	N-15	N-26
	N-16	N-27
	N-17	N-28
	N-18	N-29

Lot: Unidentified   On previous listings, but no longer found

Francis Carter   on stone with Thomas & Fannie Washington

| Jennie Corbin | B: 1882 | D: 1964 |
| | | w/o Oscar Corbin |

| Oscar Corbin | B: 1888 | D: 1975 |
| | | h/o Jennie Corbin |

| Franklin R. Grigsby | Age: 55 years | D: 17 Dec 1986 |

| Annie Corum Hatcher | B: 25 Feb 1911 | D: 27 Sep 1995 |
| | | Age: 84 years |

| Polly James | | D: 22 Sep 1885 |

| Betty F. Johnson | B: 1922 | D: 1991 |

| Albert Jones | B: 1910 | D: 1964 |

| Annie E. Jordan | B: 1905 | D: 1990 |

| Evelyn Fisher Martin | B: 1875 | D: 1955 |

G. McQuay   may be a misplaced footstone

| Wilton McQuay | B: 1911 | D: 1986 |
| | | up hill from building/driveway |

| Edith Smith | B: 1893 | D: 1967 |

| Willis Tibbs | B: 1906 | D: 1987 |

| Walter L. Trammell | B: 1911 | D: 1985 |

Fannie Washington
    on stone with Thomas Washington & Francis Carter

Thomas Washington
    on stone with Fannie Washington & Francis Carter

| Baby Wright | | D: 1993 |

| Lenny Wright | B: 23 Aug 1992 | D: 23 Aug 1992 |
| | | Age: age 5 hours |

| Robert Marvin Wright | B: 21 Dec 1893 | D: 18 Apr 1991 |
| | | CPL US Army WWI |

Lot: E- 2   Lot Owner: Wallace Robinson

| Ella M. Robinson | B: 1900 | D: 1960 |
| | | w/o Wallace A. Robinson |

| Phillip Robinson | B: 1918 | D: 1957 |
| Wallace A. Robinson | B: 1891 | h/o Ella M. Robinson |

Lot: E- 3   Lot Owner: Patricia Green

Alice Hill Green	B: 10 Sep 1910	D: 15 Sep 1963
James Vernon Green	B: 24 Jun 1908	D: 25 Jan 1958
		Virginia PFC US Army WWII

Lot: E- 4   Lot Owner: Irene Bell

Arthur W. "Pete" Bell	B: 23 Nov 1938	D: 14 Jan 1998
Irene Bell	B: 1912	D: 1972
		w/o Quillie Bell
Quillie Bell	B: 1908	D: 1957
		h/o Irene Bell

Lot: E- 5   Lot Owner: Frank Bushrod & James White

Frank H. Bushrod	B: 1904	D: 1958
		h/o Juanita W. Bushrod
Juanita W. Bushrod	B: 1914	w/o Frank H. Bushrod
Gladys W. Thornton	B: 20 Dec 1915	D: 1999
w/o Henry H. Thornton		Colonial Funeral Home marker
Henry H. Thornton	B: 22 Jun 1910	D: 18 Jul 1982
		h/o Gladys W. Thornton
James M. Whitney	B: 1925	D: 1986

Lot: E- 6   Lot Owner: Richard Washington

| Richard Bland Washington | B: 6 Oct 1918 | D: 11 Nov 1997 |
| | | US Army WWII |

Lot: E- 7   Lot Owner: Lorraine Dade

Edward T. Dade	B: 1920	D: ndd
Estelle R. Dade	B: 1897	D: 1974
		w/o Lorraine Dade
Helen R. Dade	B: 1922	D: 1996
Lorraine Dade	B: 1898	D: 1968
		h/o Estelle R. Dade
Lorraine Dade, Jr	B: 25 Oct 1928	D: 14 Nov 1991
		PVT US Army WWII

Lot: E- 8   Lot Owner: Moses Grayson

Jessie T. Cotton   B: 5 Apr 1895   D: 11 Dec 1967
h/o Viola M. Cotton   Corporal US Army WWI 1918

Viola M. Cotton   B: 13 May 1902   D: 12 Jul 1982
                                                 w/o Jessie T. Cotton

Moses Grayson   B: 3 May 1910   D: 13 Apr 1977
                                                 h/o Sarah C. Grayson

Sarah C. Grayson   B: 10 Nov 1910   D: 14 Jun 1966
                                                 w/o Moses Grayson

Lot: E- 9   Lot Owner: Lee Etta Grice

Tillie Mae Brackett   B: 17 Aug 1924   D: 27 Dec 1986

Doris H. Burns   B: 11 Jun 1926   D: 8 Aug 1987

Lee Etta Grice   B: 2 Jul 1900   D: 25 Jun 1992
                                                 w/o Lewis H. Grice

Lewis H. Grice   B: 31 Oct 1897   D: 8 Oct 1966
                                                 h/o Lee Etta Grice

Lot: E-10   Lot Owner: Russell Gaskins

Eliza G. Gaskins   B: 1907   D: 1977

Russell E. Gaskins, Sr   B: 1910   D: 1987

Lot: E-11   Lot Owner: Ernest Brooks

Ernest Brooks   B: 1880   D: 1960
                                                 h/o Nannie V. Brooks

James Brooks   B: 27 Mar 1892   D: 25 Apr 1971
                                                 Virginia PVT US Army WWII

Nannie V. Brooks   B: 1897   D: 1971
                                                 w/o Ernest Brooks

Lot: E-12   Lot Owner: Miscellaneous

Benjamin Liddon Borders   B: 6 Mar 1931   D: 16 Aug 1995
                                                                   Korea

Willie D. O'Neill, Jr   B: 1942   D: 1999
                                                 Joynes Funeral Home marker

Lot: E-13   Lot Owner: Landon Harris

James H. Harris, Sr   B: 14 Oct 1929   D: 6 Dec 1981
                                                                  PFC US Army Korea

Laura B. Harris   B: 1907   D: 1980
                                                                        nee Bolden

Lloyd Gibson Harris   B: 22 May 1925   D: 9 Aug 1970
                                     Virginia TEC 825 ENGR AVN BN WWII

Robert L. Harris   B: 1900   D: 1961

Lot: E-14   Lot Owner: Miscellaneous

Helen Brown   B: 1903   D: 1996
                                                 Joynes Funeral Home marker

Bertha B. Washington   B: 21 Oct 1906   D: 12 Nov 1984
                                                 w/o Henry J. Washington

Henry J. Washington   B: 21 Dec 1902   D: 13 Feb 1980
                                                 h/o Bertha B. Washington

Lot: E-15   Lot Owner: Golder Bridgett

Golder Bridgett, Jr.   B: 23 Dec 1924   D: 17 Jan 1999
                                                                  US Army Korea

Golder Bridgett   B: 1892   D: 1973
                                                 h/o Mary Alice Bridgett

Mary Alice Bridgett   B: 1905   D: 1969
                                                 w/o Golder Bridgett

Lot: E-16   Lot Owner: Wayland Washington

David G. Henderson

Wayland Washington   B: 9 Nov 1912   D: 27 Feb 1978

Lot: E-17   Lot Owner: Robert Woodsen

Emma Elizabeth Togan   B: 9 Jul 1935   D: 18 Jul 1987

Mary A. Washington   B: 22 Dec 1927   D: 22 Oct 1993

Lot: E-18   Lot Owner: Nancy Russell

John W. Russell   B: 1894   D: 1957
                                                 h/o Nancy E. Russell

Nancy B. Russell   B: 1913   D: 1979
                                                 w/o John W. Russell

Lot: E-19   Lot Owner: Susie Hill

| Charles R. Hill | B: 1932 | D: 1996 |

| Richard W. Hill, Sr. | B: 1934 | D: 1999 |
Royston Funeral Home marker

| Roosevelt Hill | B: 24 Jul 1906 | D: 11 Nov 1962 |
h/o Susie E. Hill

| Susie E. Hill | B: 5 Jun 1916 | D: 5 May 1983 |
w/o Roosevelt Hill

Lot: E-20   Lot Owner: Alice Green & Katherine Hill Bridgett

| Calvin Edward Hill | B: 25 Feb 1925 | D: 4 Oct 1959 |
Virginia PFC 624 PORT Co TC

WWII

Lot: E-21   Lot Owner: Delia Payne

| Delia H. Payne | B: 17 Sep 1893 | D: 1 Sep 1974 |

| Thomas R. Payne | B: 29 Aug 1909 | D: 19 May 1964 |

Lot: E-22   Lot Owner: James Brown

| James Brown | B: 29 Mar 1886 | D: 8 Oct 1975 |
h/o Louella V. Brown

| Louella V. Brown | B: 17 Dec 1886 | D: 7 Jul 1957 |
w/o James Brown

| Tony Stewart | B: 1950 | D: 1996 |

Lot: E-23   Lot Owner: Henry Stewart

| Charles H. Stewart | B: 29 Dec 1910 | D: 29 Jun 1981 |
h/o Laura W. Stewart

| Laura W. Stewart | B: 1908 | D: 1963 |
w/o Charles H. Stewart

| Calvin Leroy Turner | B: 1957 | D: 1978 |
SP4 US Army

Lot: E-24   Lot Owner: Harold Hampton

| Helen A. Barnes | B: 25 Jan 1932 | D: 24 Mar 1995 |

| Harold R. Hampton | B: 1897 | D: 1971 |
h/o Rosalie J. Hampton

Rosalie J. Hampton   B: 1893   D: 1963
                                                w/o Harold T. Hampton

Walter Louis Wilson   B: 6 Apr 1929   D: 29 Aug 1989

Lot: E-26   Lot Owner: Fred Washington

Robert D. Washington   B: 1931   D: 1981
                                                PFC US Army Korea

Lot: E-27   Lot Owner: Sandy Stewart

Pearl L. Brown   B: 5 Jun 1899   D: 18 May 1964

Charles E. Gaskins   B: 1888   D: 1926
  h/o Sadie B. Gaskins   buried in Landmark, VA

Sadie B. Gaskins   B: 1 Feb 1889   D: 8 Apr 1964
                                                w/o Charles E. Gaskins

Thomas E. Gaskins   B: 8 Nov 1912   D: 8 Jan 1965
                                                            (snail)

Marie G. Stewart   w/o Sandy A. Stewart

Sandy A. Stewart   B: 1912   D: 1975
  h/o Marie G. Stewart   CPL US Army WWII
                                        birth date is 1914 on footstone

Lot: E-28   Lot Owner: Thomas Warner

Russell Eugene Basil   B: 8 Oct 1944   D: 14 Mar 1987
                                                SP4 US Army Vietnam

Thomas Nelson Davis   B: 2 Feb 1897   D: 7 Jul 1983
                                                PVT US Army WWII

Helen L. Smith   D: no dates

Garnett M. Warner   B: 1907   D: 1978

Lot: E-29   Lot Owner: Joseph Butler

Emily Jane Butler   B: 1912   D: 1998

Joseph P. Butler   B: 1907   D: 1993

Lot: E-30   Lot Owner: Charles Smith

Rene Tootsie Marshal   B: 15 Sep 1908   D: 24 Dec 1967
                                on stone with William A. & Lettie K. Smith

Katie Smith   B: 7 May 1893   D: 10 Jun 1969
                                                w/o Wade Smith

Lettie K. Smith   B: 4 Aug 1911   D: 27 Aug 1962
              on stone w/ William A. Smith & Rene Tootsie Marshall

Wade Smith   B: 1890   D: 6 Dec 1960
                                                    h/o Katie Smith

William Smith   B: 16 Jun 1909   D: 29 May 1968
              on stone w/ Lettie K. Smith & Rene Tootsie
Marshall

Lot: E-32   Lot Owner: Bessie Wilson

Blanch Smith   B: 1896   D: 1965
                                                    w/o Thomas Smith

Thomas Smith   B: 1896   D: 1986
                                                    h/o Blanch Smith

Lot: E-34   Lot Owner: Miscellaneous

George Bland   D: 1960

Katherine B. Grayson   B: 19 Apr 1911   D: 17 Feb 1997

Robert E. Grayson   B: 2 May 1918   D: 8 Feb 1973
                        Virginia SSGT 3371 QM TRK Co WWII

Lot: E-35   Lot Owner: William Gray

*Hallie G. Bridgett   date reads 1932 +

Gilbert Gray   B: 1935   D: 1961

Hallie B. Gray   B: 1908   D: 1987

William Gray   B: 1905   D: 1978

Thomas Waters   B: 1879   D: 1959

Lot: E-37   Lot Owner: Fred Orange

Crawford Orange   B: 1892   D: 1976
                                                    PFC US Army WWII

Lot: E-38   Lot Owner: Gladys Robinson

Gladys V. Robinson   B: 16 Feb 1919
                                         w/o Norvelle H. Robinson

Norvelle H. Robinson   B: 9 Oct 1914   D: 9 Dec 1981
                                         h/o Gladys V. Robinson

Lot: E-40   Lot Owner: Miscellaneous

Annie Jackson   B: 29 Jan 1892   D: 21 Dec 1975

Bessie A. Miles   B: 1910   D: 1998
                                                     Lyles Funeral Home marker

Lot: E-41   Lot Owner: James Anderson

Annie W. Anderson   B: 1907   D: 1988
                                                     w/o James (Pat) Anderson

James (Pat) Anderson   B: 1903   D: 1960
                                                     h/o Annie W. Anderson

Lot: E-43   Lot Owner: Mrs. Wingate

Clarence P. Mcallister   B: 1911   D: 1984
                                                     h/o Stella H. McAllister

Stella H. Mcallister   B: 1920   w/o Clarence P. McAllister

Jasper "JB" Wingate   B: 28 Jan 1920   D: 19 Jul 1967

Lot: E-44   Lot Owner: Archie Valentine

Archie Lee Valentine   B: 9 Nov 1909   D: 23 Dec 1972
                                     Pennsylvania SGT Co C 1312 ENGR REGT WWII

Hilda A. Valentine   B: 1 Nov 1909   D: 25 May 1974

Lot: E-45   Lot Owner: Wyat Hall

Lloyal L. Hall   B: 1914   D: 1960

Lot: E-46   Lot Owner: Clara Gains

Eli T. Fauntleroy   B: 18 Sep 1893   D: 8 Nov 1974
                                                     PVT US Army

Lot: E-47   Lot Owner: Alex Strozier & James Royster

Arnetta M. Royster   B: 19 Jan 1925   D: 11 Mar 1985

Alexander Strozier, Jr.   B: 19 Mar 1912   D: 24 Dec 1996
                                                     US Army WWII

Lot: E-48   Lot Owner: Not Given

Eva Bridgett Anderson   B: 1896   D: 1982

Mary Jane Anderson   B: 1927

Lot: E-0-14   Lot Owner: Not Given

Welby Carter Marble	B: 1957	D: 1996
		Royston Funeral Home
Delia E. Morler	B: 18 Jan 1881	D: 14 Jun 1976
		born in Tenn, died in MD

Lot: E-0-15   Lot Owner: Lee

Chester A. Davidson	B: 1885	D: 1935
Perry S. Hall		D: 6 Apr 1890
Rosetta Lee Hall	B: 26 May 1897	D: 8 Mar 1962
Ida Lee Redman		D: 11 Jan 1908

Lot: E-0-16   Lot Owner: Scott

Dorothy E. Scott	B: 1909	D: 1976
		'Mother'

Lot: E-1- 1   Lot Owner: Jos. Waters

Carrie V. Waters	B: 1927	
Charles F. Waters	B: 1937	D: 1974
Charles W. Waters	B: 1974	
Evelyn W. Waters	B: 1918	
George H. Waters	B: 1934	
Helen V. Waters	B: 1976	
James William Waters	B: 1936	D: 1936
Joseph W. Waters	B: 1908	D: 1975
		CK3 US Navy WWII

Lot: E-1- 3   Lot Owner: Miscellaneous

Quince Finger	B: 1881	D: 1939

Lot: E-1- 5   Lot Owner: Henry Hall

Amey E. Hall	B: 1893	D: 1939
		w/o J. Henry Hall
George Augustas Hall	B: 1916	D: 1982
		next to J. Henry & Amey Hall
J. Henry Hall	B: 1884	D: 1959
		h/o Amey E. Hall

Nathan W. Hall   B: 6 Jan 1914   D: 29 Jun 1983
                                                        CPL US Army WWII

Lot: E-1- 6   Lot Owner: L. Pheonix

Aaron E. Pheonix   B: 6 Jun 1894   D: 26 Oct 1972
                                                        PVT Co M 368 Infantry WWII

Nannie Pheonix   B: 30 Mar 1894   D: 12 Sep 1973

Mamie Scott   B: 10 Sep 1875   D: 22 Oct 1932

Edwin J. Wiates   B: 27 Jun 1911   D: 2 Oct 1960

Lot: E-1- 7   Lot Owner: Emerson Smith & Doris Allen

Daisy L. Allen   B: 1888   D: 1955

J. Monroe Allen   B: 1874   D: 1940

James M. Allen   B: 24 Nov 1925   D: 15 Feb 1989
                                                        US Army

Emerson E. Smith   B: 12 Jun 1902   D: 1 Jun 1955

Wilhelmina R. Smith   B: 30 Dec 1903   D: 1 Jun 1997

Lot: E-1- 8   Lot Owner: Grayson

Annie Grooms Grayson   B: 1895   D: 1939

Lot: E-1-9   Lot Owner: Jackson

Fannie Scott Jackson   B: 10 Apr 1905   D: 5 Dec 1973

James E. Scott   B: 1925   D: 1977
                                                        PVT US Army WWII

Lot: E-1-10   Lot Owner: Berryman

Edward M. Berryman   B: 31 Aug 1928   D: 27 Oct 1958
                                                        Virginia CPL Co A 761 Tank BN

Mattie M. Berryman   B: 7 Sep 1895   D: 7 May 1976

Raymond F. Berryman   B: 25 Dec 1889   D: 23 Oct 1947

Thelma O. Berryman   B: 9 Sep 1931   D: 25 May 1985

Ethel V. Lloyd   B: 15 Nov 1910   D: 14 Jun 1972
                                                        Virginia SGT US Army WWII

Ronald W. Smith   B: 1956   D: 1999

Lot: E-1-12   Lot Owner: Jackson

Cornelia Butler	B: 1906	D: 1975
		w/o Lonnie Butler
Lonnie Butler	B: 1898	D: 1972
		h/o Cornelia Butler
Anna Gaskins		no dates
Lucius Gaskins		no dates
Nancy Jackson	B: 1820	D: 1909
		m/o Simon Jackson
Simon Jackson	B: 1858	D: 1915
		s/o Nancy Jackson

Lot: E-1-13   Lot Owner: William Gaskins

Mary Evans Gaskins	B: 1890	D: 1940
William "Wid" Gaskins	B: 1891	D: 1974

Lot: E-2- 1   Lot Owner: John Ramey

Lewis R. Ramey	B: 9 May 1911	D: 23 Aug 1979

Lot: E-2- 2   Lot Owner: Frank Smith

Ethel Lee Smith	B: 20 Apr 1925	D: 22 Jun 1953
Rachael B. Smith	B: 1901	D: 1976
Sogeolia Smith	B: 2 May 1867	D: 27 Jun 1926
Walter Smith	B: 1897	D: 1971

Lot: E-2- 3   Lot Owner: David Fisher

David D. Fisher	B: 2 Sep 1911	D: 5 Nov 1986
h/o Eliza W. Fisher		M SGT US Army WWII
Eliza W. Fisher	B: 4 Dec 1908	D: 2 Feb 1991
		w/o David D. Fisher

Lot: E-2- 4   Lot Owner: Henry Jackson

Edward Willis [Sgt] Cook	B: 26 May 1914	D: 18 Feb 1984
		SGT US Army WWII
Hortance Jenkins Cook	B: 3 Aug 1920	D: 25 May 1988
Mary Cook	B: 1892	D: 1970
		on same stone as Henry

Henry Jackson   B: 1901   D: 1975
                                              on same stone as Mary Cook

Lot: E-2- 5   Lot Owner: Hall

Evelyn Hall   B: 29 May 1892   D: 30 May 1957

Amelia H. Outram   B: 1902   D: 1990
                                              w/o Robert C. Outram

Robert C. Outram   B: 1905   h/o Amelia H. Outram

Lot: E-2- 6   Lot Owner: Cora Poles

Corrie L. Poles   B: 1906   D: 1981
                                              w/o Lovel J. Poles

Lovel J. Poles   B: 1902   D: 1943
                                              h/o Corrie L. Poles

Anthony Michael Shorts   D: 12 Nov 1994

Charles M. Shorts   B: 1947   D: 1981

Michael D. Shorts   B: 9 Jan 1952   D: 19 Dec 1992
                                 a son, brother, uncle & devoted friend

Thelma L. Warner   B: 25 May 1926   D: 9 Aug 1957

Lot: E-2- 7   Lot Owner: James Smith

James R. Smith   B: 20 Aug 1872   D: 16 Jul 1948

Johnnie T. Smith   B: 8 Dec 1916   D: 2 Nov 1922
   h/o Mollie B. Smith   marriage date, 07/02/1938

Mary T. Smith   B: 22 May 1872   D: 4 May 1951

Mary Virginia Smith   B: 18 May 1913   D: 17 Feb 1997

Mollie B. Smith   B: 1 May 1914   D: 20 May 1982
   w/o Johnnie T. Smith   marriage date, 07/02/1938

Pearl A. Smith   B: 26 Apr 1908   D: 23 Feb 1976

Lot: E-2- 8   Lot Owner: Willie Whitney

Annie M. Whitney   B: 1898   D: 1988
                                              w/o Willard H. Whitney

John I. Whitney   B: 06 Apr 1887   D: 30 May 1955
                                 PVT Co C1 SEP INF BN DC NG WWI

Willard H. Whitney   B: 1887   D: 1969
                                              h/o Annie M. Whitney

Lot: E-2- 9   Lot Owner: Foster Grant & Johnson

Edmonia J. Grant   B: 2 Feb 1893   D: 1 Mar 1985
                                                      w/o Robert A. Grant Sr

Robert A. Grant, Sr   B: 16 Aug 1889   D: 23 Mar 1978
                                                      h/o Edmonia J. Grant

Nathan Johnson   B: 1 Feb 1951   D: 24 Dec 1940

Lot: E-2-15   Lot Owner: Shed Bolden

Anna Bolden   w/o Shed Bolden   D: 20 Jan 1923

Shed Bolden   B: 31 Mar 1851   D: 18 Dec 1911
                                                      h/o Anna Bolden

Lot: E-3- 1   Lot Owner: Elton Moore

Herbert E. Moore   B: 1889   D: 1975

Sadie W. Moore   B: 1896   D: 1944

Lot: E-3- 2   Lot Owner: Willie Smith

Maggie S. Christa   B: 22 Feb 1902   D: 28 Dec 1973

R.W. Dawson   B: 21 Dec 1884   D: 13 Jan 1929
                                                      s/o Rev R.P. & Laura Dawson

Harry L. Smith   B: 1930   D: 1986

Mary T. Smith   B: 1896   D: 1951

Willie Decatur Smith   B: 23 Oct 1892   D: 12 Jul 1957
                                Virginia PVT Co F1 Chemical BM WWI

Lot: E-3- 3   Lot Owner: Walter Wright & sister

Rachel Lee Wright   B: 12 Mar 1895   D: 11 Jan 1985
                                                      sister of Walter Wright

Walter Wright   B: 30 May 1900   D: 5 Mar 1987

Lot: E-3- 4   Lot Owner: Pete Tibbs

Mary K[atherina] Tibbs Avery B: Apr 1932   D: 10 Jul 1989
                                                      Chinn Funeral Home marker

Mary Tibbs Thomas   B: 10 Sep 1918   D: 5 Jun 1987

Charles W. Tibbs   B: 2 Jun 1914   D: 19 Apr 1973
                                SSGT Army Air Force WWII

| Fannie V. Tibbs | B: 1887 | D: 1934 |
| | | w/o Peter W. Tibbs |

| Peter W. Tibbs | B: 1884 | D: 1951 |
| | | h/o Fannie V. Tibbs |

| Rosa L. Tibbs | B: 1921 | D: 1978 |

Lot: E-3- 6   Lot Owner: Hester Alexander & R. Ford

| Harry C. Alexander | B: 1883 | D: 1958 |

| Hester E. Alexander | B: 1887 | D: 1977 |

| Florence [Lewis] Ford | B: 8 Dec 1920 | D: 15 Dec 1994 |
| | | w/o Robert Ford |

| Robert Ford | B: 5 Jul 1918 | D: 8 Aug 1990 |
| h/o Florence [Lewis] Ford | | US Army WWII |

Lot: E-3- 7   Lot Owner: Charles H. Smith & Everett Smith

| Baby boy Smith | | D: 3 Dec 1954 |

| Charles H. Smith | B: 1897 | D: 1976 |
| | | h/o Emma D. Smith |

| Emma D. Smith | B: 1902 | D: 1986 |
| | | w/o Charles H. Smith |

Lot: E-3- 8   Lot Owner: Pinckney Brown

| Beatrice F. Brown | B: 4 May 1934 | w/o Earl D. Brown |

| Earl D. Brown | B: 13 May 1928 | D: 21 Jan 1971 |
| | | h/o Beatrice R. Brown |

| Ethel S. Brown | B: 1 Aug 1901 | D: 25 Jul 1976 |

| Pinckney C. Brown | B: 26 Apr 1901 | D: 18 Feb 1955 |

Lot: E-3- 9   Lot Owner: Molly Evans

| Edna B. Evans | B: 1919 | w/o Randolph B. Evans Sr |

| George G. Evans | B: 1884 | D: 1950 |
| | on stone with Mollie M. Evans & Mollie E. Wells | |

| Mollie M. Evans | B: 1888 | D: 1958 |
| | on stone with George G. Evans & Mollie E. Wells | |

| Randolph B. Evans, Sr | B: 1920 | no death date |
| h/o Edna B. Evans | | COX US Navy WWII |

Mollie E. Wells   B: 1919   D: 1975
on stone with George G. Evans & Mollie M. Evans

Lot: E-3-11   Lot Owner: Henry Ashton

Sally Gertrude Ashton   B: 23 Jul 1874   D: 24 Jun 1946
w/o Henry Samuel Ashton

Guthrie Henry Ashton   B: 25 Mar 1915   D: 30 Mar 1986
US Army WWII

Henry Samuel Ashton   B: 17 Feb 1872   D: 25 Nov 1950
h/o Sally Gertrude Ashton

Martha C. Ashton   B: 8 Jul 1916   D: 24 May 1962

Mary Frances Thornton   B: 25 Oct 1891   D: 10 Apr 1987
my loving Mother, Helen T. W.

  Blake

Imogene C. White   B: 22 Jul 1908   D: 7 Jan 1968

Lot: E-3-12   Lot Owner: Avis Dade

Avis D. Abston   B: 1925   D: 1970

Francis E. Abston   B: 1918   D: 1978
US Army WWII

Lot: E-3-15   Lot Owner: Henry Lewis & M. Grant

Henry R. Lewis   B: 1866   D: 1950

Lot: E-4- 1   Lot Owner: Wilmer Hatcher

Mozell Hatcher   B: 15 Nov 1914   D: 31 May 1978

Wilmer Hatcher   B: 1908   D: 1976
PVT US Army WWII

Edward L. Hill   B: 1963   D: 1986

Florence H. Hill   B: 1937   D: ndd

James E. Hill   B: 1931   D: 1998

James E. Hill, Jr   B: 19 Jul 1958   D: 23 Sep 1958

Lot: E-4- 2   Lot Owner: Sue Smith

Clarence Smith   B: 1 Sep 1892   D: 15 Mar 1947
PVT VET Hosp4 WWI

Lot: E-4- 3   Lot Owner: James Anderson

Irvin A. Anderson   B: 15 Jul 1912   D: 24 Nov 1971
                               Virginia CPL US Army WWII

Lot: E-4- 5   Lot Owner: Douglas Deneal

Birdie E. Deneal   B: 1890   D: 1938
                               w/o James D. Deneal

James D. Deneal   B: 1884   D: 1968
                               h/o Birdie E. Deneal

John Douglas Deneal, Jr   B: 8 Jun 1923   D: 16 Dec 1989
                               PFC US Army WWII

Lot: E-4- 6   Lot Owner: C.P. Cook, Sr.

Laura C. "Cullie" Bunn   B: 1912   D: 1985

Bithia E. Cook   B: 1892   D: 1968

Carr P. "John" Cook   B: 1888   D: 1958

Carr Philip Cook, Jr.   B: 13 Nov 1919   D: 17 Aug 1991
                               SSGT US Army WWII

Ruth A. "Jessie" Cook   B: 1915   D: 1975

Nancy Cook Cotton   B: 1917   D: 1991

Thomas W. Cotton, Jr   B: 1917   D: 1993

Lot: E-4- 7   Lot Owner: Miscellaneous

Haywood Bowles   D: 14 Jan 1912
                                                    Ames Funeral Home

F. Carl Dawson   B: 27 Sep ----   D: 27 May ----

Pauline S. Dawson   B: 25 Jul 1900   D: 26 Dec 1985

Elwood Hall   B: 1916   D: 1994
                               h/o Hattie S. Hall

Hattie S. Hall   B: 1916   D: 1982
                               w/o Elwood Hall

Lot: E-4- 8   Lot Owner: Kenneth Smith & Charles D. Smith

Charles D. Smith   B: 18 Jan 1925   D: 28 Apr 1997
                               US Navy WWII

Eleanor D. Smith   B: 23 Jan 1928   D: no death date

Kenneth D. Smith   D: 17 Jul 1950

Lot: E-4-10   Lot Owner: Harry Howard

Alice Virginia Howard   B: 11 Oct 1930   D: 23 Mar 1996

Harry John Howard   B: 26 Mar 1896   D: 9 Nov 1959
                               Virginia CPL Co A 372 Infantry

WWI

Lot: E-4-11   Lot Owner: Ashton

Annie L. Ashton   D: 15 Dec 1950

Emiley Ashton   D: 23 Mar 1929
                               w/o Lee Ashton   Age: 85 years

Leana Ashton   B: 1895   D: 19 Oct 1918

Lee Ashton   D: 3 Aug 1918
                               h/o Emiley Ashton   Age: 79 years

Lot: E-4-14   Lot Owner: Martin

E.J. Martin   B: 1859   D: 7 May 1923
                               w/o W.F. Martin   "Mother"

Lina B. Martin   D: no dates
                               c/o W.F. & E.J. Martin   Age: 7 days

Sarah Olive Martin   B: 29 Dec 1872   D: 10 Aug 1902
                               d/o W.F. & E.J. Martin

Thomas B. Martin   B: 12 Jun 1887   D: 29 Nov 1954
                               PVT Co M 808 Pioneer Inf WWI

William R. Martin   D: no dates
                               c/o W.F. & E.J. Martin   Age: 7 days

Lot: E-5- 1   Lot Owner: Louis Campbell

Elizabeth Campbell   B: 1894   D: 1944
                                              w/o Louis Campbell

James H. Campbell   B: 6 Nov 1923   D: 27 May 1972
                                       s/o Louis & Elizabeth Campbell
                               Virginia, PVT US Marine CorpsWWII

Louis Campbell   B: 1882   D: 1957
                                              h/o Elizabeth Campbell

Moses Campbell   B: 1 Jan 1929   D: 10 Sep 1995
                                              US Army WWII

Randolph Campbell, Sr   B: 9 Apr 1920   D: 14 Jul 1992
                                                       SGT US Army WWII

Lot: E-5- 2   Lot Owner: Stanley Peterson

Gaither W. Peterson   B: 1910   D: 1947

Lot: E-5- 3   Lot Owner: Miscellaneous

Barbara "Goodie" Wright   B: 18 Feb 1835   D: 16 Apr 1990

Lot: E-5- 5   Lot Owner: Robert McQuay

Nannie S. McQuay   B: 1896   D: 1977
                                              w/o Thomas C. McQuay

Robert T. McQuay   B: 15 Jul 1893   D: 1 Dec 1934

Robert Thornton McQuay   B: 1892   D: 1934
                                            h/o Myrtle Young McQuay
                             Corporal Am Expeditionary Force France
   1918

Thomas C. McQuay   B: 1894   D: 1964
                                              h/o Nannie S. McQuay

John W. Parker   B: 22 Sep 1889   D: 22 Apr 1982

Lot: E-5- 8   Lot Owner: Lemuel Thornton

Lemuel Thornton   h/o Sarah Thornton   D: 1930

Sarah Thornton   w/o Lemuel Thornton   D: 1941

Lot: E-5- 9   Lot Owner: Mary Russ

Linwood Britt   B: 24 Aug 1914   D: 8 Jul 1992
                                                       SGT US Army WWII

Mildred Maria Russ   B: 22 Apr 1915   D: 23 Nov 1986

Orlin W. Russ   B: 16 Nov 1916   D: 5 Jul 1994

Bob Russ   dates missing, funeral home name missing

William Russ   B: 1882   D: 1980

Lot: E-5-11   Lot Owner: Thomas Warner

Robert L. Basil   B: 1941   D: 1971
                                        "Vietnam era" on metal peg

Earline Grant   B: 1909   D: 1949

H. Marie Warner   B: 1922   D: 1950

Landon H. Warner	B: 1916	D: 1971
M. Mayo Warner	B: 1918	D: 1943
Olive B. Warner	B: 1904	D: 1952
Sarah D. Warner	B: 1885 w/o Thomas S. Warner	D: 1950 "Mother"
Thomas S. Warner	B: 1881 h/o Sarah D. Warner	D: 1958 "father"

Lot: E-5-12   Lot Owner: Buck Marlow

Anna Carey Marlow	B: 1867	D: 1944
James B. Marlow, Jr	B: 1893	D: 1939
James B. Marlow, Sr	B: 1847	D: 1908
Leana Davis Marlow	B: 11 Apr 1891	D: 19 Jan 1977
Mary Marlow Parker	B: 12 Sep 1890	D: 20 Nov 1957
Julia A. Summers	B: 1876	D: 1956

Lot: E-5-13   Lot Owner: Julia Grant

Charlotte A. Grant	B: 24 Jul 1906	D: 6 Mar 1924
E. Virginia Grant	B: 12 Mar 1904	D: 5 Aug 1924
Isaac Burrell Grant		D: 9 Jun 1910
O.L. Grant	Age: 61-3-8	D: 6 Sep 1908 h/o Julia A. Grant

Lot: E-5-14   Lot Owner: Washington

| Elmira Washington | Age: 72 years | D: 14 Oct 1900 |
| William Washington | B: 1876 | D: 1951 |

Lot: E-5-15   Lot Owner: R.P. Dawson

Digie Dawson	B: 9 May 1891	D: 3 Feb 1896 c/o R.P. & Laura Dawson
Esther Dawson	B: 19 Sep 1881	D: Jun 1881 d/o R.P. & Laura Dawson
Mark Hanna Dawson	B: 17 Dec 1896	D: 3 Nov 1899 s/o R.P. & Laura Dawson
Nehemiah Dawson	B: 1 Jun 1889	D: 30 Nov 1909 s/o R.P. & Laura Dawson

R.P. [Rev] Dawson   B: 4 Aug 1856   D: 23 Jan 1921
                                                        h/o Laura Dawson

Lot: E-6- 1   Lot Owner: Frank Bushrod

Earl Bushrod   B: 1913   D: 1977

Ethel B. Smith   B: 15 Jun 1910   D: 4 Feb 1989

Lot: E-6- 2   Lot Owner: Willis Adams

Willis E. Adams   B: 12 Oct 1909   D: 8 Jan 1949
                                 Virginia TEC4 1365 Engr Truck Co WWII

Essie A. Brown   B: 1930   D: 1978
                                                         "daughter"

Ruth A. Davis   B: 31 Jul 1961   D: 24 Sep 1992

Willie Davis   B: 10 May 1929   D: 22 Jan 1970
                                 Louisiana SGT Corps of Engineers Korea

Oliver B. Grant   B: 1 Jan 1930   D: 6 Aug 1962

Lot: E-6- 3   Lot Owner: Dudley Gaskins

Custis C. Gaskins   B: 1924   D: 1988

Dudley S. Gaskins   B: 1896   D: 1967
                                                 h/o Martha L. Gaskins

Martha L. Gaskins   B: 1898   D: 1978
                                                 w/o Dudley S. Gaskins

Shirley D. Gaskins   B: 1939   D: 1979
                                 Royston Funeral Home marker

Helen Mae Gaskins Petty   B: 19 Mar 1919   D: 8 May 1992

Lot: E-6- 4   Lot Owner: Bill Smith

Aubrey M. Smith   B: 1930   D: 1981

Lillian M. Smith   B: 1919   D: 1922

Marie Gaskins Smith   B: 19 May 1900   D: 25 Jan 1983

William J. Smith   D: 29 Nov 1941
                                 Virginia PVT 369 Inf 93 Div

Lot: E-6- 5   Lot Owner: James Robinson

James D. Robinson   B: 4 Jun 1876   D: 21 Jul 1955
                                               h/o Sadie E. Robinson

Sadie E. Robinson   B: 17 Mar 1884   D: 7 Jul 1966
                                               w/o James D. Robinson

Lot: E-6- 6   Lot Owner: Harry Douglas

James R. Douglass   B: 6 Mar 1926   D: 3 Oct 1966
                                               Virginia Cox USNR WWII

Nathaniel Hatcher   B: 15 Feb 1921   D: 8 Jan 1997
                                               US Army WWII

Lot: E-6- 7   Lot Owner: Alex Strozier

Carrie J. "Tweed" Donaldson   B: 1907   D: 1986

Lot: E-6- 8   Lot Owner: Polly Smith

Stanley Reid   B: 1927   D: 1996

Grace Marie Smith   B: 21 Jun 1905   D: 10 Feb 1985

Willie Arthur Smith   B: 1 Apr 1897   D: 28 Mar 1969
                                               Virginia PVT Veterinary Corps WWI

Lot: E-6- 9   Lot Owner: George Grigsby & Pierson

Archie F. Pierson   B: 1903   D: 1969

J. Edward Pierson   B: 1902   D: 1958

Josie G. Pierson   B: 1904   D: 1990

Lot: E-6-10   Lot Owner: W. Gaskins

John Carter   B: 1896   D: 1963
                           Sudduth-Moser Funeral Home
  marker

Minnie Virginia Gaskins   B: 4 Jan 1909   D: 19 May 1951
  w/o W.H. Gaskins   d/o William & Delia Johnson

Willie H. Gaskins, Sr   B: 6 Jun 1909   D: 1 Jul 1994
                                               "Father"

William D. Smith   B: 9 Sep 1927   D: 29 Sep 1958
                           Virginia CPL 2806 ENGR GEN SVC BN
  WWII

Lot: E-6-11   Lot Owner: George Marshal

Kate Henderson		D: 12 Sep 1927
George Marshal	Age: 30 years	D: 21 Aug 1908

Lot: E-6-12   Lot Owner: A. Davis

Allen Davis	h/o Bettie Davis	D: 11 Mar 1906
Arie V. Davis	B: 20 Feb 1881	D: 24 Mar 1905
		d/o Allen & Bettie Davis
Bettie A. Davis		D: 18 Mar 1920
	w/o Allen Davis	Age: 63 years
Landon H. Davis	B: 1878	D: 1958

Lot: E-6-13   Lot Owner: Pete Smith

James (Pete) Smith	B: 8 Mar 1884	D: 28 Nov 1963
Solomon Smith	B: 1867	D: 31 Apr 1904
		h/o Mary J. Smith

Lot: E-6-14   Lot Owner: George Smith

Mary Smith		Age: 11 years
	d/o G.H. & Virginia A. Smith	
Virginia A. Smith		D: 27 Aug 1927
	w/o George H. Smith, d/o Soloman & Jane Smith	

Lot: E-7- 1   Lot Owner: Mazie Bridgett

Dorothy Ann Dade	B: 14 Jan 1931	D: 27 Aug 1985

Lot: E-7- 2   Lot Owner: M. Grayson

Martha Ellen Grayson	B: 1900	D: 1953
Nellie S. Grayson	B: 8 Dec 1928	D: 12 Jan 1982
Welby H. Grayson, Sr	B: 8 Apr 1901	D: 15 Mar 1975
Mildred L. Hopkins	B: 28 Jun 1924	D: 7 Feb 1965

Lot: E-7- 4   Lot Owner: Richard Gaskins

Emma P. Gaskins   B: 7 Nov 1887   D: 3 Dec 1927
                                                  w/o Richard H. Gaskins

John Wesley Gaskins   B: 2 Feb 1902   D: 12 Feb 1972
                             Virginia TEC4 3429 OM Truck Co
   WWII

Lucious Gaskins   D: 1 Apr 1985

Richard H. Gaskins   B: 24 Apr 1870   D: 10 Nov 1966
                                                  h/o Emma P. Gaskins

Lot: E-7- 5   Lot Owner: Lee Stewart

Anna Elizabeth Stewart   B: 1900   D: 1996

Richard Lee Stewart   B: 22 Feb 1909   D: 24 Oct 1974
                                                  PFC US Army

Lot: E-7- 6   Lot Owner: Henry Artis

Bernice Artis   B: 21 Sep 1917   D: 8 Dec 1927
                                                  d/o Henry & Cora Artis

Cora Artis   B: Jan 1893   D: Apr 1943
                                                  w/o Henry Artis

Henry Artis   B: 1875   D: 29 Mar 1942
   h/o Cora Artis   b. Powhatan Co; d. Middleburg

Lot: E-7-10   Lot Owner: Kate Henderson

Jane E. Ashby   B: 1885   D: 1981

Martha P. Chinn   B: 24 Jan 1918   w/o William Chinn

William Chinn   B: 5 Jun 1909   D: 30 Mar 1968
                                                  h/o Martha P. Chinn

Julia M. Mcintosh   B: 28 Jun 1876   D: 21 Jan 1966

Viola E. McIntosh   D: no dates

Lot: E-7-14   Lot Owner: James Smith & Sam Winston

Gertrude Oliver Harden   B: 14 Jan 1933   D: 9 Jan 1998

Alcinda Smith   B: 3 Aug 1875   D: 15 Oct 1906
   10 year member of Mountville Baptist Church   w/o James Smith

Clifton Winston   B: 1890   D: 1945
                                                  f/o William Winston

Jennie Winston	B: 25 Nov 1899	D: 17 Mar 1988
William Winston	B: 1926	D: 1945
		s/o Clifton Winston

Lot: E-7-15   Lot Owner: Laura Rogers

Bernard Rogers, Sr	B: 1879	D: 1918
Eugene M. Rogers	B: 9 Feb 1913	D: 14 Feb 1970
		US Army WWII
Jessie Rogers	B: 1909	D: 1923
Laura Rogers	B: 1879	D: 1934
George F.E Rogers	B: 23 Mar 1920	D: 8 Aug 1968
		Virginia CPL US Army WWII

Lot: E-8- 1   Lot Owner: Isaac Donaldson

| John Arthur Johnson | B: 26 Mar 1911 | D: 13 Aug 1973 |
| | | Virginia SGT US Army WWII |

Lot: E-8- 2   Lot Owner: Barkley Brent

| Rufus W. Brent | B: 1926 | D: 1979 |
| | | PVT US Army WWII |

Lot: E-8- 3   Lot Owner: William Cox

| William P. Cox | B: 28 Jan 1919 | D: 2 Jul 1983 |

Lot: E-8- 4   Lot Owner: George Perry

| Viola Smith | B: 12 Jul 1907 | D: 26 Dec 1944 |

Lot: E-8- 5   Lot Owner: Mr. & Mrs. Luther Smith

| Rella V. Smith | d/o Janie T. Smith | Age: 3- 8-0 |

Lot: E-8- 6   Lot Owner: Bea, Liz & Bessie Smith

| Bessie B. Smith | B: 31 Mar 1912 | D: 8 Oct 1970 |

Lot: E-8- 7   Lot Owner: George Rich & Tom Young

| Tanesha Arnell Napper | B: 28 Sep 1974 | D: 18 Jul 1987 |

George L. Rich
    on stone with Lucy W. Rich, Thomas C. & Virgie W.
  Young

Lucy W. Rich
> on stone with George L. Rich, Thomas C. & Virgie W. Young

Thomas C. Young
> on stone with George L. & Lucy W. Rich, & Virgie W. Young

Virgie W. Young
> on stone with George L. & Lucy W. Rich, & Thomas C. Young

Lot: E-8- 8   Lot Owner: Elizabeth Howard

| Marvin Lee Grant | B: 1933 | D: 1984 |
| | | US Army Korea |

| Moses S. Grant, Jr | B: 8 Feb 1932 | D: 31 Dec 1973 |
| | | PFC US Army |

| Elizabeth T. Howard | B: 1907 | D: 1996 |

| Velma M. Peterson | B: 9 May 1930 | D: 30 Aug 1993 |

Lot: E-8- 9   Lot Owner: Julia Turner

| Burkley Turner | B: 9 Nov 1925 | D: 9 Nov 1951 |
| | Virginia PVT 24 Chemical Decon Co | |

| George Turner | B: 1909 | h/o Julia B. Turner |

| Julia B. Turner | B: 1908 | D: 1993 |
| | | w/o George G. Turner |

Lot: E-8-10   Lot Owner: Joe Booker

| Joseph P. Booker | | D: 21 Oct 1916 |
| | h/o Mary Booker | Age: 17 years |

| Mary Booker | | D: 19 Feb 1917 |
| | w/o Joseph P. Booker | Age: 37 years |

Lot: E-8-11   Lot Owner: Willie O'Neil

| Edna S. O'Neil | B: 1922 | w/o W. Dulaney O'Neal |

| W. Dulaney O'Neil | B: 1921 | D: 1979 |
| | | h/o Edna S. O'Neil |

Lot: N- 1   Lot Owner: Cook

| Alise B. Cook | B: 22 Feb 1921 | no death date |
| | | w/o Robert Douglas Cook |

| Robert Douglas Cook | B: 6 Feb 1919 | D: 23 Apr 1981 |
| h/o Alise B. Cook | | S SGT US Army WWII |

Lot: N- 5   Lot Owner: Thompson

Annie L. Farmer	B: 19 Apr 1942	D: 17 Dec 1993
Leola D. Thompson	B: 4 Mar 1922	D: 24 Oct 1976
James L. Williams	B: 3 Oct 1918	D: 22 Oct 1971
	Virginia TEC5 US Army WWII	

Lot: N- 7   Lot Owner: Mr. & Mrs. William Parker

Theodore Holmes	B: 22 Feb 1903	D: 25 Feb 1991
William R. [Rev] Parker	B: 20 Jun 1910	D: 11 Aug 1981
		US Army WWII

Lot: N- 8   Lot Owner: Vanderzee Whitney

| Gerline Powell | B: 1953 | D: 1989 |
| Vanderzee Whitney, Jr | B: 1947 | D: 1972 |

Lot: N- 9   Lot Owner: Harry Bolden

Evelyn H. Bolden	B: 5 Jun 1926	D: 16 Oct 1998
Harry M. Bolden	B: 5 Jan 1926	D: ndd
	married 9 Jul 1947	

Lot: N-12   Lot Owner: James Williams

| Robert William Thomas | B: 6 Feb 1921 | D: 12 Jun 1988 |
| | TEC5 US Army WWII | |

Lot: N-13   Lot Owner: Grant & Gardner

Augustus P. Ambers	B: 9 Jun 1908	D: 27 Oct 1984
	PFC US Army WWII	
Gloria White Gardner	B: 1940	no death date
w/o William Preston Gardner		married 12/2/1978
William Preston Gardner	B: 1927	D: 1994
h/o Gloria White Gardner		married 12/2/1978
M. Estelle Grant	B: 1899	D: 1973
		w/o Roger W. Grant
Roger W. Grant	B: 1912	h/o M. Estelle Grant

Lot: N-19   Lot Owner: George Robert Holmes

George Robert Holmes   B: 4 Jun 1926   D: 14 Dec 1995
                                                     US Army WWII

Helen M. Holmes   B: 11 Jun 1951   D: 9 Jan 1995

Lot: N-20   Lot Owner:Mary Corum

Ardella Moore   B: 1928   D: 1996
                                            Ames Funeral Home marker

Mary Julie Moore   B: 1920   D: 1989

Annbell Moore Robinson   B: 1926   D: 1985

Lot: N-22   Lot Owner: Clarence & Edith Bushrod

Clarence Bushrod   B: 1914   D: 1977
                                               h/o Rosie M. Bushrod

Rosie M. Bushrod   B: 1917   w/o Clarence Bushrod

Lot: N-23   Lot Owner: Boots White

Howard Alphonso White   B: 28 Oct 1926   D: 17 Apr 1975
                                                    TEC5 US Army WWII

Kelvin Terry White   B: 11 Dec 1954   D: 12 Nov 1987

Mattie Smith White   B: 28 Sep 1927   D: 8 Nov 1998

Lot: N-25   Lot Owner: Charlie Trammell

Charlie L. Trammell   B: 1910   D: 1980
                                               h/o Irene H. Trammell

Irene H. Trammell   B: 1915   w/o Irene H. Trammell

Lot: N-27   Lot Owner: Smith

Curl Edward Smith   B: 17 Dec 1914   D: 28 Dec 1990

Lot: N-28   Lot Owner: W. Gaskins

Annemarie G. Gaskins   B: 31 Dec 1923   D: 17 Jul 1986
                                               w/o Winston S. Gaskins

Winston S. Gaskins   B: 19 Jun 1922
                                            h/o Annemarie G. Gaskins

Lot: East - Single Graves   **Lot Owner: Miscellaneous**

Site 1   Susan H. Jackson   B: 1870   D: Oct 1959

Site 2 Harriet G. Howard   B: 4 Sep 1916   D: 4 Jul 1966
                                    on stone with Susan H. Jackson

Site 12 Jeff R. Chavis   B: 20 Feb 1906   D: 4 Jul 1965

Site 15 John Reed   B: 26 Jul 1936   D: 12 Sep 1966

Site 16 John D. Scott   B: 8 Sep 1951   D: 23 May 1967

Site 17 Audrey D. Bolden   B: 16 Aug 1919   D: 20 Jul 1976

Site 18 Clarence Jefferson   B: 1896   D: 1967
                                    h/o Louise B. Jefferson

Site 19 Louise B. Jefferson   B: 1906   D: 1993
                                    w/o Clarence Jefferson

Site 21 Luther Franklin Smith B: 1899   D: 1969

Site 24 Arthur Hill   B: 29 Feb 1908   D: 26 May 1970

Site 25 Mack Rolling Bushrod B: 1905   D: 1970

Site 26 Rochelle Smith   B: 1952   D: 1971

Site 29 Marjorie B. Hall   w/o J. Wesley Hall   no dates

Site 30 J. Wesley Hall   B: 1912   D: 1972
                                    h/o Marjorie B. Hall

Site 31 Edith E. Bushrod   B: 1911   D: 1999
                                    Colonial Funeral Home marker

Site 32 Beverly Bushrod   B: 2 Apr 1909   D: 7 Nov 1974

Site 33 Joseph N. Barnett   B: 1924   D: 1974

Site 34 James T. Grant   B: 8 Mar 1932   D: 27 Jan 1975
                                                              SGT USMC

Site 36 Louisa P. Butler   B: 29 Apr 1886   D: 26 Dec 1976

Site 38 Ella Louvenia Redd   B: 1922   D: 1998
                                    Ames Funeral Home marker

Site 39 Beatrice R. Johnson   B: 6 Aug 1908   D: 6 Jul 1977

Site 42 Evelyn Bushrod   no dates

Site 44 Collies Benson   B: 3 Feb 1906   D: 5 Mar 1982

Site 45 Rebecca A. Smith   B: 1907   D: 1982

Site 47 Jerry L. Jackson   B: 10 Mar 1963   D: 7 Jun 1984

Site 49 Blakley Isaac Howard B: 1920   D: 1984

Site 54 Franklin Delaney Roosevelt Smith
                                      B: 12 Dec 1932   D: 25 Sep 1989

Lot: West - Single Graves   Lot Owner: Miscellaneous

Site 8 Akilah Kyong Hae Grayson
                                      B: 11 Nov 1985   D: 29 Aug 1987
                                      d/o Ivan Eugene & Shin Hae Yon Grayson

Site 8 Marcia J. Hae Grayson B: 18 Jan 1984   D: 29 Aug 1987
                                      d/o Ivan Eugene & Shin Hae Yon Grayson

Site 9 Ivan Eugene Grayson   B: 6 Sep 1960   no death date
                                      h/o Shin Hae Yon Grayson

Site 9 Shin Hae Yon Grayson B: 26 Jun 1955   D: 29 Aug 1987
                                      w/o Ivan Eugene Grayson

Site 12 Richard L. Kelley   B: 23 Jan 1928   D: 22 Nov 1993
                                      h/o Mildred T. Kelly

Site 13 Mildred T. Kelley   B: 11 Sep 1945   no death date
                                      w/o Richard L. Kelley

Site 16 John E. Wilkins   B: 1943   D: 1989
                                      in mem - Fairfax VW co-workers/friends

Site 20 William H. Grant   B: 1951   no death date
                                                                        Son

Site 21 Marie E. Grant   B: 1922   D: 1997
                                                                        Mother

Site 25 Isabelle Payne   B: 17 Jan 1930   D: 19 Nov 1990
                                      Joynes Funeral Home marker

Site 27 Welby Herbert Grayson   SSGT US Air Force
                                      B: 15 Oct 1926   D: 16 Feb 1991

Site 30 Robert Sylvester Williams
                                      B: 1898   D: 1992

Site 31 Johanna Virginia Chavis
                                      B: 28 Nov 1913   D: 21 Nov 1992

Joyce E. Hinton   B: 8 Dec 1948   D: 24 Dec 1997

Site 38 Judith P. Gaskins   B: 28 Mar 1892   D: 1 Apr 1994

Site 39 James E. Smith   B: 8 Mar 1916   D: 14 Jan 1995

Site 40 Beatrice D. Payne   B: 25 Mar 1925   D: 1 Oct 1994
                                          Joynes Funeral Home marker

Site 42 Jerry Horner King   B: 1932   D: 1994
                                             Joynes Funeral Home

Site 43 Corine Frampton   B: 1915   D: 1997
                                          Ames Funeral Home marker

Site 50 Amy J. Williams   D: 18 Jun 1976

Site 51 Howard David Lloyd, Jr   US Army WWII
                                B: 21 Oct 1916   D: 30 Apr 1994

Site 53 Margaret L. Rose   B: 10 Nov 1936   D: 9 Dec 1994

Site 55 George W. Rose, Sr   B: 22 Feb 1930   no death date

Site 56 Robert Lee Smith   B: 11 Mar 1953   D: 10 Jul 1995

Site 58 Alfred Lee Marshal   B: 1913   D: 1995

Site 59 Ralph Eugene Coates   B: 1943   D: 1996
                                          Lyles Funeral Home marker

Site 62 Joe Warren Marshall   B: 16 Feb 1930   D: 28 Jan 1999
                                          Ames Funeral Home marker

Site 64 Ann Lee Hatcher   B: 16 Jan 1914   D: 5 Nov 1996

Site 67 Rev. Thomas Grant   B: 2 Apr 1923   D: 28 Jul 1997
                                                              WWII

Site 72 Herman James Carter   B: 1942   D: 1998
                                          Joynes Funeral Home marker

Rodney L. Smith, Jr.   B: 1978   D: 1998
                                          Joynes Funeral Home marker

Site 74 Caroline M. Washington   Ames Funeral Home marker
                                B: 1922   D: 1998

Site 80 Samuel Wesley Fisher   B: 3 Jun 1930   D: 1 Nov 1994
                                             PFC US Army Korea

Lot: W-1- 1   Lot Owner: **Gussie Davis**

Milton H. Ball h/o Mary R. Lane	B: 27 Jul 1910	D: 1976 on same stone as Mary R. Lane
Gussie E. Davis	B: 1888	D: 1968 stone with Albert B. Jones
Albert B. Jones	B: 6 Jul 1901	no death date stone with Gussie E. Davis
Ed Lane	B: 25 May 1889	D: 30 May 1953
Mary Lane	B: 1906	D: 1989
Mary R. Lane	B: 29 Jan 1906	D: 26 May 1989 w/o Milton H. Ball
Mary C. Valentine	B: 9 Jun 1915	D: 25 Dec 1978 Mom
Walter H. Valentine	B: 19 Aug 1907	D: 9 Aug 1985 Dad

Lot: W-1- 4   Lot Owner: **Richard Minniefield**

Annie Jones Minniefield	B: 1860	D: 23 Dec 1931

Lot: W-1- 5   Lot Owner: **Flecy Jackson & Vinnie Shorts**

John Marshall Jackson	B: 24 Aug 1920	D: 26 May 1994 TEC 4 US Army WWII
Lucille E. Jackson	B: 1927	D: 1980
Mary F. Jackson	B: 4 Mar 1881	D: 12 Aug 1956

Lot: W-1- 8   Lot Owner: **Lucy Murray**

Johanna Buckner		D: 4 Aug 1866 w/o Robert Buckner "Mother"
Randolph Buckner	B: 29 Sep 1849	D: 28 Aug 1915 s/o Johanna & Robert Buckner
Robert Buckner		D: 11 Feb 1891 h/o Johanna Buckner "Father"
Scott Buckner		D: 28 Jan 1928 on same stone as Randolph Buckner
Ella Murray	B: 20 Jan 1840	D: 15 Feb 1898
Leven Murray	h/o Lucy B. Murray	D: 30 Dec 1929

| Lucy B. Murray | w/o Leven Murray | D: 15 Jan 1932 |

Lot: W-1- 9   Lot Owner: Logan Turner

Florance E. Stoke		D: 2 Dec 1922
Elizabeth S. Turner		D: 14 Jun 1925
Hattie E. Turner		D: 13 Dec 1917
Virginia B. Turner		D: 22 Feb 1894
William B. Turner		D: 24 Jan 1901

Lot: W-1-10   Lot Owner: Willis Hansborough

Susan Hansborough	B: 10 Jun 1856	D: 14 Apr 1927
		w/o Willis Hansborough
Willis Hansborough	B: 17 Sep 1853	D: 16 Sep 1913
		h/o Susan Hansborough

Lot: W-1-12   Lot Owner: Carr Cook

Earnest N. Barnett	B: 1885	D: 1962
Edith E. Hall	B: 7 Feb 1891	D: 30 May 1967
		w/o S. Chester Hall
S. Chester Hall	B: 13 Sep 1880	D: 2 Aug 1962
		h/o Edith E. Hall
Laura F. King	B: 1913	D: 1962
Preston King	B: 1902	D: 1968

Lot: W-1-14   Lot Owner: Logan Ashby

| Mary J. Ashby | B: 12 May 1834 | D: 6 Jul 1908 |
| Thompson Ashby | Age: 76 years | D: 17 Sep 1890 |

Lot: W-1-15   Lot Owner: Martha Charity

Anna E. Charity	d/o Mary B. Charity	D: 3 Dec 1923
Mary T. Charity	m/o Anna E. Charity	D: 12 Feb 1930
Katie Turner	B: 1 Nov 1866	D: 5 Jan 1939

Lot: W-1-16   Lot Owner: Payton Taylor

Frances Taylor   D: 9 Feb 1917
                            w/o Payton Taylor   Age: 72 years

Madison H. Taylor   B: 16 Jan 1869   D: 16 Mar 1940
                                                 h/o Mary S. Taylor

Mary S. Taylor   B: 6 Nov 1872   D: 1 May 1953
                                                 w/o Madison H. Taylor

Payton Taylor   D: 29 Jun 1896
                            h/o Frances Taylor   Age: 71 years

Lot: W-2- 1   Lot Owner: Hollie Moore

Hollie Frances Moore   B: 6 Oct 1856   D: 10 Sep 1937
                                                 m/o Wade Hampton Moore

Wade Hampton Moore   B: 6 Jan 1895   D: 10 Jul 1936
                                                 s/o Hollie Frances Moore

Lot: W-2- 2   Lot Owner: Grimes & C.C. Fisher

Hattie B. Gibson   B: 1882   D: 1969
                                                 w/o Powell W. Gibson

Powell W. Gibson   B: 1875   D: 1959
                                                 h/o Hattie B. Gibson

Gertrude F. Grimes   B: 1889   D: 1966
                                                 w/o Wirt S. Grimes

Wirt S. Grimes   B: 1888   D: 1946
                                                 h/o Gertrude F. Grimes

Lot: W-2- 3   Lot Owner: Geo. Fauntleroy

Helen C. Fauntleroy   B: 31 Jan 1918   D: 22 May 1918

Rosie Anna Fauntleroy   B: 31 Jul 1881   D: 28 Oct 1918
                                                 w/o George W. Fauntleroy

Lot: W-2- 4   Lot Owner: Wilt Jones

Charles "Jack" Turner   B: 1910   D: 1991
                                                 h/o Dorothy E. Turner

Dorothy E. Turner   B: 1925   D: 1987
                                                 w/o Charles "Jack" Turner

Raymond E. Turner   B: 27 Mar 1951   D: 18 Aug 1979

| Wayne Michael Turner | B: 11 Jun 1947 | D: 21 Sep 1995 |
| | | Capt. US Navy Vietnam |

Lot: W-2- 5   Lot Owner: Fannie Garner

Fannie Garner	w/o Jackson Garner	D: 23 May 1913
Jackson Garner	h/o Fannie Garner	D: 23 Sep 1877
William J. Garner	B: 1861	D: 1938

Lot: W-2- 6   Lot Owner: Lawson Moore

Frank Moore, Sr.	Age: 76 years	D: Feb 1898
John M. Moore	B: 1886	D: 1971
s/o Lawson H. & Patsy G. Moore	on stone with father & mother	
Lawson H. Moore	h/o Patsy G. Moore	no dates
Patsy G. Moore	w/o Lawson H. Moore	no dates

Lot: W-2- 7   Lot Owner: S. Hamlin & Henry Shorts

Addie H. Hamilin	B: 29 Oct 1891	D: 30 Mar 1988
Albert H. Hamlin	B: 3 Sep 1913	D: 6 Feb 1984
		loving father son and brother
Sam Hamlin	B: 1 Mar 1883	D: 31 Jul 1954
Thomas Hamlin	B: 6 Sep 1922	D: 31 Jul 1957
Lettie Shorts	B: 13 May 1861	D: 21 Jan 1891
R. Henry Shorts	B: 1865	D: 1917

Lot: W-2- 8   Lot Owner: Joe Buckner

| Helen Buckner Crawford | B: 16 Oct 1897 | D: 2 Feb 1978 |

Lot: W-2-10   Lot Owner: Hollie Daw

Cornelious Daw	B: 7 Oct 1881	D: 19 Mar 1916
Edward Daw	B: 26 Jan 1869	D: 15 Dec 1918
Hattie Daw	B: 6 Jul 1885	D: 7 Jan 1908
Henrietta Daw	B: 7 May 1866	D: 10 Jan 1900
Hollie Daw	B: 1837	D: 31 Oct 1920
		Mother
Mary B. Daw	B: 12 Aug 1877	D: 9 Jun 1929
T.B. Winter & Son, Middleburg, VA, broken off base		

Lot: W-2-11   Lot Owner: Joe Brown, Sr.

B. Marshall Brown   B: 15 Jul 1899   D: 24 Apr 1931
                                        s/o Joseph & Pricilla Brown

Joseph Brown   h/o Sarah E. Brown   D: 12 Nov 1918

Sarah E. Brown   w/o Joseph Brown   D: 28 Dec 1920

Katie J. Clinton   B: 20 Mar 1872   D: 9 Jun 1892
                                        w/o Grant Clinton, d/o Joseph & Sarah E.
Brown
                                        on stone with Charles A. Moten

Charles A. Moten   B: 11 Feb 1860   D: 24 Jan 1891
     on stone with Katie J. [Brown] Clinton   s/o Sarah E. Brown

Lot: W-2-12   Lot Owner: Braxton Brown

Braxton Brown   B: 15 Aug 1829   D: 20 Jan 1902
                                        s/o James & Sallie Brown, h/o Martha Brown

Lot: W-2-15   Lot Owner: Thompson Washington

W. Thomas   no other information

Lot: W-2-16   Lot Owner: Carr Cook

Carr Cook   B: 1855   D: 1932

Edward D. Cook   B: 1891   D: 1933

Joanna C. Cook   B: 1858   D: 1940

Ruth A. Cook   B: 1882   D: 1949

Nancy C. Thronley   B: 1861   D: 1936

Lot: W-3- 1   Lot Owner: Kate Kendrich

Martin C. Kendrick   D: 1 Apr 1942

Lot: W-3-2   Lot Owner: Miscellaneous

Earl Grayson   B: 4 Aug 1906   D: 22 Apr 1993
                                        PFC US Army WWII

Albert J. Hall   B: 30 Sep 1885   D: 6 Mar 1962

Lot: W-3- 3   Lot Owner: Wesley Bolden

Ethel H. Bolden   B: 26 Jun 1920   D: no death date

John Wesley Bolden   B: 12 Nov 1912   D: 7 Dec 1944

| Phyllis Alea Bolden | B: 1945 | D: 1946 |
| | | d/o L.W. & E.H. Bolden |

Lot: W-3- 4   Lot Owner: Robert Doctor

| Peter Willis. Tibbs, Jr | B: 1 Apr 1928 | D: 23 Feb 1998 |
| | | US Army WWII |

Lot: W-3- 5   Lot Owner: Simms

| Clarence Fletcher | B: 18 Sep 1862 | D: 11 Feb 1925 |
| Mary Etta Simms | Age: 19 years | D: 18 Nov 1917 |

Lot: W-3- 7   Lot Owner: Hollie Alexander & Daniel Mack

Clarence W. Alexander	B: 1878	D: 1935
		h/o Hattie H. Alexander
Hattie H. Alexander	B: 1884	D: 1958
		w/o Clarence W. Alexander
Daniel Mack		h/o Harriett Mack
Harriett Mack		w/o Daniel Mack

Lot: W-3- 8   Lot Owner: Charlotte Thomas

| John Thomas | Age: 72 years | D: 26 Sep 1890 |

Lot: W-3-10   Lot Owner: John Withers

Allen J. Davis	B: 14 Feb 1888	D: 25 Jan 1923
Harry A. Davis	B: 29 Aug 1913	D: 20 Oct 1938
	s/o Allen j & Mary W. Davis, h/o Mary W. Davis	
Mary W. Davis	w/o Harry A. Davis	D: 1 Aug 1941
Curtis L. Withers	B: 14 Feb 1907	D: 27 Mar 1931
Susan M. Withers	B: Dec 1853	D: 5 Dec 1891

Lot: W-3-14   Lot Owner: Spencer Thornton

Martha Pollard	w/o William Pollard	D: 4 Sep 1910
William Pollard	h/o Martha Pollard	D: 25 Dec 1903
Ben Thornton		D: 11 Jan 1933
Daisy E. Thornton		D: 13 Dec 1884
		w/o William B. Thornton
William B. Thornton		D: 10 Feb 1885
	s/o Spencer & B.E. Thornton, h/o Daisy E. Thornton	

Lot: W-3-16   Lot Owner: S.P. Fisher

Simon P. [Rev] Fisher   B: 15 Jan 1856   D: 1 Sep 1913

Lot: W-4- 2   Lot Owner: Miscellaneous

Maria Bolden   B: 25 Sep 1881   D: 1 Aug 1929

Christine B. Wright   B: 25 Dec 1910   D: 2 Sep 1991
                                                       w/o Robert M. Wright

Robert M. Wright   B: 21 Dec 1893   D: 18 Apr 1991
                                                       h/o Christine B. Wright

Lot: W-4- 3   Lot Owner: Charles McQuay

Charles McQuay   D: 6 Jul 1936

Ella McQuay   D: 3 May 1942

James Poles   B: 1873   D: 1942

Lot: W-4- 5   Lot Owner: Joan Moten

Amanda Moten   B: 1 Nov 1871   D: 10 Jun 1898
                                                       w/o Thomas H. Moten

Fannie B. Moten   B: 1 Oct 1886   D: 4 Feb 1954
                                                       w/o John H. Moten

John H. Moten   B: 1880   D: 1961
                                                       h/o Fannie B. Moten

Lucy Moten   B: 1850   D: 6 Sep 1919

Thomas H. Moten   B: 10 Apr 1868   D: 29 Apr 1902
                                                       h/o Amanda Moten

Edwin W. Smith   B: 22 Nov 1826   D: 8 Sep 1932
                                                       h/o Josephine M. Smith

Josephine M. Smith   B: 29 Jul 1878   D: 4 May 1950
                                                       w/o Edwin W. Smith

Lot: W-4- 8   Lot Owner: Lucy Garner

Edward T. [Dr] Ford   B: 10 Aug 1843   D: 21 Aug 1926

Irene M. Ford   B: 8 Jan 1873   D: 20 Jan 1940

Lucy K. Garner   B: Aug 1819   D: Oct 1910

Eliza E. Mack   B: 20 Jun 1848   D: 29 Dec 1897

Lot: W-4-13   Lot Owner: John Bolden

Bettie Bolden	Age: 51 years	D: 9 May 1912
Frank Bolden	Age: 30 years	D: 11 Mar 1912
John Bolden	Age: 90 years	D: 26 Jun 1917

Lot: W-4-14   Lot Owner: Charles Mason & G. Douglas

Genevieve Douglas   B: 13 Jan 1895   D: 16 Mar 1943

Hannah E. Mason   B: 13 Jul 1816   D: 18 Jan 1886
                                              w/o Charles William Mason

Lot: W-4-15   Lot Owner: William Smith

Josie L. Murray   B: 18 Sep 1868   D: 18 Jan 1900
                                                   w/o S. J. Murray

Harriet Smith   B: 4 Feb 1842   D: 29 Feb 1900
                                                  w/o William Smith

Julia Smith   B: 3 Aug 1883   D: 10 Jan 1891
     d/o William & Hannah Smith on stone with brother Richard Smith

Martin L. Smith   B: Jun 1880   D: 17 Sep 1927

Richard Smith   B: 2 Oct 1873   D: 1 Jan 1884
       s/o William & Hannah Smith on stone with sister Julia Smith

William Smith   B: 10 Aug 1818   D: 3 Apr 1896
                                                  h/o Harriet Smith

Lot: W-4-16   Lot Owner: J.M. Fisher

Frances A. Fisher   D: 13 Mar 1895
                            w/o J.H. Fisher   Age: 52 years

J. Marshall Fisher   B: 16 Oct 1818   D: 2 Dec 1911

Lot: W-5- 2   Lot Owner: Laura Chinn

Ollie Bolden   B: 1897   D: 1945

Betty H. Chinn   B: 1908   D: 1939
                                     on stone with W. Ulysses Chinn

Newton Chinn   B: 1887   D: 1929

W. Ulysses Chinn   B: 1925   D: 1945
                                       on stone with Betty H. Chinn

Claudius L. Finger   stone is submerged, cannot read

Lot: W-5- 3   Lot Owner: James McQuay

Kate McQuay Brown	B: 1 Feb 1885	D: 4 Feb 1919
Fannie C. McQuay		D: 10 Sep 1928
		w/o James W. McQuay
James W. McQuay		D: 19 Oct 1950
		h/o Fannie C. McQuay

Lot: W-5- 4   Lot Owner: A.R. Smith

Armstead Smith	B: 31 May 1876	D: 28 Aug 1948
		h/o Cornelia L. Smith
Armstead R. Smith	B: 30 Apr 1902	D: 16 Feb 190-
		s/o Armstead & Cornelia L. Smith
Cornelia L. Smith	B: 4 Dec 1882	D: 30 Sep 1911
		w/o Armstead Smith
Fannie Smith		D: 8 Feb 1901
w/o Thomas Smith	'our mother'	Age: 65 years
J. Woodie Smith	B: 18 May 1857	D: 8 Jan 1933
		on stone with Julius T. Smith
Julius T. Smith	B: 1900	D: 1981
		on stone with J. Woodie Smith
Thomas Smith		D: 25 Jan 1912
h/o Fannie Smith	our father	Age: 90 years

Lot: W-5- 5   Lot Owner: French Whitney

Rosalie Richardson	B: 1903	D: 1960
Annie Fisher Whitney	B: 1859	D: 1936
French Whitney	B: 1853	D: 1918
French Whitney, Jr	B: 13 Apr 1885	D: 21 Mar 1973

Lot: W-5- 6   Lot Owner: Robert Douglas

Arthur L. (Buster) Douglass	B: 16 May 1915	D: 15 Mar 1965
Mary L. (Sister) Douglass	B: 23 May 1914	D: 17 Feb 1997

Lot: W-5- 7   Lot Owner: John Hall

Annie Hall Carter	B: 20 May 1900	D: 14 Feb 1952
John H. Hall	B: 1870	D: 1935

| Mary J. Hall | B: 1868 | D: 1940 |
| Nathaniel Hall | B: 1906 | D: 1938 |

Lot: W-5- 8   Lot Owner: Charlie Bolden

Fannie T. Barrett	B: 18 Dec 1821	D: 13 Mar 1892
Nellie Turner Bolden	B: 28 Jan 1860	D: 16 Mar 1922
		w/o Charles L. Bolden
Willie H. Bolden	B: 16 Mar 1902	D: 27 Oct 1918
Fannie B. Stewart	B: 18 Feb 1899	D: 27 Jun 1975

Lot: W-5- 9   Lot Owner: H.J. Corum & James H. Corum

Henry James Corum	B: 1918	D: 1986
		PVT US Army
Lucy S. Corum	B: 1937	D: 1978
Wade H. Corum, Jr	B: 9 May 1911	D: 26 Aug 1989
		S2 US Navy WWII

Lot: W-5-10   Lot Owner: Miscellaneous

Arthur Green		D: 24 Nov 1880
	h/o Cary Green	Age: 44 years
Cary Green		D: 30 Jul 1930
	w/o Arthur Green	Age: 98 years
David E. Milberrie	B: 1897	D: 1977
		h/o Ruth W. Milberrie
Ruth W. Milberrie	B: 1902	w/o David E. Milberrie
Gurley H. Wanzer	B: 13 Apr 1890	D: 4 Jul 1974
		PVT US Army

Lot: W-5-11   Lot Owner: Henry Robinson

| Lucy E. V. Robinson | B: 24 Dec 1866 | D: 26 Sep 1899 |
| | | d/o Henry & Susan |

Lot: W-5-12   Lot Owner: N.N. Hall

Catherine E. Hall	B: 28 Aug 1882	D: 1 Feb 1931
		d/o Nathan N. & Cornellia Hall
Cornellia Hall		D: 29 Oct 1911
	w/o Nathan N. Hall	Age: 56 years

| Evvie Hall | | Age: 8 years |
| | | d/o Nathan N. & Cornellia Hall |

| Infants Hall | | c/o Nathan N. & Cornellia Hall |

| Nathan N. Hall | B: Mar 1859 | D: 30 Apr 1939 |
| | | h/o Cornellia Hall |

| Thomas Hall | | s/o Nathan N. & Cornellia Hall |
| | | Age: 1 years |

| Maria Turner | | D: 9 Oct 1886 |

Lot: W-5-13　　Lot Owner: N.N. Hall

| Etta Hall | B: 1893 | D: 1969 |
| | | w/o William N. Hall |

| William N. Hall | B: 1890 | D: 1985 |
| | | h/o Etta Moore Hall |

| William N. Hall, Jr | B: 1916 | D: 1947 |
| | | "Buddy" |

Lot: W-5-16　　Lot Owner: S.V. Fisher

| Benjamine H. Fisher | Age: 7- 3-0 | D: 4 May 1896 |
| | on stone with Maynard D. Fisher & Edward Gibson | |

| C. Clarendon Fisher | B: 1890 | D: 1954 |

| Douglas R. [Rev] Fisher | Age: 58 years | D: 24 Jan 1912 |
| | | h/o Lucelia Jane Fisher |

| Lucelia Jane Fisher | Age: 58years | D: 12 Feb 1905 |
| | | w/o [Rev] Douglas R. Fisher |

Maynard D. Fisher	Age: 28 years	D: 21 Jul 1911
	on stone with Benjamine H. Fisher & Edward	
Gibson		

| Edward Gibson | Age: 7 years | D: 30 May 1905 |
| | on stone with Maynard D. & Benjamine H. Fisher | |

Lot: W-6- 1　　Lot Owner: Wm McK. Jackson

| Charles W. Foster | B: 24 Mar 1923 | D: 13 Feb 1995 |
| | | US Army WW II |

| Ethel J. Foster | B: 1924 | D: no death date |

| Mildred L. Jackson | B: 1902 | D: 1971 |

| William McK. Jackson | B: 1900 | D: 1970 |

Lot: W-6- 3   Lot Owner: Love & Methodist Church

Mary Carr
w/o Shedrick Carr

D: 14 Feb 1898
Age: 75 years

Shedrick Carr
h/o Mary Carr

D: 17 May 1898
Age: 81 years

Lot: W-6- 4   Lot Owner: Charles Fisher

Fannie Fisher Colston

B: 9 Jan 1914

D: 11 Jul 1937
w/o Charles E. Colston

Arthur Randolph Fisher

B: 20 Sep 1909

D: 14 Aug 1983
US Army WWI CPL

Charles F. Fisher

B: 5 Oct 1886

D: 24 Sep 1955
h/o Hannah E. Fisher

Edward Mason Fisher

B: 8 Aug 1908

D: 12 Sep 1936

Hannah W. Fisher

B: 5 Apr 1887

D: 11 Oct 1979
w/o Charles F. Fisher

Robert Thomas, Jr

B: 21 Sep 1928

D: 7 May 1979
CPL US Army

Robert P. Thomas

B: 2 Mar 1901

D: 7 May 1953
h/o Willie F. Thomas

Willie F. Thomas

B: 16 Aug 1905

D: 2 Nov 1985
w/o Robert P. Thomas

Lot: W-6- 5   Lot Owner: John Fauntleroy

Caroline Mason Fauntleroy
w/o John Fauntleroy

B: 12 May 1829
top off base

D: 20 Oct 1926
Age: 97 years

John Fauntleroy

B: 15 Jul 1831
top off of base

D: 1 Jul 1908
Age: 77 years

Lot: W-6- 6   Lot Owner: Joseph Milstead

Devin Maurice Newman

B: 15 Dec 1991

D: 21 Feb 1992
"infant son"

Lot: W-6- 7   Lot Owner: Marie Thornton

Maria Thornton Howard

Age: 51 years

D: 29 Dec 1918

Josephine Thornton
w/o Robert Thornton

D: 24 Oct 1920
Age: 22 years

Robert Thornton   Age: 25 years   D: 9 Apr 1918
                                                h/o Josephine Thornton

Lot: W-6- 9   Lot Owner: Geo. Pinkett

Randolph T. Hatcher   B: 1932   D: 1999
                                        Ames Funeral Home marker

Lot: W-6-10   Lot Owner: Wesley Wanzer

Frances H. Wanzer   B: 1890   D: 1964

Lot: W-6-11   Lot Owner: Kate M. Scott

Archie K. Scott   B: 1956   D: 1987

Joyce E. Scott   B: 29 Jul 1947   D: 12 Sep 1998

Lot: W-6-12   Lot Owner: Geo. Berryman

George H. Berryman   B: 16 Aug 1856   D: 4 Nov 1923

Parmelia E. Berryman   Age: 10- 8- 8   D: 12 Nov 1896

Sadie Berryman   B: 1886   D: 1960

Thomas J. Berryman   Age: 94 years   D: 10 Mar 1891

Lot: W-6-14   Lot Owner: Thomas Washington

Hannah V. Fisher   B: 6 Mar 1907   D: 26 Jun 1907

Alfred Lee   h/o Hannah Lee   no dates

Hannah Lee   w/o Alfred Lee   no dates

Hallie Washington   B: 25 Jun 1885   D: 17 Jan 1882

Harry Washington   B: 28 Mar 1883   D: 13 Jul 1906

Lucy F. Washington   B: 27 Nov 1890   D: 25 Mar 1909

Lucy Virginia Lee Washington B: 2 Mar 1851   D: 6 Oct 1929
                                        w/o William Henry Washington

William Henry Washington   B: 28 Aug 1818   D: 12 Dec 1904
                                        h/o Lucy Virginia Lee Washington

Lot: W-6-15   Lot Owner: A. Lee

Mary Lee Jetton   no dates, inside Lee family plot

Mary Jones   B: 1830   D: 1900
                                        on stone with Alfred & Mildred

Alfred Lee, Jr   s/o Alfred & Mildred Lee   D: 1894

Alfred Lee, Sr	B: 1852	D: 1899
		h/o Mildred Lee
Braxton Lee	s/o Alfred & Mildred Lee	D: 1897
Charles Lee	s/o Alfred & Mildred Lee	D: 1902
Gertrude Lee	d/o Alfred & Mildred Lee	D: 1893
Mildred Lee	B: 1856	D: 1922
		w/o Alfred Lee Sr
Thomas Lee	s/o Alfred & Mildred Lee	D: 1896
Louise Lee Meredith		no dates

Lot: W-6-16   Lot Owner: Arch Jackson

| Sadie B. Scott | B: 12 Oct 1904 | D: Jun 1959 |

Index

Licklider
Elva Pearson 177
Lighliter
Ann Presgraves ... 167
Linkins
Caroline C. 137
Carrie Elizabeth .. 137
H.B. 137
James Dallas 137
Mary E. 137
Linville
Elijah. 193
Lipps
Cicero 135
Elbert B. 135
Jonathan 135
Sue Kirk 135
Lisenbee
Forrest S. 64
Littleton
Catherine M. 88
F. 88
Fielding 88
Hannah 88
John K. 88
Richard C. 88
Lloyd
Alice D. 49
Aubrey E. 63
Bessie Lee 63
Calvin C. 47
Ethel V. 209
Gladys R. 47
Howard David, Jr 229
Thomas Alvin 63
Wilmer L. 49
Locke
Edward F. 65
Lucy L. 65
Lodge
William 22
Logan
Laura V. 102
Pat 193
Samuel. 102
Sarah D. 102
William John 7

Loughborough
Augustine 121, 122
Caroline Virginia
Fauntleroy 121
Louise D. 121
Turner F. 121
Love
George 95
Jane L. 106
Mary S. 95
Lowe
infant 172
infant daughter.... 172
Jos 172
R.T. 172
Raymond T. 172
Luck
Drusilla A. 95
John M. 95
Lucile Ashton 78
Marion C. 79
Nancy Swain 178
Roberta R. 79
Roszier R. 79
S. Preston 78
Samuel Preston Jr
.... 178
W. W. 79
William J. 79
Luckett
Ann C. 80
Evalina 80
F. W. 79
G.T. 80
Ludwell 80
Ludwell H. 80
Lynch
J. A. 193
Lynn
Carrie W. 91
J. Humphrey 90
Leslie A. 90
Parilia F. 90
T. Noel 91

M

MacDougall
Hugh Adams 68
Mack
Daniel 235
Eliza E. 236
Harriett. 235
Mackethan
Ellen Seipp 20
Madden
Bertha V. 48
William F. 48
Maddox
Dorothea I. 78
Robert M. 53
Maddux
Hannah. 13
William 13
Mancuso
Joe 116
Mattie L. Adams .. 116
Manierre
Cyrus E. Jr 5
Mannings
George 194
Manuel
Caroline V. 77
Elmer 77
Marble
Welby Carter 208
Marders
Catherine Isabella 134
Lovell. 134
Marlow
Anna Carey 218
James B. Jr 218
James B. Sr. 218
Leana Davis 218
Maroney
M. 193
T. B. 194
Marshal
Alfred Lee 229
George 221
Rene Tootsie 205, 206